UFO VISITATION

UFO VISITATION

Preparing for the Twenty-first Century

ALAN WATTS

BLANDFORD

A BLANDFORD BOOK

First published in the UK 1996 by Blandford
A Cassell Imprint
CASSELL PLC
Wellington House
125 Strand
London, WC2R 0BB

Reprinted 1996, 1997

Distributed in the United States by Sterling Publishing Co., Inc.
387 Park Avenue South, New York, NY 10016-8810

A Cataloguing-in-Publication Data entry for this title is available from the
British Library

ISBN 0-7137-2600-8

Illustrations by Dave Johnston

Typeset by York House Typographic, London
Printed and bound in Great Britain by
Biddles Ltd, Guildford and King's Lynn

CONTENTS

INTRODUCTION

PERSONALLY, I think it can be safely said that the visitation of this planet by extra-terrestrial intelligences is now a confirmed fact. For one thing, mankind at large continually sees their vehicles in the sky and on the ground and calls them UFOs (Unidentified Flying Objects). Literally hundreds and hundreds of books and articles have appeared, describing sightings and their ramifications. If there is nothing in this, then I feel that vast numbers of people have been fooled. Highly respected and intelligent people in government departments which have been set up to investigate the UFO phenomena have, when free to do so, come down heavily on the side of the existence of the UFOs.

It is because of the continued presence of UFOs that a great change has come over us since World War 2. They have contributed immeasurably to our interest in, and knowledge of, worlds other than our own. We are, indeed, being subtly but surely converted from a species which imagined it was alone in space to the realization that we are just one of a vast assemblage of intelligent beings. However, there is reason to believe that the human race on Earth is unique. There are many other intelligent beings spread throughout the Universe but none of them seems to be quite like us.

Opinion polls carried out in recent years show that a majority of the population of most developed countries now believe that UFOs exist and that they come from somewhere outside Earth.

People may be unable to fully understand how that is possible, seeing that light years separate us from the nearest stars that may have planets, but, in many ways, the twentieth-century public is in advance of its media mentors. People have seen so many marvels that they are often fully prepared to believe that what is considered impossible today will become reality tomorrow. They can well believe that Albert Einstein did not have the last word about what is or is not possible in the Universe. And they are not surprised to find evidence that these visitations have been going on for as far back as anyone can probe.

Many books have been written about the 'impossible' things that ancient peoples seemed to be able to do. Some of these things we have only recently relearned and, in some cases, still cannot fathom. But the research that has unearthed the details of what our forebears were capable of makes me increasingly certain that we have been the recipients of knowledge and advancement from entities outside Earth – entities who have been through the mill of civilization in the past and have, we must hope, a benevolent interest in our continuing welfare.

It now appears that, for over 20 years, and largely unbeknown to the vast majority of humanity, we have been receiving direct communications from deep space. The communicators call themselves the Council of Nine and it all started with Uri Geller and his companion and mentor, Andrija Puharich. After that, the 'window' through which the communications have come shifted to one selected person, Phyllis Schlemmer. Phyllis is a deep-trance medium who has had to surrender the whole of her personality to the communicators during the sessions when the messages were being received.

I was aware of the original communications from the Nine through reading Andrija Puharich's book *Uri* (1974), which recounts some of the amazing things which happened when he was with Geller. But I was not aware of the wealth of information about the past, present and likely future on this planet that has been coming in from the Nine since then. Much of this intelligence has been gathered into a book called, for reasons which will become apparent, *The Only Planet of Choice* (Schlemmer, 1994).

This book had me on the edge of my seat with the excitement of revelation. What I was reading seemed like something I had always known but which was now being confirmed for me by the very entities who had overseen the developments. What is more, they seemed to be a very level-headed and sensible set of 'Nine Principles and Forces, personalities if you will, working in complete mutual implication'. This was how their first spokesman, M, described the Nine. The communications came through a Hindu sage in trance and were, it was said, directly from those nine deep-space entities who were conjoined to overlook the development of the Universe and were second only to the Supreme Being.

I have always been a UFO buff and have studied the UFO scene since soon after 1947, the very beginning of the modern era of sightings. For some reason, while there had been spacecraft visiting us for all of time, 1947 seems to have been selected as the year when the reality of the visitors was to be brought home to the developing awareness of the human race as a whole.

This was the year of Kenneth Arnold's encounter with a flight of luminous craft near Mount Rainier in Washington State. Suddenly the world's media began to realize that something was afoot. Within a few days one of these spacecraft 'crash-landed' in the desert of New Mexico. Many who have studied the information that has leaked out believe that this crash was no accident but possibly a way for the space denizens to invade the American top brass in order to establish a direct line of communication with the then most powerful government in the world. Since then, others have come forward with information about other such incidents.

However, whatever may or may not have come of these alleged contacts, it is quite obvious that the citizens of the world have been deliberately kept in ignorance of the true facts of the visitations from space.

Yet the vast majority of people now believe that we are receiving extra-terrestrial visitors, or ETs – and they are not afraid of the idea. The true fear still lurks in the corridors of power and yet the great and the powerful know full well that, in denying the reality of space visitation, they have a tiger by the tail. One day the truth will out and what will they, who have pooh-poohed the idea for so long, then have to say? Again I, although not the confidant of any government or military personage of any kind, do not know. But what I suspect – and what many other observers of the UFO scene also suspect – is that they are already preparing the ground.

Thus we are seeing, and shall continue to see as we advance into the twenty-first century, a new approach by those government agencies whose brief has been, in the past, to denigrate and deny. It is what I can only describe as 'drip-feed'. The American Freedom of Information Acts may have precipitated this slow but sure release of previously classified information on UFOs and their doings but I am fairly certain that it goes considerably deeper than that.

There are indications from the Nine, via Phyllis Schlemmer, that it may not be too long before there is a direct form of contact with us from space. Covert probings in that direction may have already taken place and we do not know how long it may be before something more open occurs. It may not be dependent on the attitudes of governments and military powers. It may not even happen, because the reason for it may disappear, or the intransigence of the power-hungry may preclude it.

What is remarkable, and what singles out our time as one of the most potentially important periods in Earth's history, is that, for the first time, we are being spoken to person to person. No messiahs are being sent. We have grown up enough to be spoken to directly, without parables and sermons. Father is giving us the benefit of his wisdom but, like a wise parent, he is saying that we do not have to follow his advice. At the same time, he is saying that, if we do not follow it, potential disaster looms. Personally, I cannot help feeling proud that such an elevated set of entities consider we are important enough to be spoken to and to benefit from knowledge that previously we only suspected was the truth.

In writing this book, I have first of all looked at the UFOs from their aspects as advanced machines and what we have observed about their behaviour in close encounters of every kind. There are space beings to be seen on many occasions when UFOs land and these beings have missions. The missions are many and varied and often we have no inkling of why they are undertaken. However, one type of mission which deeply affects humanity is when the beings select individuals and abduct them under strong forms of mind control. We may not like these abductions but it is a fact of life and the only way to overcome fear is to confront it and learn what it is that makes us fearful.

UFOs and their world are deeply grounded in the scientific and, if people are to understand that world better, they must confront some of things that have been learned about the physical and subphysical Universe through the rigour and discipline of scientific method. Indeed, I will go further than conventional science allows. I will probe the world that makes the Universe a great cosmic computer, able to act and remember, and show how this may supply the answers to impossible events that science has not yet investigated.

This will help you to understand some of the curiosities of UFO behaviour – things that seem to go against common sense. For example, I will look into what is known about the structure of space. Not from the inconceivable standpoint of the mathematician's five or more dimensional spaces but from our knowledge of the physical realm in which we exist. I will introduce the remarkable work of a retired engineer, R.D. Pearson, who has confronted the problem of what lies under the most fundamental particles we know. He has discovered a universal 'superhighway' of communication channels that may well be the one which allows minds to communicate with each other without the aid of the five senses. Moreover, it is this superhighway which allows psychics to receive knowledge and wisdom from elsewhere of which we would otherwise be ignorant or perhaps only suspect as being the truth.

I will explore the beginnings of the Nine's communications through Uri Geller and follow them with a resumé of relevant communications from 'Tom', as the spokesman for the Council of Nine wishes to be called. This takes us back into important events in Earth's history, particularly the history of ourselves. You will see that the sudden flowerings of civilizations have come about through the direct intervention of representatives of the Twenty-four Civilizations who work as the executives of the Nine. Those representatives have arrived in the kind of vehicles we now call UFOs and they have flitted in and out of our ancient civilizations at will.

Today, intervention from space is more subtle than it seems to have been in ancient times. Then, spacemen – some called prophets – came and led the people directly. That is not the way it is now. Everyone is more scientifically aware. Even without a specifically science-based background at school, we know, and can comprehend, the import of scientific and technological matters. After all, we live with technological marvels and need an understanding of them in order to get the best use out of them. In particular, we are able to appreciate, probably better than career scientists, that space beings must be coming here from elsewhere.

The question most often asked of people who give talks on UFOs is: 'Where do they come from?' The answer has to be: 'From many places.' That is why the phenomenon is so varied and apparently random. However, there is now a considerable literature concerning the planets belonging to the star systems from which some of the visitors come.

Finally I cannot help but address the undoubtedly seamy side of the UFO phenomenon. There is evidence that infiltration of individuals and society as a whole is going on and even becoming more widespread. Again, while such intervention may have changed in detail, it appears that it has been with us throughout recorded time.

Sometimes the UFO scene gets a bit ugly. Domesticated animals are visited by 'vets' with such amazing surgical abilities that those who know about veterinary medicine are amazed. Yet no one sees it done. Only the carcases, often fully drained of their blood, remain as mute testimony to those who have come in the night. We cannot, however much we might wish to, ignore such things. They happen, and often on a massive scale, as between 1975 and 1979 in the USA, when over 7,000 individual cases were reported. Likewise, we cannot gainsay the fact that certain women are made to be the reluctant carriers of space hybrids. They are mothers by proxy but the embryos implanted in their wombs are whisked away to some unknown intensive care unit before they come to term.

5

We are told by the spokesman for the Nine that these less savoury things are the work of 'the opposition' – those who are not exactly committed to the ongoing welfare of Earth's inhabitants. There are, it seems, both goodies and baddies in space but the only way we can defeat the latter is through knowledge. This book is designed to be a small contribution to the growth of that knowledge.

NOTE

Converting Imperial measurements to metric

Throughout this book measurements are mainly given in Imperial. Those readers who are more familiar with metric might find the following useful:

To convert in to cm: × 2.54
(e.g. 2 in = 5.08 cm)

To convert ft to m: × 0.30

To convert yd to m: × 0.91

To convert miles to km: × 1.60

To convert oz to g: × 28.34

To convert lb to g: × 453.60

ONE

VISITORS FROM SPACE

MOTHER EARTH, that keeps us and feeds us, is a ball floating in space. It is just one of countless similar balls throughout the Universe which must harbour life and must therefore be populated by intelligent beings. These beings will not necessarily be like us, although many will be humanoid in shape because that is the shape best adapted for living on the surface of a ball with gravitational attraction. Where they will differ is in their mental and psychic development. Many will long ago have mastered the necessary technology to leap into space and thus discover what lies beyond the confines of their planets. These races are not acting independently. They are part of a master plan and often their 'work' consists of preparing planets for colonization with intelligent creatures, akin to ourselves, and accelerating their development so as to further a plan for the Universe, the final outcome of which we are quite unaware.

However, information that is now being gathered via unconventional sources indicates that Earth is possibly a unique planet whose inhabitants are different from any others in the Universe. Earth is very beautiful physically, as are many of the human beings who live here. Or at least they have the capability to be beautiful. Unfortunately they also have free will, which allows them to be as ugly as sin in body and soul if they so choose. Our new awareness indicates that other space races may not have this choice, nor are they as physical as Earth people. Therefore they have developed their mental powers to make up for their lack of physicality. It is members of some of these races who are visiting us today, and who have been visiting us for as far back as can be probed.

You may not yet be able to accept some of the premises of the last paragraph so let us get onto more familiar ground. Earth is certainly unique in the kingdom of the Sun. No other planet of the solar system can, for one reason or another, support life as we know it: Mars, even if it once had life, is now a largely barren orb; Venus is too hot; Mercury is too close to the Sun; Jupiter is a mass of liquid gases; and so on. Only Earth possesses an environment that has encouraged the development of physical creatures whose intelligence and desire for knowledge and adventure makes them yearn for the stars.

Thus, while we cannot rule out the prospect that other planets are populated by humanoid entities, it would seem that Earth is the only one of the Sun's planets which would truly attract creatures similar to ourselves on journeys through space. This is why we see their spacecraft in our skies, on the ground, and entering and emerging from our oceans. Earth must be a fascinating place for space denizens and they come here year after year, for reasons that make sense to them but which to us are usually meaningless.

We call their craft UFOs, a term used by the military authorities to differentiate them from e.g. aircraft, balloons, airships, which can be identified on their radar screens. It is not a good term because the number of radar contacts with these extra-terrestrial spacecraft is legion and the radar operators have now become very adept at identifying the traces that UFOs make. They have had to become so, because recognizing that an incoming blip was a wayward UFO and not an IBM (Intercontinental Ballistic Missile) was, during the Cold War, a matter of life or death on a grand scale.

Sometimes identification is a simple matter for the radar operators. On 13 August 1956, the crew of a C-47 transport plane sighted a UFO below them and estimated its altitude as about 6,500 ft. At the same time, Lakenheath airbase in Suffolk, UK, was informed by a ground-control station that they had the object on radar and it was moving at over 4,000 mph. Other radar units confirmed the position and speed of the object.

Even today 4,000 mph is, at above Mach 5, an as yet unattainable speed for aircraft and, in 1956, when jet fighters were in their infancy, it was unthinkable. Thus it had to be a UFO.

As it was, around 10.00 p.m., a De Havilland Venom nightfighter was sent up and vectored onto a course to approach the UFO. The Venom also got the object on its own airborne radar (photo 1).

The UFO not only approached the Venom but then manoeuvred into a position on the aircraft's tail and stayed there, mimicking the latter's every move. Both the Venom and UFO were seen on the ground radars as they played out this follow-my-leader game, which went on until the fighter had to land because it was short of fuel. A further Venom was then scrambled and the whole episode eventually occupied some 5 hours.

During all this time, the object was visible from the ground as a brightly shining disc. Thus we had an object in the sky which was seen by the crew of an aircraft, then by several radar stations, and then by an interceptor's radar, as well as by direct observation. At the same time it was visible from the ground.

Such a consistent testimony from competent observers shows that this was some form of rigid craft. It was indeed a flying object, but one that could travel some five to six times faster than the airspeed record of that time. It was not a figment of the imagination. It returned electromagnetic radar waves and so was metallic, or at least surrounded by some kind of aura that reflected such waves. At the same time it generated very bright light but this was no will o' the wisp effect. The light was definitely and clearly being produced by the UFO.

That was some 40 years ago but UFO visitation has by no means ceased. Indeed, sometimes remarkable things happen in your own back yard.

Prior to this book, I wrote another called *UFO Quest* (Watts, 1994) and, as part of the publicity campaign, I appeared on Anglia television on the evening of Friday 2 December 1994. After the programme there was a knock at the door. 'Are you the man who has just been on the TV about UFOs?' asked the teenage boy who stood there, clutching a piece of paper. It appeared that the previous Monday, 28 November, he had been 'buzzed' by a triangular-shaped UFO (fig. 1.1) when cycling with a friend not far from his house. Being boys, they flashed their cycle lights at the thing and, in response, it came and hovered no more than 30 feet above this boy's house. He had drawn a picture of the silent object and wanted to tell me what he had seen. What upset

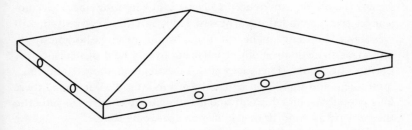

Fig. 1.1   This is roughly the shape of the UFO which was seen low over houses of an estate in Elmstead Market, Essex, UK on 28 November 1994.

me was that he lived just over my back garden fence and I hadn't seen anything!

He was just one of hundreds of other people who saw UFOs over my home area of northeast Essex that evening. One of the most awesome of these encounters that Monday night occurred around 5.00 p.m., when many people on their way home from work saw a vast, low-flying, totally silent craft, estimated to be no less than 1,000 ft long and half as wide, only 100–150 ft above them. It was not the familiar circular form of the traditional 'flying saucer' but triangular and exhibited different combinations of coloured lights.

When the local Essex UFO Research Group collated replies to a questionnaire, they had to sift through reports from no less than 165 people and, while most sightings had occurred around tea-time, many others did not. Nor did they all tally with the vast craft mentioned above. Other, smaller, but still usually triangular UFOs were also reported, including the one which had hovered over the boy's house in the Elmstead Market estate.

The UFO scene is full of oddities. People report what they have seen but that does not mean that it is necessarily what was there. In my previous book, I explained how UFOs could, by means of their surrounding magnetism, apparently change shape and size. It is possible that the UFO which was reported as being 1,000 ft long only appeared to be that size, its image being distorted by the refraction effects induced by its magnetic aura. This is a rather advanced case of the oddities which affect things under water. For example, sticks appear to develop an abrupt bend when they are put into a pail of water and a coin at the bottom of the pail appears to increase in size.

John Ross is a relation of mine by marriage. One Saturday morning in 1974, while living some 5 miles south of Hamilton City, New Zealand, he experienced a classic UFO sighting under circumstances that precluded what he saw being anything conventional. It was about 11.30 a.m. and he was eating brunch when he became aware of a cigar-shaped silver object hovering over a field of maize to the north of his house. The object was, he estimated, about 100 ft long, quite silent and some 25 ft above the ground (fig. 1.2). It stayed there long enough for him, his wife and his two young children to gather in the garden and confirm that John was not seeing things.

This phase lasted some 2 or 3 minutes and then the object began to drift slowly away from them, stopping over a gully, through which ran a stream. It stayed there for a minute or so before resuming its northward flight but, by now, it was slowly gaining height. It stopped again, but this time over the high-tension power lines which lay $\frac{1}{4}$ mile from the house. After a short while it moved away more quickly and climbed into the sky at an angle of about 20 degrees until it disappeared from view.

The above is just one good example of a contact with the spacecraft that visit the skies of the world on a regular basis.

A similar contact, from ancient history, which to me is the best and most detailed, was the sighting of many bright discs in the sky during the reign of the Pharaoh Thutmosis III sometime around 1500 BC (Trench, 1960). According to the translation by Prince Boris de Rachewiltz, the first appeared as a 'circle of fire' in the sky. It was an object 'as wide as it was broad', i.e. either a square or a true circle, and it had no appendages. The report even estimated the diameter as 'one rod'. If this rod is the same as the accepted measurement then the object was 15 ft across, although that could have been its apparent diameter. It must have come close because, according to the scribe of the *Royal Annals*, 'the breath of its mouth had a foul odour'. Now, while modern reports seldom mention smells from UFOs, they certainly do occur.

For example, a 1964 report from a Mr B.E. Parham, who was driving between Gainesville and Lavonia in Georgia, USA, tells of an

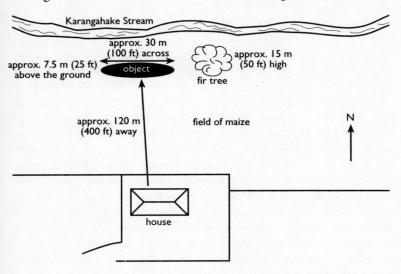

Fig. 1.2   Plan of the encounter which John Ross and his family had with a cigar-shaped UFO in New Zealand in February 1974.

amber-coloured object resembling a flattened cone that flew over his car. It was close to midnight on 29 June and the object not only 'jumped' over his car but also jumped ahead of it and seemed to be interested in his headlights. The object made a noise like 'a million hissing snakes' and left behind an odour similar to embalming fluid. The terrified Parham was subjected to a great wave of heat during the encounter, in which he was followed for 2 miles, but, when he eventually stopped and doused his headlights, the object seemed to lose interest and rose into the sky with a motion like a pendulum (Vallée, J. & J. 1967).

A week later, there was such intense interference on the television set of Mr J. Iveston of Tallulah Falls, Georgia, that the family could not watch it. So they went outside, which is when they saw an object flying at tree-top height within a few hundred metres of the house. It was 9.00 p.m. but this time the object was quite silent and hovered over a neighbour's garden. It was, according to nine witnesses from three houses, a cup-shaped object of which only the lower part was truly visible. It had blinking red lights as well as a steady white one.

As it lifted away, the lights disappeared but a powerful green light shone down and illuminated the surrounding countryside. This object also left behind an odour comparable to that of 'brake fluid or embalming fluid'. Whether this was the same object that Parham had seen a week earlier is difficult to ascertain because, exactly like terrestrial aircraft, UFOs can exhibit many different aspects. We only have to compare a helicopter with a fixed-wing aircraft to realize that, while both use the same medium, air, for support and both may be equipped with forms of jet engine, they are very different. Indeed, terrestrial aircraft are possibly more diverse than other kinds of technological devices. The same seems to apply to extra-terrestrial spacecraft. Yet the most common form is the inverted saucer shape with some kind of dome or cupola. Small UFOs are more often circular than any other shape and Thutmosis' sighting was no exception.

As far as the Ancient Egyptian scribe who recorded the sightings around 1500 BC was concerned, he was careful to state (and probably highly surprised) that the fire-circle 'had no voice' and one of the things which astonishes many UFO observers is the fact that such large craft, with amazing flying abilities, make no noise. In the northeast Essex sighting of the vast triangular craft in November 1994, what staggered the witnesses most was its ability to fly so low and make not a sound.

Yet silence is not a universal rule, as the Parham encounter shows. What we do not know is whether UFOs make noises voluntarily or whether they cannot help it. Having looked at many reports, I tend to support the view that most of the time the latter is the case.

Just as with modern 'waves' of sightings, the one fire-circle in Egypt did not make a wave and 'after some days had passed these things became more numerous in the sky than ever'. They apparently covered the sky from horizon to horizon and were more brilliant than the sun itself. In the translation the fire-circles are quoted as ascending higher in the sky towards the south which is similar behaviour to that which we often observe today (Watts, 1994).

Similar events were recorded over Nuremburg, Germany, on 14 April 1561 (photo 2) and over Basel, Switzerland, just over 5 years later. In the drawings made at the time, the face of the sun has been used to indicate the excessive brightness of the large object which occupies the top centre of both drawings. Having no technical knowledge, the artists have drawn either what they themselves saw or what was described to them by what must have been a very large number of witnesses.

The UFO phenomenon is a very complex one but we do find a consistency in some of their ways of operating and there have been similar reports from all over the globe for many years and, it seems from ancient writings, many millennia.

It is now firmly established that some of the UFOnauts operate their craft in much the same way as we operate aircraft carriers. Very large, usually cigar-shaped craft transport smaller, usually saucer-shaped craft and 'fly them off' to create, in a particular locality, what is called a 'wave' of sightings.

One such well-documented wave provided the main subject for Jacques Vallée's book *Anatomy of a Phenomenon* (1966). This was the flood of sightings that occurred over a large part of France during 1954. Vallée tells us that: 'Dozens of reports were made every day in September, October and November.' A second book, *Challenge to Science* (Vallée, J. & J., 1967) shows that, during the 1954 wave, there was an increasing ground swell of sightings throughout August and the first half of September amounting to an average of four or five a day. Towards the end of September and into October, the numbers grew dramatically until, on many days, between 30 and 60 sightings were being reported. Then, from the middle of October into November, the numbers dropped until there were just the same few reports a day, as there had been in the summer.

This is how UFO waves occur. The numbers of reports may be small initially but they reach a peak and then die away. This is what one would expect if a naval task-force visited a particular portion of the globe and then flew a number of sorties for a period before steaming off for home and shore leave. Anyone living inland from a coast where the task-force was operating, who had maybe no knowledge of its mission, would see aircraft suddenly appearing in their skies. Then the number of sightings would increase to a peak while the task-force carried out its mission, only to be followed by the inevitable run-down before the force left for other waters.

In my previous book, I christened the big carrier-craft 'Leviathans' and I am convinced that it is Leviathans which create waves of UFO sightings. Back in the days when jet fighters were in their infancy, and ground-to-air missiles were either unknown or far less lethal than they are today, the Leviathans would often be able to come relatively close to the ground to despatch their saucers.

There were many great sightings of Leviathans close to the ground, e.g. the Oloron and Gailac sightings in the 1950s and 1960s (see page 15), but they are things of the past, except in areas remote from fighter bases and missile sites. The UFOs are very advanced technologically but they must still respect the modern firepower of our militarists. They also take care not to get involved in close encounters with our aircraft, in case the aircraft are inadvertently destroyed. Nowadays, if a Leviathan expedition is mounted, the mother-ship stays at high altitude. At the time of writing, the sheer number of UFO sorties has diminished. It may be resumed in the future but I wonder whether those who mount these worldwide visitations have mainly accomplished the task which they set themselves and so now only need to keep us under a much lower level of surveillance.

The great carrier craft have been observed under perfect conditions by airline pilots on innumerable occasions. An estimate by Dr Richard Haines (Good, 1992) puts the figure at over 3,000 in the years 1945–90, although I consider that to be an underestimate. We do not know precise figures because, in recent years, airline crews have not been allowed to tell the truth about any UFOs that they may see. This has not always been the case and this is why some of our best reports come from the 1950s.

One such sighting (Buttlar, 1979) involved the BOAC (British Overseas Airways Corporation) airliner *Centaurus* which was on a routine flight from New York's Idlewild Airport to London on 29 June 1954. The flight took off at 5.00 p.m. Eastern Standard Time but, 4 hours later, the Captain, James Howard, at that time one of BOAC's most experienced pilots, had his attention drawn by his co-pilot to a large object surrounded by a number of smaller ones. This group of UFOs was estimated to be some 5 miles away from the *Centaurus* but was flying on a course parallel to the plane. The small objects were holding a circular formation about the big craft and they maintained this position for some 8 miles. The crew described certain changes in shape of the big craft which coincided with changes in the position of the small ones. In the end the whole crew of seven, including the stewardess, plus 14 passengers, observed the formation.

Changes of shape are often reported by reliable witnesses of UFO events and they have been recorded on film. In the *UFO Annual* (Jessup, 1956) there are two photographs taken over a 15-minute interval by a press photographer. To the photographer it was a 'strange light in the sky'. The first picture shows a capsule-shaped object just three times longer than it is broad. In the second picture it has transformed into a rod-like device standing at the same angle in the sky but now over ten times longer than it is broad. Such seemingly impossible changes can be accomplished if the device is surrounded by a very strong magnetic field (see page 60).

To return to the *Centaurus* incident, the Captain radioed Goose Bay, Labrador, for a plane to be sent to investigate but, before it arrived, the large craft absorbed the smaller ones and then took off at what was described as 'a fantastic speed'. All told, the formation had flown parallel to the airliner for no less than 18 minutes, which represented 50 miles. In his summing up of what they had witnessed Howard said:

> It was a solid thing, I'm sure of that, manoeuvrable and intelligently controlled – a sort of base ship linked somehow with those smaller attendant satellites. There is no rational explanation – except on the basis of spaceships and flying saucers.

This is the kind of description given by most people who have clearly witnessed the operating patterns of Leviathans. It appears that, somehow, the mother-ship maintains an automatic hold over her brood so that the whole formation acts as one. When no other consideration obtains, the satellite saucers slave to their parent craft but, when the latter wishes to move away at high speed, the small craft are flown into the maw of the parent.

Another Leviathan event was recorded by Vallée (1966). It took place at Oloron, some 16 miles southwest of Pau in the Département of Bearn in southern France, at about 12.50 p.m. on 17 October 1952. A teacher, M. Pringent, among a number of other witnesses, describes what he saw.

There was a white cylindrical object, long and thin, standing at a 45 degree angle. It was surrounded by about 30 yellow discs with domes. These discs travelled in pairs, maintaining a constant distance between each other. When they came close to one another a kind of electric arc, or discharge, suddenly appeared between the two objects.

This event was followed on radar by the station at Mont-de-Marsan while the witnesses saw 'white smoke' emerging from the top of the cylindrical object. This may have been the source of the 'angel hair' that fell in large amounts.

Angel hair is a well-documented accompaniment to some UFO sightings and consists of white fibres that usually dissolve spontaneously on touching the ground. Vallée suggests that the fibres must be made of ionized atoms. However, it seems to me that a similar thing happens when ball lightning earths itself and it has been suggested that, in this case, anti-matter (see page 55) is involved. A photograph of angel hair that fell over half a square mile at Horseheads, New York, on 23 February 1955, can be found in the *UFO Annual* (Jessup, 1956). A local chemistry professor identified it as 'radioactive, heavily damaged cotton fibre'. Radioactivity would be associated with anti-matter but not with ionized atoms.

Ten days later the same kind of event occurred 140 miles to the northwest, at Gaillac in the Département of Tarn. This time a Leviathan, its outer surface wreathed in what looked like wisps of cloud, stood on end for 10 minutes over the town, surrounded by 16 saucers. Again angel hair fell. The 'cloud-cigar' was also sighted by observers at a meterological station at Brives-Charensac, who saw it remain motionless for half a minute before moving off. At the same time they observed a silvery metallic disc that crossed their sky towards the southeast.

In *UFO Quest* (Watts, 1994) I detailed several other observations (including personal ones) of the Leviathan type of carrier craft and its mode of operation. There seems no doubt that, among a welter of apparent one-offs, this is something we do know about the way in which waves of sightings are generated. Or maybe we should be cautious and say *were* generated because this form of overt visitation seems, since about 1980, to have been replaced by a more subtle form of intervention. There are still many, many craft to be seen but they come and go much more stealthily.

TWO

ENCOUNTERS, CLOSE AND OTHERWISE

IN THE OPENING chapter I recounted some typical reports of UFOs. They were selected from sources which even the sceptical reader might find acceptable because this book is not intended to be a catalogue of UFO observations. Such reports are legion and the reader will find many other books full of them. In this chapter, I want to put the UFO phenomenon in context as far as our sketchy knowledge of space visitors allows.

It may help those who are not too familiar with the UFO scene if I categorize the UFO reports. The most widely accepted classification is that due to J. Allen Hynek and made familiar to most people by the Stephen Spielberg film *Close Encounters of the Third Kind*. Hynek started off gamekeeper and turned poacher in that he was once the official astronomical consultant to the US Air Force's 'Project Blue Book'. It was to Blue Book that all the official UFO reports filtered and Hynek was in a privileged position and able to see them. His scientific credentials are impeccable. Some time Director of the Lindheimer Astronomical Research Center at Northwestern University as well as Chairman of its Astronomy Department, he was also Associate Director of the Smithsonian Astrophysical Observatory in Cambridge, Massachusetts, and headed its NASA-sponsored satellite tracking programme. Like many other scientists, he has become convinced that UFOs exist and feels that we must confront this visitation from space and not, as the US Air Force and other authorities try to do, sweep it under a carpet of denial and ridicule.

Hynek's classification is as follows:

1   Distant UFOs:
(a) Nocturnal lights.
(b) Daylight discs.
(c) Radar-visuals.

2 Closer UFOs:
(a) Close encounters of the first kind.
(b) Close encounters of the second kind.
(c) Close encounters of the third kind.

NOCTURNAL LIGHTS

Lights in the sky doing odd things are the most frequently observed phenomena, if only because such a light immediately attracts the eye. Such lights command attention when they remain stationary for minutes on end, are too big or the wrong colour to be a star or a planet, or do not act as a terrestrial aircraft would do, i.e. they move on the kind of erratic courses which aircraft are incapable of taking.

I remember once looking up at the constellation Ursa Major (Great Bear) and being intrigued to find that there were not four stars in the 'body' of the bear but five! Then, as I watched, this fifth star moved slowly away. Not a mind-blowing observation but the kind of experience that thousands of people must have had over the years. This happened in the days before earth-satellites so it could not be attributed to any such cause. In any case, when first seen, the 'star' was stationary.

However, nocturnal lights are the least satisfactory when you are trying to find out the nature of the visitation from space but they do prove how very prevalent UFOs are. Often a UFO that would go unnoticed by day will be reported by night.

DAYLIGHT DISCS

Hynek (1972) quotes the following as a typical example of this category.

What I saw was a small silvery white disc of unknown diameter, unknown altitude, but definite physical existence; it first appeared stationary, under visual observation, for about ten minutes. Then it moved across the sky, visually passing under the clouds and finally disappeared into the white clouds. No sound could be detected.

The white dot stood still too long and moved too silently to have been an aircraft; it appeared to travel in a direction distinctly inconsistent with the direction of the clouds so as to preclude . . . that it was a balloon.

As with most UFO reports from ordinary people it is obvious that this observer has already considered the possible natural causes and it is only because there is no alternative that has he decided that the object must be a UFO. The vast majority of those who observe UFOs are able to give a fairly accurate and detailed account of what they saw. They are people who, in their daily lives, perform complex and responsible tasks in the community and are not to be fooled by the debunkers making out that what they saw was a balloon, or a bit of fluff illuminated by the sun, or some other equally stupid suggestion. A typical daylight disc observation is shown in photo 3.

Those observers of UFOs whom the debunking authorities fear most are the open-minded scientists and the aircrews. This is why no aircrew, either military or civilian, now dares risk giving a detailed account of the many UFOs they encounter. It may be more than their jobs are worth.

RADAR-VISUALS

We have already given a really excellent example of this category (see page 8) with the UFO which was intercepted by the Venom night-fighters and so we will pass on to the 'close encounters'.

CLOSE ENCOUNTERS OF THE FIRST KIND

Hynek considers UFOs that come close to the observer but which do not produce any physical effects, either on the observer or the environment, to be in this category. Nevertheless, such events are in essence no different from those in which a close UFO causes, say, the faces of witnesses to redden, as if sunburned, or induces nausea. However, such cases show that, if you should be close to a UFO, it is not necessarily going to affect you in any apparent way. I say 'apparent' because there can be subtle after-effects of which the witness may not be aware.

A good example comes from an experienced observer, Raymond Fowler (Hynek, 1972). It happened at Beverly, Massachusetts, USA, and the object was described as a 'luminous platter' which hovered over a schoolhouse. However, it not only hovered but approached the watchers more than once in a manner that made them think it would descend upon them personally. During one of these very close encounters, a witness said:

All I could see above my head was the blurry atmosphere and brightly lit-up lights flashing (not blinking) slowly around. I was very excited – not scared – very curious. I would not have run at all except for the fact the object got too close and I thought it might crash on my head.

Another witness describes how the object was directly over them and at rooftop level. He described it as being like a plate but solid and yet totally silent. He said that he was 'fascinated, stunned, unable to think' and he automatically ran away.

The object was still there when the police arrived and they described it in the same general terms but gave more details. They said it had three lights – red, green and white – and commented on the craft's silence. The object moved back and forth over the school at least twice and then went away but the duration of the sighting was a full 45 minutes.

Hynek, from his extensive experience of reading Blue Book reports, says that the similarity of the close encounters' reports is remarkable. If, as has been suggested, the witnesses are experiencing some sort of hallucination, he would have expected the differences in reported events to be much, much greater. As it is, the differences often lie in the inability of the witnesses adequately to describe such strange experiences.

CLOSE ENCOUNTERS OF THE SECOND KIND

Although he introduces this category as different from the one above, Hynek still does not consider that they truly differ in kind. It is just that, in first kind encounters, there is nothing to show for the UFOs visitation while, in the second kind, there is. However, the usefulness of the second kind encounters lies in the proof that the phenomenon was real and not some figment of the imagination. Not that I personally think many of the reports are made up. The witnesses are affected too deeply for that and anyone interviewing them is usually struck by their obvious, sincerely held belief that they are describing what they actually experienced.

One of the effects which falls under this category is the so-called electromagnetic (EM) effect. The EM effect is one which stops vehicles which have spark-plug ignition and is thought to be due to some form of electromagnetic radiation or aura from a nearby UFO. There have been several cases where both diesel- and petrol-engined vehicles have been approached or overflown by UFOs and, while the petrol engine was either drastically reduced in power or stopped altogether, the diesel continued to function (Lorentzen, 1969).

It has to be said here that this is not the only way in which UFOs can control vehicles. There is evidence for an 'inertial' effect, which in some cases places a restraining force on the vehicle over and above what may happen to its engine power.

The EM effect is thought to be caused by magnetism broadcast from the UFO. One of the most consistent emanations from UFOs is a strong magnetic field. It may well be alternating and can, by acting on the ignition coil, reduce the efficiency of the sparks at the plugs, thus lowering the power of the engine. In some cases this only makes the engine sluggish while, in others, it kills the engine stone dead (Watts, 1994).

In some cases, the battery is affected and there are cases where the battery has in fact boiled. The latter indicates an alternating magnetic field entraining the ions in the electrolyte (battery acid) and so inducing an alternating current which, acting against the internal resistance of the battery, generates a great deal of heat and so leads to boiling.

However, UFOs affect the electrical system of vehicles in various ways: sometimes ignition fails while lights remain as bright as ever; in other cases, both ignition and lights fail.

One of the latter cases is reported by Hynek. Three women in a car saw a lighted craft to their left which at first they took to be a helicopter. The driver (Kim) told how, as they drew close to the object, the car would not accelerate and lost power as if 'it wasn't getting enough juice'. Then the engine stalled and the lights and radio went out. The craft hovered close to them while Kim tried vainly to re-start the car. Then the object began to move rapidly away, after which the car started quite normally. There was no noise from the UFO and the street lights were not affected. From the witnesses' descriptions it appears that the craft was lens-shaped (or maybe egg-shaped) with something resembling car headlights around its surface.

Then, under this category, come the landing marks. On 24 April 1964 an egg-shaped object landed in the New Mexico desert at a place called Socorro (for map, see fig. 14.1). A state policeman, Lonnie Zamora, saw an object emitting a bright light coming down onto the desert. It did not appear to be far from a dynamite store and Zamora was understandably concerned. So he drove after it, in time to see a white or silvery object standing on four unequal legs in a gully. Two 'large kids or small adults' were standing near it, dressed in white coveralls. By the time Zamora had driven around a hill to get a closer look, the two figures had disappeared and the craft took off with a thunderous noise. (Stanford, 1978).

When other police, alerted by Zamora, arrived at the place where the craft had been, they found deep marks in the ground and traces of calcination. A photo of one of the imprints can be found in the above reference.

So here we have one of many reports of physical effects left by UFOs on the ground but we also have a new dimension – figures are seen near the craft.

CLOSE ENCOUNTERS OF THE THIRD KIND

On the night of Sunday, 21 August 1955, a landing event occurred at Kelly, Kentucky – a small town some 80 miles northwest of Nashville, Tennessee. At about 7 p.m., Billy Sutton, the teenage son of the household, went out to get water from the well and came back to report that some kind of flying object had landed behind the Sutton's farmhouse. None of the eight adults (there were also three children) in the house took much notice but, an hour later, a 'little man' was seen coming towards the house. The creature came with its arms raised and, when it came too close for comfort, two of the men blasted it with shotguns.

The creature's response was to somersault backwards and disappear into the darkness. Then, when the men had returned to the house, another creature appeared at a window and again the men fired at it through the flyscreen. It also appeared to have been hit and disappeared.

Outside, the men found another creature on the roof and shot at it, apparently knocking it over the roof. There was another in a tree at some distance but, when this one was shot at, it 'floated' to the ground.

The entities were impervious to the bullets and, after being knocked down, were immediately up again, only to disappear. One of the creatures was knocked off a barrel by a 0.22 round, which was heard to strike it, but all it did was to tumble off and roll along the ground.

By about 11.00 p.m., having expended some four boxes of 0.22 shells, the family decided that they had had enough. For one thing the children were extremely frightened, not to mention the adults. They piled into cars and headed for Hopkinsville police station.

The police were convinced by the family's state of terror that there was something to be investigated and, summoning help, arrived at the farm around 12.30 a.m. However, all they could report by that time was several 'strange meteors' that passed over their vehicles with a loud swishing sound.

The entities themselves were described as $3\frac{1}{2}$–4 feet high, with huge eyes and hands, large, pointed ears, and arms that hung almost to the ground (fig. 2.1). Their suits gave them the appearance of being 'nickel-plated'. It was their eyes, however, that commanded most attention. They were large and sensitive, apparently programmed to make the entities retreat when bright lights were trained on them. They had no pupils and no eyelids.

Maybe whoever programmed these creatures – because they were almost certainly some form of advanced robot – had been watching Westerns because the 'men' always raised their long arms in the air as they approached. However, this supplicant posture did nothing for the trigger-happy Sutton household, who described how the creatures, whenever they were hit, floated to the ground. They also seemed to float as they approached.

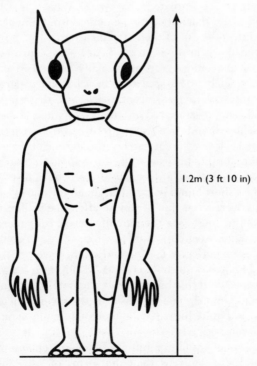

1.2m (3 ft 10 in)

Fig. 2.1   Sketch of humanoid seen at Kelly, Kentucky, on 21 August 1955, based on witness's accounts. (After Bowen, 1969)

This is a well-documented and investigated incident and it illustrates the class of event which Hynek says he would rather not have included in his book. This shows the resistance there is, even amongst experienced investigators, to the idea that UFOs are craft with occupants. Yet, at the same time, Hynek quotes Vallée's catalogue of close-encounter cases. Vallée lists 1,247 cases, of which 750 were actual landings; of these landings over 300 (around 40 per cent) had reported humanoids with them.

As an example of a reliable report of humanoid UFO denizens, I will paraphrase a long chapter in Timothy Good's *Alien Liaison* (1992), which deals with the ordeals of 'John', 'Barbara' and 'Jim', who collectively owned a ranch in Colorado. They experienced many strange effects after moving to the ranch, including electrical failures and someone, or something, walking around the house, which might have been of the type of hairy humanoid creature called a 'Bigfoot' (see page 199 and photo 16). They saw UFOs and humanoids and some of their cattle were mutilated (chapter 18). What was strangest of all were the 'messages' that at one time emerged from nowhere and at another seemed to come out of their stereo system.

Jim had previously been a US Air Force security officer and public relations man and was professionally trained in psychological and biological sciences. He seemed to have become programmed during an encounter with a translucent black box that hummed. This box mysteriously disappeared in the short interval between him first approaching it and then, having returned to his car, coming the short distance back to where it had been. Later, he observed a light in some trees and, despite his fear, walked towards it to find two men waiting for him. They were $5\frac{1}{2}$ feet tall, dressed in tight-fitting 'flight suits'. They had short blond hair and large but normal eyes. However, their features were very fine – almost effeminate. The thing which impressed Jim most was their totally relaxed manner; they addressed him by name, opening with 'How nice of you to come'. They seemed to Jim to be perfectly normal and might have been simply acquaintances that he had stumbled on, had it not been for a slightly glowing disc-shaped craft that he could just see some 50 ft from them. The men apologized in colloquial English for the inconvenience that they had caused and told him that 'a more equitable arrangement will be worked out between us'.

It is much rarer for human beings to encounter these human-looking UFO denizens than the forms of small humanoids called 'Greys', but George Adamski (Leslie & Adamski, 1953) was ridiculed for daring to state that he also met such an entity at 12.30 p.m. on

Thursday, 20 November 1952, 'on the Californian desert just over ten miles from Desert Center toward Parker, Arizona' (for map, see fig. 14.1).

Even so Good (1992) records several similar meetings with ETs which were quite human in appearance. One of these occurred in the north of England in 1963 when a close friend of Good's made contact with two human-looking ETs after he had witnessed the landing of a disc. According to this contactee, there were telepathic communications between the ETs and a small group of scientists who 'were liaising with the aliens'. In this case, as in others yet to be considered, information was passed, together with demonstrations of out of this world abilities. The contactees were told that the ETs had bases on Earth and had been responsible, over a very long period, for the genetic upgrading of the human race. We shall see that there is more evidence for this contention as we proceed.

In this survey of the breadth of the UFO observations I am only including a few of the myriad cases which could be cited but we will look more deeply into the 'third kind' cases in the next chapter.

There are at least two more categories of encounter which Hynek, in an attempt to keep his feet somewhere on the ground of scientific enquiry, could not bring himself to add to his list.

CLOSE ENCOUNTERS OF THE FOURTH KIND

The ordeal of Betty and Barney Hill (see page 157) is just one example of an increasing number of cases of abduction that are coming to light. In these cases the unfortunate victims are not harmed physically but their nightmare is often written deeply into their subconscious and surfaces later as psychological problems.

The UFO denizens induce a form of amnaesia in their abductees, who are then led or, in some cases 'floated', from where they are into the maw of a waiting space vehicle. There they are subjected to various forms of medical investigation. Afterwards, they are returned more or less unharmed but find, when they 'wake up', that some time has passed. They are unable to account for this missing time, nor for the fact that, in some cases, if they have been abducted from cars, they are no longer in the same place. In some classic instances, they are hundreds of kilometres from the last place they remember.

On 5 November 1975, a team of tree fellers came across a UFO hovering in a clearing. They had finished work and were driving home, the location being 11 miles south of Heber in Arizona, USA. They said that the disc-shaped object was hovering some 16 ft off the ground and was only a matter of 30 ft away from them when the driver brought the truck to a stop (Buttlar, 1979). The light from the UFO spread a golden glow over the whole area surrounding it.

Spontaneously, one of the gang. Travis Walton, jumped down and ran towards the UFO, totally disregarding the entreaties of his work-mates to came back. He approached the craft closely by crawling through the undergrowth but then stood up in response to a shrill noise. The craft shot a dazzling beam of blue light at his chest and he lost consciousness.

Meanwhile the driver had panicked and driven off at high speed to observe the events from a somewhat safer distance. The light from the UFO disappeared and the others, when they thought it safe, went back to find, to their consternation, that Walton had completely disappeared.

It was 5 days later, and not far from where he had been abducted, that Walton reappeared. He was totally exhausted by what had happened to him in the intervening period but he did not know what that was. However, he showed signs of having been injected in the arm.

Under regression hypnosis, he recalled thinking he was in hospital because he was lying on a metal table with severe pains in his head and chest. However the 'doctors', who were observing him with large oval brown eyes, were figures about 5 feet high, with narrow faces and bald heads. They had no nails on their fingers and their skin was a shade of chalky white. The description fits the kind of extra-terrestrials which have become known as Greys although not all Greys have five fingers as these did (compare fig. 3.1).

At one stage Walton was so incensed by his predicament that he was preparing to throw himself at his captors. However, they ob-viously read his intentions and withdrew, leaving him alone. He was then able to walk around the craft. He described a curious chair whose arms supported a console and a screen. As he drew closer to it, the room became progressively darker and he then found himself looking, apparently into space, through the wall of the craft. On playing with the console he discovered that it was a form of navigation device in that it indicated motion of the craft against the stars. He was then con-fronted by a tall human-like man in a blue one-piece suit with a transparent helmet. The man was tanned but had strangely bright golden-hazel eyes. Walton remembers being struck by his hairlessness, even though he sported a good head of sandy-blond hair.

This man took Walton on a guided tour outside the craft, which was now apparently at some space port. He was shown several other craft, similar to the one which abducted him but smaller. There were also two other men and a very physically attractive woman in a room that they entered. These people had the same colour hair and in many ways resembled the first man almost as if they were members of the same family. Eventually he was placed on a table and the last thing he remembers is the woman approaching him with what looked like a tubeless oxygen mask. He woke up on a pavement west of Heber but recalls seeing a circular object departing into the sky.

What happened to Walton during all those 5 days of his 'captivity' is unknown because it seems that he was kept under very deep sedation. In this, his case is atypical. Normally, abductees are given a medical examination, much of which they can recall under hypnosis, and are returned to *terra firma* once this has been accomplished. In Walton's case the details were all recalled through the conscious mind, and hypnosis produced no further information. During those 5 days he could only have been a passenger on the UFO while it performed whatever tasks it had to do because, if not, where was he all that time? It would appear therefore that he was one of that select band who have been taken for rides in UFOs. The trouble is he could recall nothing about the journey. And this leads us to the fifth category.

CLOSE ENCOUNTERS OF THE FIFTH KIND

These are the relatively rare events where contactees or abductees are actually taken on flights by their 'captors'. A fair number of them have now come to light and thus when George Adamski claimed to have such an experience back in the 1950s (Adamski, 1956), he could possibly have been speaking the truth. At the time, and even since his untimely death, he has been held up to ridicule for suggesting that anyone could travel in a flying saucer. We shall look at some of these out of this world experiences in chapter 14.

Thus, in the light of our developing knowledge of the phenomenon, and with the general public's much higher level of acceptance of what and what is not possible as far as space visitors are concerned, two more classes have been added to Hynek's famous list of categories. We shall look into these in later chapters.

THREE

MODERN INTERVENTION

IN DAYS OF OLD, beings who had their roots in deep space, came and manifested themselves as human. They walked as men, with men, but their abilities made those they came to help believe them to be gods, if not God himself.

Ordinary people then lived much simpler lives than we do today. They had little or no knowledge of technology beyond that which they needed to perform their daily tasks. Now all that has changed. The explosion of information which washes over us today, as well as universal education, has seen to that. Whether we are basically happier than our forefathers is open to question but we are certainly vastly more aware of what is going on around us. We have also been subjected, over the last 50 years or so, to an exact but subtle change in our thinking about the space that surrounds us.

Not very long ago the sky was just a place in which clouds rode, from where bolts of lightning struck, and in which stars and planets shone like jewels in the firmament of night. The planets could possibly influence us but the stars were totally remote and could not conceivably have any involvement with human life on this planet. Earth was an island in space and nothing that really concerned humanity was in that space. Space was empty and devoid of life forms of any kind. Even reports of rains of frogs and fishes from the skies did not dent the conception that such things could not happen because there was nothing up there to make them happen.

Then, in 1947, just 2 short years after the end of World War 2, came what was, for most, another impossible event. Otherwise stable people, including pilots, reported seeing discs and other strange objects in the sky. Brave, trusting souls actually came forward to report even stranger manifestations and had to suffer the subsequent ridicule. Now we know that 1947 was not the beginning of the UFO saga, although it is often taken to be the horizon year for the opening of mankind's eyes to the evidence that we are not completely alone in the Universe.

Since then, millions of people have seen UFOs and dozens of books have been written describing their more spectacular manifestations. Slowly and inexorably the drip-drip-drip of publicity about flying saucers has had its effect and we have gone from a situation where very few people believed that there were flying saucers to one where the majority are quite convinced of their existence. They may not wish to be UFO buffs themselves but they are fully prepared to believe those who say that UFOs represent intelligences visiting us from space. From being what were thought to be figments of deranged minds, the UFOs have become solid objects which ordinary level-headed people occasionally see.

This is a great step forward in mankind's collective consciousness and it provides a solid and developing foundation for whoever, or whatever, may visit us from space in the twenty-first century. This growing awareness, this raising of the majority's acceptance level from negative to positive, may not simply be a chance event. It could well be the UFO denizens themselves who have set it in motion so that eventually we will all come to accept them. Not in the way portrayed by Hollywood movies, where little green men land and say 'Take me to your leader', but in much subtler guises.

In this way, as in many others, UFOs are affecting us and the way we think about our world and the possibilities of worlds beyond. Our own faltering first steps into space have helped this new awareness tremendously but we have had to call a halt to space exploration because we have found that the space we thought was ours is actually someone else's and has been since time began. We have invaded what we thought was a desert island and found it full of natives who are vastly more at home in it than we are. A chronological list of encounters between astronauts and UFOs on the Mercury, Gemini and Apollo missions between May 1963 and December 1972 is given in *The Roswell Incident*, by Berlitz and Moore (1980).

Perhaps the greatest leap forward in our acceptance of the UFO phenomenon lies in our recognition that UFOs are vehicles for ETs. Often, when a UFO touches down on Earth, humanoid beings are subsequently seen near it. These beings do some things which we may recognize as the kind of things we might do if we dropped in on an unfamiliar planet.

For example, in 1954, the owner of a farm near Campo Grande, in Brazil, reported that he was fishing some 400 yards from his house when his dog began to howl. This drew his attention to a strange object which looked like two spheres, a tiny one rotating around a much larger one, hovering some 6 ft above the ground.

The witness was staggered to see three creatures descend from the large sphere. He described them as very small humans whose movements were somewhat like the Kelly ETs described in the previous chapter: rather rapid and agile as if they had little weight.

One of them held in his arms a roughly basket-shaped object, which glowed, while the other wielded a metallic tube with a type of funnel at the end. Using the tube like a vacuum cleaner, the two creatures collected material from the edge of the river and this went into the basket. This was taken into the sphere, after which the ETs re-emerged and repeated the operation. Once the operators had returned to the large sphere, it took off at high speed and disappeared into the sky, accompanied by the smaller object.

When he went to look, the witness found man-sized square holes had been created in the ground and enquiries revealed that similar holes had been found by other people in the locality (Lorentzen, 1969).

In November 1967, a very similar incident occurred near Fording-bridge, Hampshire, UK, when Karl Barlow's truck was immobilized by a UFO which came down in the road some 45 ft ahead of him. Out of a port-hole in the bottom of the object emerged a kind of vacuum-cleaner hose which proceeded to suck up grass, gravel and dead leaves from the sides of the road (Lorentzen, 1969).

During the years 1988–90 the island of Puerto Rico was the scene of many UFO encounters, some of which were quite spectacular. One encounter, on 31 August 1990, involved a typical sighting of aliens.

Miguel Figueroa, who owned a small café not far from the Laguna Cartagena, seems to have been contacted via a dream because he got up at 3.30 a.m, worried that someone had broken into his café. When he arrived something was certainly going on because there were no less than ten cars parked in front of it and a knot of people were obviously alarmed about something.

His enquiries revealed that the occupants of the cars were driving down Road 101 when they were confronted by a bunch of strange little men with big heads. Certain that they had all been seeing things, despite one woman being hysterical and the men nervous, Figueroa drove down the road in the direction which little men were supposed to have taken.

About a kilometre further on he was astounded to see that the group at his café had been telling the truth. As quoted in Good (1991), Figueroa said:

They were five of the strangest creatures I have ever seen. The biggest was about 5 feet tall and the smallest about 3 feet tall. They were skinny, with large pear-shaped heads, long pointy ears, big slanted eyes and almost no nose – only small holes. Their mouths were almost like a slit – very little. They all had long arms with three fingers on each hand and three toes on their feet.

He went on to say that he could not make out whether they had one-piece suits on or were naked but that they were greyish in colour from top to toe (fig. 3.1).

They were about 50 ft away when first sighted and Figueroa wanted a closer look so he drove after them. He got so close that the group were alerted and turned to look at him, whereupon a very bright light 'like a welding light' shot from their eyes and temporarily blinded him. He was then apparently telepathically told not to go any closer.

As soon as his sight returned he once again followed the creatures down the road but this time he kept his distance. He saw them jump

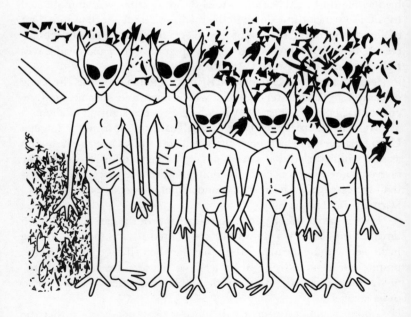

Fig. 3.1 Impression of the 'Greys' encountered by Miguel Figueroa in Puerto Rico, on 31 August 1990. (After Good, 1991)

over a bridge and into a river gully leading to the Laguna Cartagena and he watched them go down it until they were out of sight.

Next day he went back to the same place and proved to himself that he had not been dreaming because there were three-toed prints in the river mud. To be quite sure, he went away and came back again in the middle of the day, and was relieved to find that the tracks were still to be seen.

Figueroa was deeply affected by this encounter and went so far as to say that it had ruined his life. He could not get the faces of the ETs out of his mind. However, there was more to contribute to his distress.

Late the next day he received a phone call that threatened him with 'something bad' if he talked to anyone about what he had seen or where the creatures had gone. The man spoke in Spanish with an American accent but what upset Figueroa was how the person obtained his phone number, which was not only on a private line but listed under someone else's name!

Here we have a description of 'Greys' which tallies well with similar testimony from many other parts of the world. Not all Greys have three digits and toes but their facial features are very similar, especially the very big slanted eyes and the lack of nose. They are obviously not of normal flesh and blood because eyes designed to receive light do not have the capacity to project it. Greys are undoubtedly some form of very advanced robot capable of a great deal of independent action but possibly under an external control.

Receiving a phone call from someone who somehow knows your restricted phone number is not an isolated occurrence. In *The Warminster Mystery* Arthur Shuttlewood (1967) describes the amazing wave of UFO events that occurred around the small Wiltshire town of Warminster, UK, between Christmas Day 1964 and April 1966. The latter date was chosen by Shuttlewood simply because he had to wind up his book somewhere. The UFOs that plagued Warminster and its surroundings did not go away on that date.

Among the events that changed local paper reporter Shuttlewood into a UFO buff prepared to relate, if not to accept, the weird happenings of that unearthly period, was one relating to Figueroa's phone call.

During September–October 1965 Shuttlewood was the recipient of some strange phone calls. He would like to believe that they were hoaxes but knows full well that they were not. They came from beings ostensibly from the planet Aenstria (which they called the Cantel Aenstria). They gave their names as Caellsan, Selorik and Traellison and they interestingly gave their number as that of a public telephone kiosk at Boreham Field, east of Warminster town centre. Yet Shuttlewood never once heard the unmistakable sound of coins being inserted and dropping into the box when the button was pressed. The calls came in rapidly and clearly but with a certain amount of crackling, resembling electrical interference. In other words the calls were not coming from a caller, human or otherwise, in a phone kiosk but by some direct intervention into Shuttlewood's telephone line, which would account for the electrical interference sounds. Such an intervention would account for Figueroa's mysterious caller being able to tap into his line without having to know his number. We have already been told by some of our visitors (Puharich, 1974) that they are able to use any of our means of communication and sending messages down telephone lines is probably child's play to them. They have shown us many times that they can speak to us in versions of any language they choose.

The general thrust of the messages received by Shuttlewood was in the same vein as that given through many other people ostensibly contacted by ETs. They warned against the wholesale destruction of Earth's resources. They cautioned against the lust for power and domination but said they were unable to make humanity follow their dictats. They, in fact, gave much the same message as has been bequeathed to us via other channels, including psychic ones. Humanity has free will and that cannot be interfered with. Only by reason can the governments and peoples of the world be made to see the errors of their ways. Yet the path that is being trodden by the majority of the Earth's inhabitants is still downhill towards eventual destruction of the civilization which they and their forebears have struggled, suffered and died for. In that message may rest one of the major reasons for the intervention of UFOs in our lives.

FOUR

POWERFUL ABILITIES

O N THE AFTERNOON of Saturday, 4 April 1992, Alan Hilton, a homeopath and UFO researcher, was worrying about why friends he expected had not arrived. They were driving from Peterborough to his home in Kent but were already over 2 hours late. Eventually the party, consisting of Alan's friend John, his wife Susan and their baby daughter Samantha, plus Pamela, a business colleague, arrived.

Alan was surprised to find that the party showed no awareness of having arrived some 3 hours later than anticipated. However, late that night, John confided that there was something odd about his milometer. It should have registered 200 miles but it showed 300 miles and his petrol tank was all but empty.

As Alan specialized in psychological regression techniques, he took John back to when, having driven across country to Leicester to pick up Pamela, the whole carload of people came under some strange influence. This led to John driving not south from Leicester to London but in the opposite direction and no one in the car, including the driver, was aware of it. They eventually ended up in a remote country area of central England, although John had no idea where.

It was then that he recalled the amazing thing that happened to them. Without any of them feeling the least degree of panic the car was wafted bodily upwards into the clouds and into the maw of a waiting 'spaceship'. This is not the first time that vehicles and other heavy objects have been made to overcome gravity in the presence of UFOs but it is certainly rare for a 3-month-old baby to be included in the party.

It must be stated here that John, while not being exactly a UFO sceptic, had no prior interest in the subject and had never read anything about abduction cases. Yet the entities who escorted them from the car were, from his description, typical of the extra-terrestrial

Greys. They were, he said, friendly in nature, 3–4 feet tall, with large heads and slanted eyes.

Once inside the craft and out of the car, they were placed on tables and given various forms of medical examination. John describes a dome-shaped device being placed over his head which, he surmised, was to check his 'brain waves'. The Greys showed a particular interest in the baby but did not pick her up or treat her any differently from the adults.

John said they were given explanations of certain things after the examination but, even under hypnosis, he could not recall what had been said.

They came back to reality with a jolt as if they had suddenly been let down from above. Astoundingly, they were now on the M25 and the party thought they had travelled straight from Leicester and had no recollection of the length of time that the journey had taken.

Next day John's account was relayed to the women. When prompted, they also recalled aspects of the encounter, including the weightless lifting of the car and the placing of domed devices on their heads but they declined regression hypnosis. They seemed to want nothing whatever to do with the matter.

We can quote one other case of a whole car abduction. It is given by Budd Hopkins (1988) in his book *Intruders*, which largely concerns the abduction experiences of the girl he calls Kathy Davis and her elder sister Laura. I shall use Hopkins' pseudonyms although the real names are now known.

While driving home one Sunday afternoon in the autumn of 1965, Laura was compelled to leave the main road and park behind a church. The next thing she knew was that it was dark, she saw a brightly lit UFO rising away from the car, and she had lost 2 hours of her life. Under subsequent regression hypnosis she recalled having been lifted up in her car into the UFO. She could see the parking lot below her and her car was not in it. She has vague recollections of a table and shadowy grey figures inside the UFO but nothing else has been reported.

Apart from the amazing car abduction, there is another curious twist to the John and family encounter. On the way home, when they were discussing these 'impossible' events, they suddenly felt that they should look for something in the car. What they found was a strange cube of metal with sides about 1 in long (photo 4). I have personally handled this cube and must confess that the granular structure of its faces is different to any piece of metal I have ever seen. Because of its odd appearance, I cannot discount John's regressed explanation that it is a 'power cell' from the UFO's lighting system. John also gave other technical details of the device used to generate power for the lighting system (Hilton, 1993a & b). Later investigation gave the specific gravity (relative mass) of the metal as 5.25, somewhere between titanium and antimony, but my book of physical constants yields no metal with this value. What we do not know is whether the cube is solid throughout, and an alloy, or whether it is of a metal of higher specific gravity with something else inside it.

Afraid that the artefact would disappear without trace if handed over for analysis, as so many other artefacts have done, Alan Hilton did not send the strange cube for analysis. Instead he tried psycho-metry. This is a form of extra-sensory perception (ESP), whereby psychics obtain impressions when they handle an artefact. It is most often performed for individuals, who surrender a favourite piece of jewellery, e.g. a watch, for examination. The psychic then relates details of the life and personality of the owner. I have seen this done and it is remarkable how much information previously unknown to the psychometrist stems from holding the object.

In this particular case, one of these psychometric experts received a direct communication, describing the Greys involved and confirm-ing that they were friendly and from another part of our galaxy. It is possible, as we shall see in the Hill's case (see page 157), that some, if not all, Greys stem from a planet of the star Zeta Reticuli and there is evidence that, while they appear friendly at this point in time, this could be to lull us into a false sense of security.

Greys are very active on this planet and we have to ask: Why? Why do they continually tag and abduct certain people? There is, un-fortunately, no answer to that at present but certainly they are always subjecting their abductees to medical examinations, which indicates some form of in-depth surveillance of the human race. Their methods of mind control are very subtle and they can even take people from double beds without the partner being aware that anything untoward has happened.

Now we need to take the story of John and his family further. The abduction and time loss events described above took place in April but, in the following November, John, his wife Susan and their baby daughter once again came from Peterborough to stay at Alan Hilton's cottage.

At about mid-day on Saturday, 7 November 1992, John left the house for a quiet smoke in the lane that runs past the cottage. He was greeted with a 'Hello' from a man who was walking up the lane. At first John did not find this man very strange, except that he was wearing the kind of dark suit and trilby hat that American gangsters once wore. The illusion was completed by the man's white shirt, dark tie and highly polished black shoes. He seemed to John to be in his late thirties, stood some $5\frac{1}{2}$ feet tall and walked quite normally. He spoke good English and they had a friendly conversation for several minutes. What did make John curious was the man's knowledge of his family and also of Alan Hilton. In fact, he described himself as 'an old friend of Alan's from the past'. The stranger knew that Alan was not at home and he knew Susan's name and the fact that they had a child. The 'gangster' left with a message for Hilton that he 'was just passing by and to tell him that Peter Dankin called'.

Now this Man in Black (MIB) is just one of a long series of such entities that are well known to UFOlogists. MIBs have been reported since at least 1947 and have, in the past, been known to threaten and intimidate witnesses to UFO events in an attempt to prevent them telling what they have seen. To find a friendly one is unusual. However, there was more to come.

On the following Tuesday afternoon, John once more went out for a smoke but this time he found that Peter Dankin and another man (who was apparently called Neil O.) were there waiting to speak to him. The two men were, as far as John could tell, identical. They seemed to be clones of one another. The one who called himself Peter Dankin did all the talking but the conversation was brief and, while friendly, seemed rather pointless. Dankin was particularly interested in whether Hilton had been informed of the previous encounter. Finally, Dankin said they had to go but John had been warned by Hilton that, if these were MIBs, they might well vanish before his eyes. That certainly was the case, for the men had hardly gone a hundred metres before John, who was following, saw them disappear on the spot. Obviously, he was somewhat unnerved by this series of events. But even stranger things were yet to happen.

On regaining the house, and lost in thought, John had the urge to open up his lap-top computer and he automatically typed a message which was destined for Hilton's attention. A full transcript can be found in Hilton (1993b) but, selecting relevant points, the automatic communication said that, in our form, they (the MIBs) can only persist for somewhere between 10 and 20 minutes, although they can manifest in dreams for much longer. We cannot see them, nor their vehicles (UFOs) unless they choose to allow it. They said that the meetings about UFOs that Hilton had organized at his house were necessary to make people aware and to dispel fear. More information would come via John (their 'subject') if it were requested. They finally said that they came from the planet Ionunca in the star system Zeta Reticuli.

The constellation Reticulum has 34 stars and is known as the Rhombus or the Rhomboidal Net; it lies north of the constellation Hydra in the southern hemisphere.

Credence is given to this strange testimony when we realize that the message stated that Zeta Reticuli is a double star system, which we know it to be. John, however, is not an astronomer and was not previously aware of the name of the star, nor that it was a double system.

In recent years, there has been an intense amount of UFO activity in Puerto Rico. One of these incidents involves a form of intervention that has been recorded before – sometimes with wide-ranging consequences.

In the town of Trujillo Alto, the night of 17 March 1992 (Good, 1991) was at first quiet and normal. But, just after midnight, this tranquillity was shattered by a strange sound and a sudden eruption of light that was described as being of incredible proportions. The sky took on an intense blue colour and, at the same time, there were some widely dispersed failures of the electricity supply system. The blue light changed to green, and then to orange, while bright searchlight-like beams were projected from the sky and waved around in a fan-like motion. There were literally thousands of people all round Trujillo who watched this aerial display.

This great display of illumination was produced by an immense flying saucer that hovered over an electricity substation lying close to the El Conquistador urban development. The saucer was huge, as big as the urban development over which it hovered, and was surrounded by an orange-tinted cloud. The lights that had turned night into day came from intense light sources on its underside and the bright orange and green lights came from around its rim.

However, the most amazing thing about this event was that the UFO appeared to draw electrical power from the substation. Witnesses said that a funnel-like beam of electrical rays was attracted from the substation into the craft above. Thousands of minute electrical 'capillaries' rose from the station while, at the same time, there was a 'chh, chh, chh' sound akin to the discharge of static electricity.

A psychologist resident in Trujillo, who is a personal acquaintance of Timothy Good's, describes it thus (Good, 1991):

> That thing I saw was not anything I know of from earthly
> technology. The lights were so intense, like spotlights shining
> downwards, really intense and blinding. To me what I saw was
> an alien craft that visited us, absorbing the station's electrical

energy, then charged whatever they wanted to recharge in their ship – maybe they had an energy problem – then left.

The engineers who next day had to start to repair the $355,000 worth of damage were quite nonplussed as to how the transformers had burned out, as well as their terminals being fused by the intense amount of current that had somehow flowed through them. An automatic breaker system should have turned off the current and, if it failed, a back-up system should have operated. Neither happened because the UFO somehow prevented the breakers from activating while it drew on the substation's power.

The Trujillo substation incident was not the only one of its type. An unidentified employee of the Puerto Rico Authority of Electrical Energy described a similar incident in Barceloneta, in which a UFO came down and drew energy from a substation.

That the Trujillo UFO was surrounded by strong electromagnetic fields seems to be confirmed because ceiling fan blades in houses over which the immense craft hovered bent upwards. Some people's table fans began to run backwards under the influence of the UFO but returned to normal once the craft had departed. There was even a case of a 17-year-old girl who, the day after the incident, began to levitate. Another strange occurrence involved dogs and roosters which, although normally noisy, were rendered totally silent throughout the night and until late the following day. This is in direct contrast to the normal reactions of animals when close to UFOs. Dogs, for example, usually howl and try to run away. Other animals seem to panic in various ways, as though frightened out of their wits.

Some of these reactions may stem from the magnetic field fluctuations which occur near many UFOs but which usually go otherwise undetected. An example from the former USSR (Good, 1991) took place one night in 1976. Doctor Dmitriev of the State University at Novosibirsk was on a field expedition studying the geomagnetic characteristics of the Earth and so had sensitive magnetometers, which were able to record local fluctuations in the magnetic field when a UFO hovered nearby. The sighting of the chevron-shaped object lasted some 14 minutes, during which six consecutive photographs were taken. However, the UFO's magnetic field must have bent the light from the object because, despite the photographer aligning the light centrally with the camera, the resulting prints showed it displaced some 30 degrees to the side of where it had appeared to be. Two other cameras were also used to photograph the object and, in all, there were nine scientifically trained witnesses to the event.

There have been other spectacular electrical interventions (Keyhoe, 1957) but nothing as amazing as the US Great Northeast Blackout. On the evening of 9 November 1965, UFOs, described as huge fire-balls or flame-coloured globes, interfered with the Clay electrical substation that automatically feeds power from Niagara Falls to New York and surrounding areas. A pilot, Weldon Ross, and his passenger, James Brooking, reported seeing a round object, some 100 ft in diameter, hovering over the substation. They were forced to land blind at Hancock Airport because, over an area of 80,000 square miles, covering the most densely populated regions of the eastern USA, the lights had gone out.

It seems likely that globular UFOs have also interfered with other substations. Certainly they have been reported over Manhattan and other places at times consistent with one or more being responsible for massive breakdowns in electricity supply. It is supposed to be impossible for this kind of event to occur, for the prospect has been envisaged and the grid system designed to eliminate the kind of power surges that could trip the breakers over such a vast area.

In one incident, it took just 4 seconds for the Canadian Adam Beck 2 plant to start a chain reaction which somehow bypassed all the safety devices built into the US–Canadian grid system, sending massive power surges southwards and tripping out stations serving Connecticut, Massachusetts, Maine, New Hampshire, New Jersey, New York, Pennsylvania and Vermont.

This could have been a tremendous disaster as the blackout occurred during the evening rush hour and approaching 0.75 million people were trapped in the underground and in lifts. Yet, strangely, one might think, there was hardly any panic, although obviously some people entombed for several hours in lifts from which they could not escape were hysterical or in various states of shock. One decidedly human reaction to this unprecedented event occurred some 9 months later when the obstetric services were overwhelmed by a vastly increased number of births in the areas affected.

There have been other, less publicized blackouts across the USA, as well as in Mexico, Peru and Brazil. Similar unexplained blackouts associated with the sighting of UFOs have also occurred in Europe, including the Netherlands, England, Finland, the former USSR and Italy.

Are these wanton acts of aggression? Some might think so but there is another way of looking at it. Could the UFO denizens be pointing out to us that we are relying too heavily on electricity and that, when it fails, our civilized lives will come to an abrupt stop?

Certainly one of the reactions to the Great Northeast Blackout was to install emergency plant and equipment in hospitals and other vital services so that, should the same thing happen again, some semblance of normality could be preserved. I realize, sitting here at my word-processor, that, if the power fails, for whatever reason, I might lose all these words of wisdom. This would never happen if I was still using a typewriter.

A remarkable event occurred in the former USSR (Buttlar, 1979) but, at the time of writing, I was unable to discover the date or place. It was an 'attack' on a factory producing missile-firing devices and witnesses described a 'fire-ball' that came down on the factory at daybreak. There was a very loud explosion which created a strong shock wave and the whole area was lit up. After the dust had cleared, where the factory had stood, there was nothing but a rubble-filled crater. The usual precautions had been taken; the factory siren had been sounded a few minutes before the event and the work-force had taken cover. However, when inspected, the switch which activated the siren was found to be still in the off position.

Cigar-shaped and disc-shaped UFOs had been seen over the area in the previous week and, after the explosion, a disc hovered over the site, apparently inspecting the results. However, when Soviet fighters appeared, it flew off at high speed.

Now what produced this intervention is obviously impossible to say but Soviet anti-aircraft batteries are known to have fired on UFOs in the past. Perhaps, the missiles, despite their apparent inability to affect the UFOs (in one case they all exploded well before they could have struck the UFO targeted), were a sufficient nuisance to necessitate the removal of the means by which they were fired.

The ill-fated Chernobyl reactor may have been the recipient of outside intervention on the night of 11 October 1991, when there was, apparently, a further potentially catastrophic incident at the plant. At 8.09 p.m., the hydrogen gas used to cool the generator began to overheat. The result was an explosion and a subsequent fire, which was not brought under control until 2.00 a.m. the next day. The fire and explosion destroyed the roof of the building and all four electrical generators were put out of action, although there was no damage to the reactor itself. Nikolai Lebedev, in contributing a chapter on the UFO scene in the former USSR to *Alien Update* (Good, 1993), indicates that the relatively harmless explosion and fire may have been induced by a UFO.

A bright light was observed hovering over the complex just prior to the explosion. Apparently the high-voltage switch, which should have been in the off position, somehow spontaneously set itself to the on position. This led, in the operating situation extant at the time, to the overheating and subsequent complete shut-down of the reactor. This total shut-down should have been implemented after the disaster of 26 April 1986 but the reactor had been put back into service because of the hardship its closing would have caused to those reliant on its electricity during the Russian winter.

So, did our space 'friends' induce one form of relatively minor disaster in 1991 in order to force the closure of an unsafe plant and so eliminate the prospect of another, much greater disaster, on the scale of that in 1986? Vladimir Savran, a journalist on the *Chernobyl Echo*, visited the site next morning and took photographs of the scene. Good reproduces one of the photographs taken by Savran which shows a disc-shaped object hovering over the reactor site. As has happened with UFO pictures in the past, Savran was not aware of the disc when he took the photographs. It only appeared on the film when it was developed.

We could go on with a long catalogue of events where UFOs have intervened in our affairs. However, it would not necessarily elucidate the problems that face us. There is no doubt that the space denizens know all about us and what they do not know they have the means of finding out. Whenever there is intervention which threatens life, every precaution is taken to ensure that no casualties occur. If there are casualties then it is usually due to unforseeable circumstances resulting from the intervention.

An example was the tragic event in 1954 when two aircrew from an F. 94 Starfire jet, which had been ordered to pursue a UFO over New York State, were forced to bail out by a furnace-like heat that emanated from a UFO. While the pilot and radar-observer were unharmed, the jet itself crashed into the town of Walesville, killing four people. The crew members were not aware that they had bailed out at the time when they activated the mechanism (Keyhoe, 1957).

THE APPLIANCE OF SCIENCE

I T HAS ALREADY become evident to most students of the subject that there are real extra-terrestrial spacecraft, i.e. the majority of UFOs that visit Earth are machines with form and dimensions. They have interiors within which are compartments and, from this point of view, they are akin to terrestrial aircraft.

Timothy Good (1992), in *Alien Liaison*, recounts what a retired US Rear Admiral, Sumner Shapiro, told the researcher, Bob Oeschler. Apparently some of the spacecraft which have been studied were built of interlocking components that had to be taken apart and reassembled in an exact sequence. Without the key, it became an impossible puzzle. Where they differed fundamentally from terrestrial aircraft was in the materials used in their construction and in their modes of propulsion. An early book by Frank Scully (1950) called *Behind the Flying Saucers*, had already stated this and added that mechanical strength was achieved by having grooves into which the component pieces fitted together. The Brazilian investigator, Dr Olavo Fontes, was told by Brazilian naval officials in 1958 that a total of six discs had, at that time, been recovered worldwide (including one in the UK) and that all of them were made of very light metal. Fontes confirmed the method of construction and added that the components were then locked in by a system of pins around the base.

As I demonstrated in my previous book (Watts, 1994), some strange UFO observations may be explained when we realize that one of the most prevalent emanations from UFOs is magnetism. Magnetism, moreover, that is vastly stronger than anything we can as yet produce in our laboratories. Indeed, fields that are 1,000 million times stronger than those of a really strong domestic magnet.

In deducing a possible cause for that magnetism, I was forced to introduce the concept of anti-matter. Indeed, leaked information on captured UFOs insists that the basis of their propulsion system is an

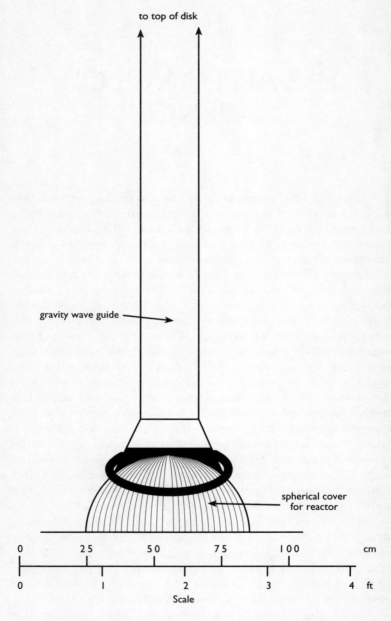

to top of disk

gravity wave guide →

spherical cover
for reactor

Fig. 5.1 The anti-matter reactor as described by Bob Lazar. (After Good, 1992)

46

anti-matter reactor incorporating the *trans*-uranic element 115. The atomic number, 115, identifies the element as having 115 protons in its nucleus and an unspecified, but larger, number of neutrons if it is to be in any way stable.

Uranium (element 92) is the heaviest element naturally occurring on Earth. Elements heavier than uranium have been created artificially by bombarding the nuclei of natural elements with protons and getting them to accept some of these protons. In this way, we have created minute quantities of elements up to, and including, 109, but it is a difficult and expensive business.

It is perfectly possible that elements such as 115, that are impossible on Earth, will be found on other planets in the galaxy. Our heaviest element is 92 simply because Earth condensed out of the remains of a less than super-hot supernova. This exploding star was, during its life, only hot enough to 'cook' the nuclei up to atomic number 92. That does not preclude heavier elements being cooked in hotter stars which, when they explode and their remains condense into planets, deposit veins of *trans*-uranic elements. With spacecraft that can range through galactic space, it should be possible to find planets, cooled out of such cataclysmic explosions, where deposits of 115 can be mined.

An argument against the existence of elements such as 115 is that they would be so highly radioactive that they would quickly decay into much longer-lived isotopes, such as those of uranium. Some uranium isotopes have half-lives which are commensurate with the accepted age of the Universe so they are, to all intents and purposes, stable. We cannot yet make elements as heavy as element 115, but theory suggests such superheavy elements may lie on a 'plateau of stability' and so be much longer-lived than otherwise thought.

According to Bob Lazar (Good, 1992), who claims to have worked on alien spacecraft at a secret base called S-4, the anti-matter reactor, whose power source is about 8 oz of element 115, has a hemispherical cover that is the size of a basketball. From this a central column, which he calls a 'gravity wave guide' goes right up the centre of the craft (fig. 5.1).

Element 115 is bombarded with protons and becomes element 116. The 116 emits anti-matter, which annihilates on contact with matter, and this is the source of the propulsion. Lazar alleged (Good, 1992) that some 500 lb of element 115 were available on Earth in 1990, and that he has handled it and performed some simple experiments with it. Such a quantity of an extra-terrestrial material could only have come here in alien spacecraft.

Now none of this is sufficiently understandable to allow us to make a reactor ourselves. What is remarkable is that Leonard Cramp (1954), in *Space, Gravity and the Flying Saucer*, made a drawing of what he thought the general arrangement inside Adamski's saucer looked like. As photo 5 shows, he drew a central column very closely resembling the one in the diagram which Lazar contributed to *Alien Liaison* (Good, 1992). When I asked Cramp why he drew this, and where his inspiration came from, he said it was intuition aided by his training as an engineer.

When he briefly met Adamski, the latter commented something to the effect that, for someone who had never been inside a saucer, Cramp's intuitive drawing was about as close as you could get. Adamski had, I believe, been inside one but, unfortunately, I also believe, as many others do, that he was fed disinformation along with true facts. Thus it has since been easy for those opposed to the facts to fasten on the probable absurdities and so rubbish the truth.

Modern physics has, through its exploration of the fundamental particles and forces of nature, learned many things about the relationship between these forces but, as yet, it has not managed to bridge successfully the gap between electromagnetism and gravity. We still cannot link gravity with the other forces, even though we know that both strong magnetism and strong gravity can, for example, bend light beams (Watts, 1994).

In the following pages, I will refer continually to communications from deep space transmitted to us through certain trance mediums. One of these is Phyllis Schlemmer (see page 93) who is in contact with elevated entities that style themselves 'The Council of Nine', or simply 'the Nine'.

The Nine have previously spoken through other mediums (see chapter 9) and their spokesmen at that time gave themselves simple identifying letters or names. The later communications are summarized in *The Only Planet of Choice* (Schlemmer, 1994) and they are a true two-way dialogue. Questions are asked and answered and the replies are highly illuminating, giving us a new insight into our present position in the Universe, our past and our possible future.

At one point in the book the spokesman for the Nine (who, when speaking through Phyllis Schlemmer, calls himself Tom) is asked to explain how the alien vehicles operate by controlling gravity. He replies that it 'has to do with the discharge of magnetics. It has to do with creating a magnetic field'. As magnetism is not usually associated with gravity, we may be able to understand more fully what is involved if we describe some of the concepts of modern physics.

The world of modern physics is very strange and many of the things we now take for granted would never have seen the light of day without the discipline of scientific method to back them up.

I will start with something very familiar. Most people, whether scientifically trained or not, have heard of the electron. On the concept of the electron, and humanity's understanding of it, rests the invention of radio, television, camcorders, calculators, computers, and all the thousand and one other electronic devices in use today. The twentieth century is indeed the age of electronics and electronics has transformed our lives.

When something becomes familiar we tend not to doubt its reality but we must realize that no one has ever seen an electron. No matter what high-powered microscopes are produced, they cannot enable us to see electrons. Electron microscopes can see the sites of atoms but not how those atoms are constructed and so our whole concept of atoms (and the electrons and nuclei that make them up) is based on theory. It is only because that theory so accurately predicts what will happen when electrons are used in various situations that we are able to believe that we know what an electron is.

And what is it? Basically it is the lightest fundamental particle of matter to possess an electrical charge. There are particles with less mass – maybe no mass – but, from a practical point of view, the electron is the lightest particle in the Universe and it has a negative charge. Electrons exist in all matter and they occur throughout the Universe. Should you wish to make some kind of approach to an alien, to help bridge the great divide between his knowledge and yours, then you could do worse than draw the structure of an atom, with its minute positive nucleus and a number of electrons, equal to its position in the table of the elements, revolving around it.

In 1871, a builder, cabinet-maker and undertaker of High Wycombe, Buckinghamshire, UK, called William Loosley, had a strange meeting with what he described, in the notes he left to be discovered on his death, as 'denizens of another world'.

Briefly, Loosley was apparently mentally summoned to a wood near his home. There he encountered a small robot-like device which he associated with the landing of a brightly lit UFO which he had witnessed earlier. The small robot led him to a larger robot waiting in the depths of the wood. This latter device proceeded to give Loosley what would, in these days, be recognized as a holographic show. Certain that, should he communicate what had happened to him to any living soul, his business would be ruined, Loosley secretly wrote down his account as soon as he could and put it away in a drawer.

Thus he was not seeking publicity – quite the reverse – and this gives his testimony the ring of truth.

An Honours physicist, David Langford, wrote a commentary on the notes that William Loosley left (Langford, 1979) in which he recognized how these robots were giving the bemused undertaker important facts of science and mathematics. It was an exercise doomed to failure because Loosley, although quite well educated for his time and station, was neither a scientist nor a mathematician. In any case, this would not have mattered because some of the images that the robot gave to this chosen Earthman were not to be understandable for another 60 or more years.

From his vantage point of being well-versed in twentieth-century physics, Langford could see that along with a description of a well-known mathematical series of numbers, there also appeared to Loosley

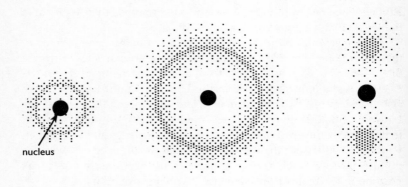

nucleus

Fig. 5.2   The shape of the 'probability atom' as shown to William Loosley. The shapes are generated by the probability that electrons, which appear and disappear continually around the nucleus of the atom, will be found in any particular place. The density of dots in these fuzzy diagrams indicates where the electrons are most likely to appear. The distribution shown left is that of a solitary hydrogen atom when left to itself. The centre diagram shows the same atom which has been energized by collision with another atom. In a more complex energized atom (right) the electrons may be found in lobe-shaped pairs of spaces (orbitals) as well as the sphere and shell orbitals shown left and centre. These shapes control how atoms join with others to form molecules.

what can only be interpreted as the shape of the so-called 'probability atom' in its first three states of energy (fig. 5.2). The theory for this was not put forward until 1926 and involved an image of the atom radically different from the one current at that time.

Thus, the concept of a hydrogen atom, for example, changed from a small point of negative charge (an *electron*) whirling around a point of positive charge (a *proton*) into a more or less fuzzy smear that expressed the chance of an electron being found in any particular position around the proton.

The most likely place for the electron to be was where the smear was densest, and it was thus liberated from being in a fixed and unchanging orbit, which was where earlier theories had placed it. It could now wander but, in 99 per cent of experiments, it was where previous ideas had said it should be. These ideas had shown that, in its lowest state of energy, the electron whirled in a spherical orbit and, according to the new theory, the lowest probability state for the H atom also became a sphere. However, it was now a fuzzy sphere of probability density. The next energy state was a sphere surrounded by a shell. These images are just as described, in his own words, by William Loosley.

Another of Loosley's descriptions of the holographic show must also represent the six electrons of an atom of carbon (fig. 5.3), the element most basic to terrestrial life. And this was some thirty years before the first description of the electron by J. J. Thomson in 1897!

The charge of the electron itself is the smallest quantity of electricity that exists and when we switch on, say, a 100 W lamp, it is only because an immense number of electrons move that 100 joules of light and heat energy can be suddenly delivered to us every second. Each individual electron's contribution is minute but, together, they can make up a mighty electrical effect.

Hydrogen is the lightest atom and has a single positively charged nucleon (a proton) at its centre and a single electron in an orbit about it. The positive charge of the proton is equal to the negative charge of the electron but the proton has nearly 2,000 times the mass of the electron. When we weigh, for example, a pure copper bracelet we are only really determining the force which gravity is exerting on the nuclei of the copper atoms.

Hydrogen (H) is number 1 on the atomic scale and helium (He) is 2. Thus, helium has two electrons and, one might think, just two protons to balance out the negative charge on the electrons. But things are never quite that easy. Chemists showed very early on that the mass of a helium atom was not twice but four times that of a hydrogen atom.

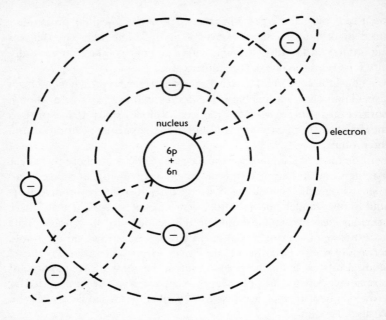

Fig. 5.3 The way in which six electrons arrange themselves to form a carbon atom. The six electrons arrange themselves into two spherical orbitals plus two lobe-shaped orbitals. The nucleus of this isotope of carbon (Carbon 12) contains six protons and six neutrons. This was another configuration shown to William Loosley many years before scientists discovered it.

We now know that, as well as the protons (whose number is always equal to the number of electrons), the nucleus has a 'weight maker' – the *neutron* – which has about the same mass as the proton but no electrical charge. Uranium (U) is well known because it is the atom which splits (undergoes fission) to provide the power for nuclear reactors. Uranium is 92 on the atomic scale. So it must have 92 protons; however, a well-known isotope of uranium (U235) has no less than 143 neutrons in its nucleus.

The three atomic building blocks – protons, neutrons and electrons – are the most familiar of a whole range of fundamental particles but most of them would never have been discovered were it not for the so-called 'atom smashers'. These started out as quite small cyclotrons, which were easily housed in laboratories. Over the years, they have been developed and, nowadays, the most powerful consist of ring-doughnut-shaped race-tracks for protons which occupy several square kilometres of land and involve billions of dollars in their construction and upkeep.

They are more or less circular tubes in the ground, surrounded by very powerful magnets. Magnetic forces bend the paths of charged particles, such as protons, and the magnets are cunningly contrived to confine the beam of particles to the centre of the highly evacuated tube in which they are accelerated. In this way, the particles acquire the kind of energies which have only appeared in the Universe once before. That was in the so-called Big Bang, with which it is believed the Universe started. The Universe we see today is the end result of the explosion, some 15,000 million years ago, of a minute but incredibly dense lump of primeval energy. Scientists now recognize that what they have been doing with their proton synchrotrons, etc. is to recreate the conditions of the Big Bang.

When the protons, travelling almost as fast as the speed of light, strike target nucleons (both protons and neutrons), very complex transformations occur. Amazingly, particles (called *hyperons*), which are much heavier than the nucleons involved in the collisions, may be created.

Thus, in accordance with Einstein's law, matter is created out of energy. These exotic particles do not last long (in the order of 1,000 millionths of a second) and they decay into a cascade of lighter particles. The end result of all such collisions are the familiar particles, protons and electrons, plus packets of electromagnetic waves (*photons*) which might be gamma rays, X-rays, light or radiant heat.

In order not to complicate matters, I have ignored a whole group of particles which, without the discipline and drive of modern science, we might never have known about. These particles occupy the world of anti-matter and will be the subject of the next chapter. Suffice it to say that, for every particle, there is an anti-particle which is its mirror image. Only two of the whole gamut of particles do not care if they are matter or anti-matter. One of these is the photon, which not only brings us light and heat from the Sun but is also responsible for holding material things together. It is the means by which electrons bind to atomic nuclei and, in so doing, form atoms.

The other is the *pion*, which has the task of holding the nucleons together to form the nucleus of an atom. These two particles – the photon and the pion – make it possible for a physical world to exist.

The UFOnauts, whatever the conditions may be on their home planets, cannot ignore the fundamental laws of the Universe. If they wish to exist as material entities on this planet they must make their bodies out of atoms and molecules. Those atoms and molecules must be held together by electromagnetic forces, and the same goes for the alien craft. Any light they emit must be composed of photons, produced by electrons changing their energies, and, as I pointed out in my previous book, *UFO Quest* (Watts, 1994), we may already know a good deal about the way in which this is achieved.

SIX

WHAT'S IN A VACUUM?

O NE OF THE MOST amazing pieces of deduction in modern science occurred when I was a mere tot of three summers. It was in 1928 that an English physicist, P.M. Dirac, published his theory that if there were negative electrons there had to be positive ones as well. This work stemmed from Einstein's theories of relativity but it hit the scientific world like a bombshell. How could there be positive electrons? No one had ever seen such an entity. The chances of encountering a man from space were much higher than ever finding traces of a positive electron. Indeed, at that time, no one had ever found even a hint of this positive electron. Yet the theory seemed to be cast-iron.

So a few researchers began to look for signs of this particle, which eventually became known as the *positron*. It was a further 4 years, in 1932, before the track of a positron was identified in a cloud-chamber photograph. After that, confirmation came thick and fast and the world of *anti-matter* was revealed to us for the first time.

No one had ever suspected the existence of positrons because, if they should be produced (and they are, for example, produced naturally by cosmic rays and some kinds of radioactive isotopes), they normally last for only a matter of millionths of a second before they contact an electron and cease to exist. A kind of minute atomic explosion (called *annihilation*) occurs and the electron, as well as the positron, disappears, leaving pure energy in the form of two or three gamma rays.

Because positrons annihilate almost as soon as they are produced, it took first a theory and then some sophisticated apparatus to reveal their existence. Yet we now realize that all the particles we know have their anti-particles. There are anti-protons and anti-neutrons, as well as anti-particles of other more exotic particles, such as pions and muons, not to mention those of the strange heavy particles, such as hyperons. Here, however, it is sufficient to talk only about electrons and positrons. There is no need to delve into the deeper realms of matter/anti-matter science.

It is important to realize that positrons – if you can keep them away from electrons – are just as permanent as electrons. It is only because there are so many electrons in everything around us (including the molecules of air) that a positron is doomed to die in such a short time. However, in the vacuum of space, positrons are able to travel very long distances before a chance meeting with an electron leads to annihilation. Anti-matter in any quantity will vaporize any material so an anti-matter 'gun' can be a potent space weapon and an important component of 'space wars'.

It has been found possible to combine anti-protons with positrons and so make anti-hydrogen, and anti-hydrogen behaves in the same way as hydrogen. Indeed, there is no way of telling whether the light from distant stars is coming from hydrogen or anti-hydrogen because both give out the same spectrum of colours. Thus we cannot rule out the possibility of an anti-Universe in which all the physical laws would be the same as in this Universe but all the particles would be anti-particles. If this anti-Universe and ours should intermingle, the result would be an immense and on-going 'explosion' as the particles of our Universe met and annihilated with the anti-particles of the anti-Universe.

This discussion of electrons and positrons is relevant because both particles exist in apparently empty space. You may say that there cannot, by definition, be anything in *empty* space.

That depends on what you mean by 'anything'. What science means by empty space is a vacuum with no matter in it – no atoms, no electrons, etc. Deep space is a vacuum and yet light travels across it from as far afield as our telescopes can reach. Something which itself is electric and magnetic must fill that space so that the light can be transported to us.

To fill this apparent emptiness, modern theory populates a vacuum with a seething assemblage of matter and anti-matter. It is only because of the anti-matter that what appears to be empty can be full of particles. This requires some explanation and will stretch your powers of visualization to the full.

Following his prediction of the positron, Dirac came up with the concept that has been called *Dirac's Sea*. Through the medium of this 'Sea', he was able to explain how energy, in the form of a high-energy gamma ray, could disappear and, at the point where it vanished, matter, in the shape of an electron and a positron, could be created apparently out of nothing (fig. 6.1). This was directly as predicted by Einstein in his famous mass-energy equation.

Dirac said this could only be explained if the electron was there all the time but 'invisible', because it was existing in a positive 'hole' which nullified the electron's electric charge, its magnetism and its mass.

To demonstrate this, take an egg box and a table-tennis ball. The ball represents the electron and the egg box represents the holes in which the electron can nestle. Under normal circumstances an electron in a hole cannot be detected because any test is nullified by the hole's properties. In particular, the hole has a positive electrical charge and represents a positron. In the analogy, any ball in the box cannot be detected, and it is referred to as 'virtual'. Once lifted out of the box, however, it becomes 'real' and can be detected.

Now imagine that a gamma ray gives its energy to the 'electron' in

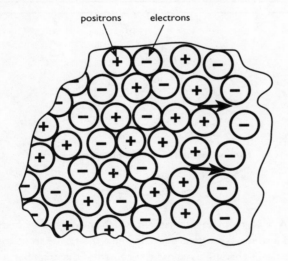

positrons   electrons

Fig. 6.1 The modern concept of a piece of 'empty' space. The electron–positron pairs appear and disappear continually and there is always an equal number of each. Together they cancel each other's attributes, e.g. electrical charge, magnetism and mass. On the right-hand side a strong field of magnetic or gravitational force has pulled the particles apart somewhat, allowing their electromagnetic attributes to be revealed. This way electromagnetic (EM) fields (indicated by the arrows), which are powerful enough to bend light, can be produced in apparently empty space.

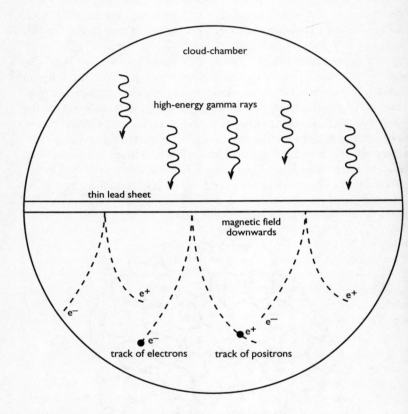

Fig. 6.2 A drawing of an experiment which shows energy being converted into matter. We are looking into the transparent top of a cylindrical cloud-chamber. Across the centre of the chamber a thin sheet of lead has been placed. High-energy gamma rays from a radioactive isotope are directed against the lead sheet. The cloud-chamber enables us to see the tracks of any charged particles that result. We see the tracks of electron–positron pairs (matter) which are formed when the gamma photons (pure energy) annihilate in the sheet (which serves only to facilitate this effect). The tracks are bent equally in both directions under the influence of a strong magnetic field that has been arranged to thread through the chamber from top to bottom.

the box. Lift the 'electron' out of its hole and put it on the mantel shelf. The energy required to lift it out and make it 'real' comes from the energy of the colliding gamma ray. And what is left? A hole which acts like a positive charge. That hole is a positron.

This is how matter, in the shape of an electron, and anti-matter, in the shape of a positron, can be created (fig. 6.2). Einstein's equation, $E = mc^2$, is perfectly obeyed because the energy (E) of the gamma ray that vanishes is exactly the same as the mass (m) of an electron and a positron multiplied by the speed of light (c) squared.

This is how an e–p (electron–positron) pair can be created. But what happens to the electrons that are constantly being born in the sea of the vacuum? They cannot escape like the one described above because they do not have the energy of gamma rays. They are still, however, constantly appearing and disappearing in immense numbers. The analogy using the table-tennis ball is to roll the ball over a hump into the next hole without taking it out of the egg box. This only requires a small amount of energy.

To envisage a vacuum, imagine a seething assemblage of electrons and positrons constantly being born in pairs and annihilating in pairs almost as rapidly as they are born. The times involved are so short that no apparatus can detect them and so the electrons in the vacuum cannot be 'seen', nor do they create any forces. We therefore say that the vacuum is *empty*.

It is this matter–anti-matter sea which is strained and distorted by very strong magnetic or gravitational fields. In the case of gravity it has been proved during total eclipses of the Sun that light from stars, which should be obscured by the Sun's disc, can be seen because the light is being bent round the edge of the Sun by the latter's immensely strong gravitational field.

That there must be a connection between magnetism, gravity and light can be appreciated once it is realized that light is an oscillation of the matter–anti-matter sea. This is where it acts like the real sea. Waves travel across the sea because the molecules of water oscillate to create them. Light travels through Dirac's Sea because electrons and positrons oscillate to carry the EM energy. These oscillations are photons, which travel at the speed of light, and any normal light beam contains vast numbers of them.

Light passing through a vacuum travels in straight lines but, if you make light pass through a vacuum which has been 'strained' with a high magnetic or gravitational field, it will be bent. The nature of this bending can best be understood by considering some familiar transparent materials.

Light is bent (refracted) by glass because such a dense transparent material is basically a mass of strong electromagnetic fields. These interact with the EM waves and the light slows down to about two-thirds of its speed outside the glass. We know that, if we create a super-strong magnetic field in air (which is near enough a vacuum for this purpose), this will also slow down any light that passes through it. We cannot yet create such fields, but UFOs can. They can also wind up their magnetic fields to strengths that bend light vastly more than the best glass available. Indeed, they can use the magnetic fields that surround them in such a way that their own light is turned back on itself and, in this way, a UFO may become invisible. Such effects are due to *vacuum refraction*.

Two men fishing on a reservoir at Haslingdon, some 20 miles northwest of Manchester, UK, had a very curious experience. As they gazed into the water they could see the reflection of a huge disc-shaped object. On looking up, expecting to see a UFO, they were astounded to see absolutely nothing. Then even the image in the water vanished, only to reappear soon after, but pulsating rather than being steady as it had been before (Randles & Whetnall, 1977).

Such an 'impossible' observation becomes possible if we consider that there could have been a UFO above the reservoir whose magnetic aura was shaped in such a way that the light from it was projected straight down but no light was able to reach the fishermen (fig. 6.3). It is also likely that the UFO was not as big as it appeared in the reflection. We see in the drawing how the rays can be funnel-shaped and therefore may appear to be coming from a much bigger object. The fact that the light was steady at first and pulsated later is probably related to the UFO's propulsion system, which projects apparently steady light when at high power but which can become rhythmically unsteady when at low power.

Vacuum refraction occurs because the magnetic field is heavily 'straining' the matter–anti-matter sea and so the electrons and the positrons are being pulled apart, allowing their magnetic properties to become evident rather than invisible. What the UFOs may be able to do, which we have consistently failed to do, is to manipulate the sea in such a way that only one magnetic pole appears. To most people who have had any scientific training at school this will seem impossible; whenever any magnet is broken the pieces still show two poles and no scientist has been able to detect single magnetic poles, even in space, where they might possibly exist.

Yet herein may lie the answer to the riddle presented to us when we are told that a UFO travels from a distant planet to Earth by

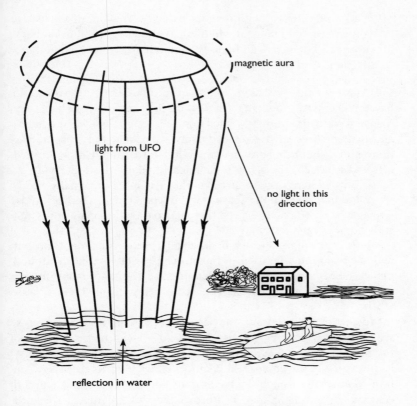

magnetic aura

light from UFO

no light in this
direction

reflection in water

Fig. 6.3   This diagram shows how a strong magnetic aura could have
bent the light from a UFO in the Haslingdon case, thereby allowing the
fishermen to see the UFO's reflection in the water but not the UFO
itself.

'drawing space' towards it as if it were an elastic membrane. The UFO
is fixed in the membrane and, when the membrane is released, travels
with it. In this way, there is no relative motion between the UFO and
the space through which it apparently moves, and so Einstein's laws
are not broken.

Looked at in a slightly different way, if a UFO, by manipulating
the matter–anti-matter sea, is able to create one pole of a magnetic field
outside and another within itself, then it could be attracted towards
the external field. This may be what Tom meant when he said
(Schlemmer, 1994):

61

When you function with the magnetic you draw all things to you. When you know how to discharge then the propulsion is reversed. To operate and release gravitational fields is related to magnetic fields.

Bob Lazar (Good, 1992) says that the captured UFOs he worked on had three 'gravity amplifiers' (fig. 6.4) on their underside, which they focussed on the point they wished to reach. Using the idea of matter–anti-matter space as a stretched membrane, one can imagine the destination point being drawn to the UFO. If the amplifiers are turned off or discharged, the space springs back, taking the UFO with it. Lazar says: 'There's no linear travel through space; it actually bends space and time and follows space as it retracts.' Which, in other words, is just what Tom says, except that the role of the magnetic is not stressed in Lazar's testimony.

This is an interplanetary or interstellar mode of propulsion but another form must be used in the strong gravitational fields around planets. This could involve something like the matter–anti-matter propulsion system which I envisaged in my previous book (Watts, 1994).

In an attempt to unravel the bases of these scientific conundrums, scientists today are trying to develop a unified field theory. If successful, they should be able to discover how gravity is related to magnetism. At present we do not really know. All we know is that there can be a connection through the medium of Dirac's Sea of positrons and electrons. Some light may be thrown on this enigma in the next

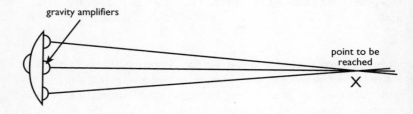

Fig. 6.4 Gravity amplifiers must have the ability to concentrate on a spot and to 'pull' the intervening space towards them. How this is possible may be understood in some measure from fig. 6.1, in which the electron–positron 'sea' of particles can be imagined to be distorted by the amplifiers.

chapter, when I will consider the even deeper realms of energy that may underlie the invisible realm visualized by Dirac.

The object of these brief explanations is to make it evident that empty space is not empty and that there is something there to be manipulated. The UFOs know how to manipulate space in a way that, as yet, we do not. Until we do, it is rockets for us!

SEVEN

THE BRAIN OF THE UNIVERSE

THERE ARE PEOPLE who believe that the Universe is a great cosmic computer. Indeed, they not only believe it but are prepared to give us visions of the mechanism by which it works and to back up those visions with hard mathematics and physics.

One of these is R.D. Pearson, who has an Honours degree in Engineering and who switched to being a physicist on his retirement. Pearson's ideas give us new insights into how the Universe functions and, at the same time, make us realize that there is a network of fundamental communication channels by which intelligence can flow back and forth across the depths of space. Our nearest equivalent to this is the computer buff's Internet or information superhighway, which allows computer users worldwide to communicate with each other by using modems to link their computers via telephone lines and satellite links.

In the previous chapters, I introduced several fundamental particles. However, many students of physics suspect that there must be even more deeply fundamental particles out of which these more familiar fundamental particles are made.

Big fleas have little fleas upon their backs to bite 'em,
And little fleas have lesser fleas and so *ad infinitum*.

But it may not be *ad infinitum* when it comes to the basic particles that build the structure of the Universe. Pearson calls his deeply fundamental building blocks *cosmons* and there are just two types.

There is a positive cosmon (C+) and a negative cosmon (C−), each of which, on its own, would occupy a space 100,000 times smaller than an electron. It is possible that, when, in the remote past, advanced 'teachers' came from space to instruct mankind in the basics of science and technology, they tried to tell us about these primaries, and yin and yang and similar dualities are still remembered today, even if their original meaning has been forgotten.

You have to imagine cosmons as minute, spherical liquid drops which can flatten against others when they collide or, under other circumstances, can pass right through one another.

Like all particles, cosmons possess energy, not only when at rest (what we call *mass* when referring to more familiar particles) but also when moving (an additional amount called *kinetic energy*). In Dirac's Sea, cosmons occur in vastly greater profusion than electrons and positrons and it is calculated that, if each type of cosmon existed without the other, there would be astronomical amounts of energy in any small portion of space – $10.^{75}$ W of power in 1 cubic metre to be precise.

However, just like the electrons and positrons in Dirac's Sea, the cosmons are in equilibrium and cancel each other out – almost. The C+ cosmons are slightly 'heavier' than the C– cosmons, and, to compensate, the latter move a little faster. According to Pearson, it is because of this extra speed that the C– cosmons provide the force we call gravity, which is therefore due to a minute disparity between two almost equal forces. That, argues Pearson, is why gravity is such a small force as far as ordinary lumps of matter are concerned. Gravity

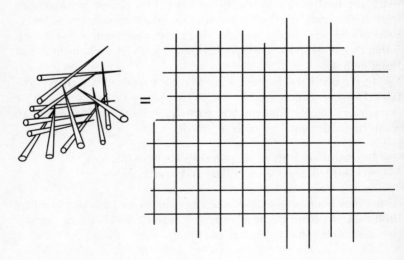

Fig. 7.1 R.D. Pearson's theories lead to the concept of a grid of communication threads filling all space. We will represent this by a conventional square grid (as in fig. 7.3).

only becomes sizeable when the great masses of stars and planets are involved.

The immense number of collisions between C+ and C− cosmons leads to the creation of filaments (*flow cells*) and these flow cells lie across one another at random like unkempt hair (fig. 7.1). Sometimes they form T-junctions where they contact other flow cells and these junctions act like on/off logic switches in a computer. Pearson likens them to the synaptic junctions between neurons of the human brain and so begins to indicate that, at this level, there could be a Universal consciousness.

The appearance of the equivalent filamentary structure in the brain is shown in fig. 7.2. The curiously egg-like entities are neurons (*neuron* is Greek for 'nerve'), which are specialized cells transmitting nerve impulses. Neurons receive signals via masses of very fine filaments, called *dendrites* (because they resemble the branches of a tree) and, when a neuron is sufficiently stimulated, it transmits spikes of electrical activity through long extensions of itself called *axons*. The axons themselves split into thousands of branches and, at the end of each branch, a kind of on/off switch appears called a *synapse* (from the Greek *synapsis*, meaning 'junction'). Synapses convert the activity from the axon branches into electrical signals which, in their turn, stimulate connected neurons. A certain level of stimulation is required before a neuron will pass on the information it has received via its own axon. In this way an initial stimulus, such as a pin-prick on the skin, is registered in the brain. Memory of the event will come about because the synapses can change their effectiveness. Some of this is not yet very well understood, even by those working on the frontiers of research into brain function.

The flow cells postulated by Pearson are like the branches of the axons and, in his theory, the switching on and off of flow cells triggers others to do the same and ripples of energy spread through the flow-cell network. Pearson likens these to the alpha rhythms of the resting brain. The brain broadcasts its alpha rhythms and other activity via electromagnetic waves which can be picked up by encephalographs. Thus it does not take too great a leap of the imagination to see that the thought patterns of the mind can broadcast into, and receive signals through, what I shall call the *Nuether* (new ether).

The idea of the Nuether is new because it replaces the concept of the ether that was current in the early years of the twentieth century. Then, science envisaged the ether as a type of fluid which filled all space and through which the Earth and all other cosmic bodies had to travel. It's existence was dismissed because the experiments set up

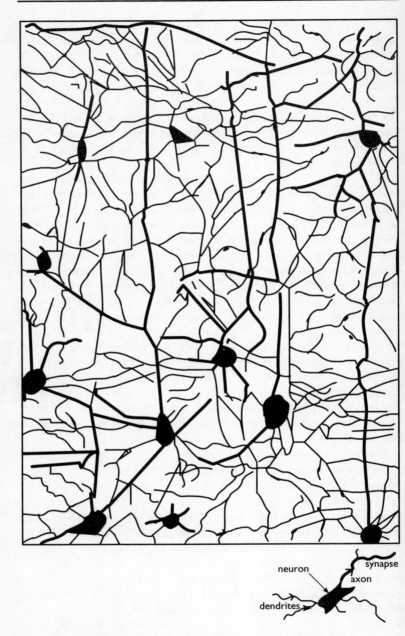

Fig. 7.2   A drawing of a very small part of the communication structure of the brain. It is this which the grid of fig. 7.1 emulates.

to detect it failed. There is now reason to suspect that the major experiment – that of Michelson and Moreley – was flawed. These two researchers found no relative movement between the Earth and the suspected ether. Some modern experimenters have since discovered that the Earth is moving through the Nuether at a speed approaching 250 mph (Marinov, 1992).

Pearson shows that the interaction of cosmons results in the formation of something resembling the neural network of the brain and scientists are programming computers to emulate this in very elementary ways (Hinton, 1992).

However, if this network *is* like the brain, it must be able to store information and learn, to ingest information as well as transport it. Therefore it should be able to manipulate its wave actions to constructive purposes. We are seeing here a vast consciousness underlying the material world which we observe. In the past, many thinkers have suspected the existence of this consciousness but Pearson's theories show us how it can communicate with the world of matter and energy as we see it all about us. Even more to the point, he indicates how our minds can be linked into and receive information from the immense 'superhighway' of intelligence flowing back and forth through the Universe (fig. 7.3).

Pearson states that, basically, Nuetheric vibrations are all there is and everything else is the result of the interaction of such waves.

This means, for example, that the electrons and positrons of Dirac's Sea must be produced by the focussing of Nuetheric waves, and this leads to increased collisions of cosmons and so to the creation of matter. Knots appear in the Nuether (what Pearson calls *density humps*) and these knots are observable particles. That they are mainly electrons and positrons is because these particles are light and so need the least energy for their formation.

We can perhaps understand this matter creation a little better by imagining that we have a sort of Nuetheric plasticine. We can model objects out of this lump of basic material but the box in which the plasticine came tells us that we are only permitted to make certain bodies. There are rules which preclude us from making just anything. Smaller things are easier to make, and we can make more of them, but we can only make things in pairs. Each time we make a negatively charged electron, we have to make a heavier particle – a positively charged nucleon – a proton. Both electron and proton are made of the same basic material but, because we have made two opposites that attract, they are bound to form stable atoms. In their turn, these atoms combine to form the material objects that make our physical world.

At the same time, the basic law that the sum total of electrical charge in the Universe must be zero is not broken. In this way, nature provides electrical balance and, at the same time, creates mass which gravity can act upon. However, not enough mass is made in this way and other electrically neutral nucleons – neutrons – nestle in the nucleus of atoms to make up their mass. How many nucleons there are in a nucleus is governed by laws too complex to discuss here but, in the nuclei of normal atoms, there have to be as many protons as there are electrons. How the electrons arrange themselves around the nucleus is also subject to definite laws, as are the ways in which the atoms combine into molecules and all larger assemblies, such as solids, liquids and gases.

As well as the familiar electrons and nucleons, we are, providing we have enough energy available, allowed to make certain medium-weight particles called *mesons* and heavier particles called *hyperons*. However, the rules of the creation game say that, once we have made these particles, we must immediately break them up into the more familiar and stable particles, such as electrons and nucleons. As well as this, some of their mass/energy substance has to return to the cosmon lump of plasticine.

Whatever you may learn to the contrary, the small packets of light that we call photons are not particles. They are little groups of EM waves travelling through the electron–positron sea and are merely the oscillation of other particles. To understand this, just think of the ocean. Waves are not the ocean, but simply the oscillation of the ocean and, in the same way, photons are oscillations of Dirac's Sea.

It is Dirac's Sea which we can call the *Electromagnetic Ether*. It is waves (photons) in this EM Ether which glue the material world together. Without the glueing effect of this aspect of nature no material world could exist. It does, for all the things we can see and feel, what gravity does for the Universe at large. It provides cohesion so that things can come to a stable state and thus make life possible.

In fig. 7.3, I have represented the grid that builds and nurtures the Universe as a simple square grid which interpenetrates and links everything else, whether material, mental or spiritual. All entities in the Universe, however advanced, have to function within the confines of this grid and within the effects that it allows to occur.

The Universal Grid supports the Universal Mind and also contains the Universal Memory Store. In Aspect 1, the Mental World, it provides all forms of mental communication. It is through this Aspect that mind can interact with mind and therefore, via the brain, make us aware of psychic and other communications.

UNIVERSAL GRID CARRIES UNIVERSAL MIND AND UNIVERSAL STORE

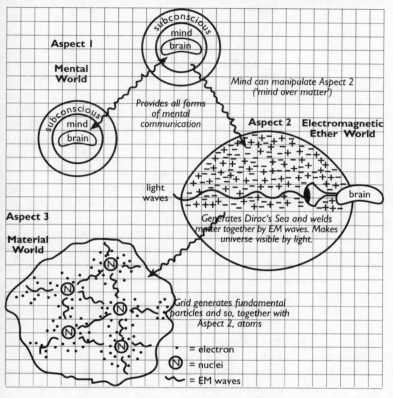

Fig. 7.3   How the Universal Grid underpins all the physical and mental effects that exist. In Aspect 1 (Mental World) the Grid connects one brain to another thus allowing for telepathy and other psychic manifestations. It allows minds deep in the Universe to communicate with our minds. In Aspect 2 (Electromagnetic Ether World) the Grid generates the boiling assemblage of electron–positron pairs (Dirac's Sea) that fills all space. This can be manipulated by Aspect 1 and one of its major functions is to convey light and thus make the Universe visible. The coarsest aspect is Aspect 3 (Material World) where the Grid generates observable matter, such as nucleons and electrons, and so forms, together with Aspect 2, atoms and everything made from atoms. Aspect 2 is essential here as it provides the cohesive force that binds all material objects together. As well as these major aspects the slight imbalance in the underlying cosmons generates gravitational forces thus holding the Universe together.

The majority of people are protected from the flood of unwanted psychic information stemming from the Universal superhighway by an information filter/barrier in the mind that rejects incoming psychic information but allows self-generated information to flow out. This barrier is sometimes lowered in those vivid dreams which we seem to realize are more than the mind playing with its own images. Psychic mediums either have a lowered barrier already or can train themselves to lower the barrier, thus allowing the mind waves of spirit entities to communicate through them. Almost everyone, at some time, will have a psychic experience which they cannot explain in rational terms. It seems that, for reasons which are unclear, the mind's barrier can occasionally be breached. From information that constantly accrues about ETs and their interactions with us, it is quite evident that many of them are fully able to breach the mind's barrier and so communicate directly with us without the need for vocalizing.

It is by this means that alien entities program our minds, thus accessing those parts of our brain that store our experience of language. In this way, through our speech centres, we are 'spoken to' in our own language. However, the human mind can also influence Aspect 2, the Electromagnetic Ether World.

The Electromagnetic Ether is spontaneously generated by the grid, thus creating the electron–positron Sea (Dirac's Sea), whose role is to carry the forces which weld the material world together and, at the same time, allows us to be aware of it by being the carrier of light. It is this Aspect which is manipulated by psychics such as Uri Geller when they mentally 'soften' the otherwise very strong bonds that hold metals together, thus allowing e.g. the handles of spoons to bend.

Aspect 3 is the Material World that we experience. It is the world of atoms and molecules, of the paper on which this is written, of living organisms, organs and bodies. It is made of the nuclei and electrons generated by 'knots' of focussed energy in the grid, welded together by the EM waves carried through the world of Aspect 2.

To sum up, and to take our ideas down in layers from the Material World, we have an invisible Electromagnetic Ether whose particles are those of Dirac's Sea. They lie in the first layer below 'reality' but are still absolutely essential because they provide the means by which radiant light, heat and the forces that hold atoms, molecules and all material things together can be transmitted. No physical Universe would be possible were it not for the binding actions of the Electromagnetic Ether. It is this layer that allows us to see the Universe via light transmitted from stars and galaxies through the vast depths of space.

When a UFO shines in the sky and is seen by many witnesses simultaneously, this has to be real light and shows the UFO to be a real object. This is a material UFO, acting normally, and anyone can see it, but of course you do not need multiple witnesses to confirm such real events. However, having many witnesses who describe the same object, with the slight variations which arise from their being in different places, simply makes it more certain that the light is being projected from a real UFO.

There is evidence to suggest that, sometimes, when it suits their purpose, those behind these visitations can project the image of a UFO directly into the mind so that only one person 'sees' it. Or they can impose one or more images on a photographic film – an image that the camera cannot have accepted through its lens.

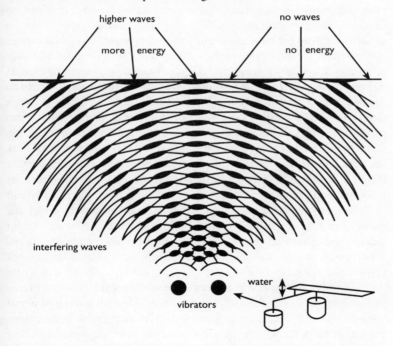

Fig. 7.4 To illustrate interference of waves – an essential part of Pearson's theories – we can make a pair of vibrators just contact a water surface and so create what are called trains of 'coherent' waves. The latter have the same size and wavelength and must travel at the same speed. Where two crests coincide there will be enhanced waves and where crest and trough coincide there will be no waves.

Then, below the Electromagnetic Ether, there is the layer of the cosmons (the Nuether), which is the basis of all things. The Nuether's function is, among other things, to balance the Universe and provide a 'neural network' for other more subtle forms of communication. It is the Nuether that makes the Universe alive and conscious and turns it from a dead assembly of orbs, held together by gravity, into something much more vibrant. This may be why gravity cannot be made to fit the otherwise all-embracing unified field theories of today. It is because gravity is due to a slight imbalance in an octave of nature below the one below the observable Universe.

When we read, in Genesis, about how the Universe began, we find references to 'waters'. It seems very likely that 'waters' is an analogy for waves. After all, in trying to explain the ideas behind invisible electromagnetic waves, teachers use the effects seen in water to illustrate similar properties in light (fig. 7.4). Using water tanks on which vibrators create wave trains, they can show how two sets of waves which are out of step by half a wavelength can produce virtually no waves where they intersect. This is known as destructive interference (fig. 7.5a). This idea of interfering wave trains may be used to explain how two intersecting light beams can, in places, produce darkness. Only energy in the form of interfering wave motions can produce regions of no energy. Where the wave crests coincide (fig. 7.5b), increased energy appears (constructive interference) and, according to Pearson's theories, it is the constructive interference of Nuetheric waves which leads to the creation of particles such as electrons and protons.

Therefore, strange statements such as 'and the waters under the earth' now take on an understandable meaning. 'Earth' is a term for matter and therefore the waters (Nuetheric waves) are 'under' the earth, being at the same time below the physical level of matter but responsible for its creation.

The statements made in ancient documents must be re-interpreted in the light of modern scientific knowledge. What was recorded was sometimes what had been imparted by ET teachers who had done their best to describe concepts far in advance of the level of understanding of their 'pupils'. The chroniclers faithfully wrote down the analogies but later generations did not comprehend the deeper meanings behind them. Uniquely today, in what is perhaps only the second technological civilization that has occupied this planet, we can at last begin to make sense of some of this preserved ancient wisdom.

As an example, there are ancient Sanskrit texts which describe in considerable detail aerial machines, called *vimanas*, that were used in

A

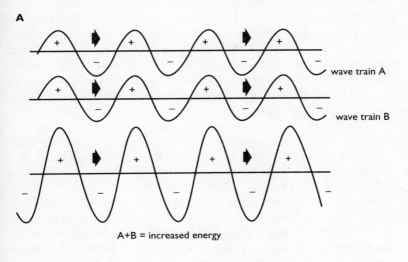

A+B = increased energy

B

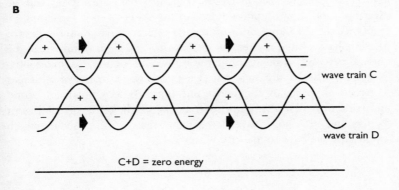

C+D = zero energy

Fig. 7.5 To illustrate interference, two pairs of wavetrains are shown. In (a) wavetrains A and B are in phase and so the result is a bigger set of waves. This is constructive interference. In (b) the two wavetrains, C and D, arrive together but with the crests of C coinciding with the troughs of D. This is destructive interference. Amazingly, we have added two trains of energy and achieved no energy as a result. Waves that are out of step in this manner are, as far as we know, the only way in which two energies can combine to produce no energy.

the Rama Empire at a time commensurate with the latter days of Atlantis. The technological works are known as *Manusa* and the more poetical ones as *Daiva*. The early twentieth-century Sanskrit scholars who attempted to interpret these works about vimanas and their abilities (Childress, 1991) could only do so in the light of the flying machines of their time. Now that we have had some instruction on the construction and propulsion systems of certain ET spacecraft, we would undoubtedly interpret the Sanskrit texts differently – more like spacecraft and less like aeroplanes.

From these late twentieth-century ideas of what makes up the basics of our Universe, we can postulate a Cosmon (or Nuether) Continuum which, because of its essential balance, could have been created from the void by separating nothing into two equal and opposite halves. In Genesis, we read that, in the beginning, 'earth [i.e. matter] was without form and void; and darkness was upon the face of the deep'. This 'deep' must refer to the void before the creation of cosmons because the Electromagnetic Ether was a natural consequence of their creation, as were the EM waves of light that enabled the developing Universe to be seen. This act of creating two almost equal and opposite cosmon 'halves' could be what is meant by 'And the Spirit of God moved upon the face of the waters'.

Once the Cosmon Continuum had been created the interactions of these halves created matter. As well as this, the Continuum created a 'neural network' which became the vehicle for a Universal consciousness. It is akin to our own neural network which conveys messages between all parts of the body and brain. The Universe's neural network provides communication between all kinds of intelligent beings and ultimately to and from the 'master mind' itself, which eventually we have to identify with God.

EIGHT

UNDERSTANDING THE IMPOSSIBLE

THERE ARE MANY strange manifestations associated with UFOs and some of them overlap with things we otherwise experience as psychic phenomena. The sudden appearance and disappearance of entities such as the 'Men in Black', which Alan Hilton's friend John encountered in the lane outside Hilton's house (see page 38), are an example of apparently human creatures which just cannot be subject to the same laws of permanency as we are. Often in such encounters only one entity speaks, as was the case with John's contacts. Similarly, when Kathy Davis (see page 166) and her girlfriend's family were visited by three strange boys when on a camping trip, only one boy spoke. The others seemed to be there as make-weights, or maybe as relays for whatever means of communication was involved in the whole bizarre episode.

Certain psychics have been known, when in trance, to materialize whole entities, including people, the spirit effigies being clothed in *ectoplasm* (see photo 15). This is a form of transitory matter and was named by Professor Charles Richet, an eminent psychical researcher around the beginning of the twentieth century. Richet witnessed on several occasions materializations of what he was convinced were living beings and wrote:

> A living being, or living matter, formed under our eyes, which
> has its proper warmth, apparently a circulation of blood, and a
> physiological respiration, which has also a kind of psychic
> personality having a will distinct from the will of the medium,
> in a word, a new human being! This is surely the climax of
> marvels! Nevertheless, it is a fact.

The lore on materializing entities goes back as far as there are records. Even Socrates believed in sylphs, which are well described as 'Men composed, as it were, of air, and subject to birth and death'. Sylphs, gnomes, undines and salamanders comprised the four categories of elementals or nature spirits. It was once firmly believed that these elementals could be summoned up by magicians. The Swiss philosopher and physician, Paracelsus, wrote:

> They are beings occupying a place between men and spirits. Resembling men and spirits, resembling men and women in their organisation and form, and resembling spirits in the rapidity of their locomotion.

Elementals, when they die, are said simply to disintegrate back into the matrix from which they emerged so that no individual consciousness endures (Holroyd, 1979). Yet sylphs will have more substance than some of the other misplaced entities that are encountered.

Only just recently, as if to give me firsthand experience of such things, I had a curious experience. It was early June and I was driving along an open stretch of country road in that area of the Suffolk–Essex borders which is known as Constable Country because the great painter created some of his most famous canvases there. There was, on my left, a part-grown crop of wheat and over its top I suddenly saw the heads and backs of two large sandy-coloured dogs. Well, I thought they were dogs – they were certainly not deer, of which there are a certain number living wild in the area. I stopped the car because they looked so out of place, being so big and both so immobile. One behind the other, they were looking in my direction. I stopped and watched them for maybe a minute before any movement was made. Then the front one moved his head and both of them turned and slunk back around the corner of the wood on whose edge they had been standing. By subsequently measuring the height of the crop, I found that these animals must have been over 2 feet high at the shoulder and therefore, if they were dogs, then they could only have been Great Danes or maybe large German Shepherd dogs. But who could have lost two such animals? There is no public footpath there. It is a particularly unpopulated area.

Small dogs get lost and no one may notice but really big dogs cannot hide so easily. Yet enquiries in this very rural area failed to reveal anyone who owned such a pair nor anyone who had seen any dogs fitting this description.

Was I looking at 'real' flesh-and-blood animals? I had a feeling I was not. It all seemed so odd and I cannot discount the idea that I was maybe seeing, in my case for the first time, examples of a class of entities which may not be entirely of this world. I shall discuss these out of place animals in chapter 19. There seems to be a form of visible animal-like entity that hovers between reality and holographic projection and the lore on these animals is so large that we have to consider its validity seriously.

In his book *Communion* (1987), Whitley Strieber tells of hearing a wolf howling and seeing one by the roadside. Yet he somehow knew that he had not actually seen a wolf or even heard one howl. He considers that the sound and the image of the wolf were just another part of his communion with space visitors that gave the book its title. It was the same with the owls. On Boxing Night 1985, Strieber had, for him, a very significant interaction with space visitors, who came into his bedroom and abducted him for, among other things, medical examination. On the following morning, he awoke with a very powerful recollection of seeing a large barn owl staring at him through the window at some time during the night. But when he checked there were no owl tracks in the virgin snow on the windowsill.

In his follow-up book *Transformation* (1988), Strieber states that, in his experience – and that of many others – owl imagery is somehow connected with the experience of being visited by alien entities – visits which usually involve abduction. Both he and his sister had had several strange encounters with owls and the circumstances surrounding these encounters led them to conclude that the owls, whatever they were, were not real. The owl imagery even went back to his childhood where regression hypnosis had convinced him that he had been contacted since he was quite young. He was persuaded, as others who see them are, that these images that look like owls are no more real than my dogs in the Suffolk countryside probably were. In the case of Andrija Puharich and Uri Geller in Tel Aviv (Puharich, 1974), it was hawks, but hawks which would not have built nests, had mates and reared young any more than Strieber's owls would have done. They would probably have been what I called in *UFO Quest* (Watts, 1994) *molographic projections*, i.e. they were more substantial than an image that is formed from light but not as real as the natural creatures that we know.

A good example is the 'black-dog' phenomenon. Reports of phantom black dogs abound across the UK and have done so for as long as we have reliable records. The number of people who have encountered Black Shuck in Norfolk, or the Gurt Dog in Somerset (known as the Pooka in Ireland), must run into thousands.

There are similarities in many black-dog reports. All seem to haunt certain stretches of road and travellers encounter the same kind of entity over long periods of time. Typical of the experience is that of the Dartmoor farmer who, hearing an animal coming up behind him, turned to find it was a large black dog. The dog must have resembled a real dog for the farmer went to stroke it, only to find that his hand passed straight through it. The farmer followed the animal to a crossroads where it exploded in a blinding flash of light which was so intense that it threw him to the ground (Michell & Rickard, 1977).

In another case in Norfolk, a dog approached a woman and seemed relatively normal until it got near to her, whereupon it suddenly blew up like a balloon in front of her eyes and dissolved into thin air. Can such apparitions be in any way understood and what may they have to do with UFOs?

I began to get the glimmerings of an answer after reading and ingesting the substance of Robert Pearson's theories outlined in the previous chapter. Let us remind ourselves of what was said there. The ideas predict an intelligent Universe which is based on a 'cosmon grid' (Nuetheric grid), which is responsible for the creation of matter.

It was while I was working at my computer that I suddenly realized that I had something like a black dog or maybe a Man in Black before me on the monitor. I was looking at one of the icons which represent the names of disks on the computer screen.

It was when I was using the mouse to move an icon that I suddenly realized where Pearson's ideas were leading.

The icon, when stored on the floppy disk, was invisible and irretrievable. Without the means to retrieve it, as far as I was concerned it might as well have been on Mars. Yet slip that disk into a device called a computer and the icon became a set of electromagnetic signals that could be fed to a visual display screen and rendered visible as a recognizable entity. An entity, moreover, which I could recall at will, but only when I had a need to.

I saw that the monitor screen with its raster of pixels was a two-dimensional analogy of Pearson's three-dimensional cosmon grid. Each of the multitude of little dots (pixels) which made up the icon was being energized to form a unique but recognizable pattern. Yet, because of the ability of the computer to 'memorize' items programmed into it, the information for making that pattern was always there. It only needed me – the intelligent [sic] part of the set-up – to do certain things and, hey presto, there it was – something apparently created out of nothing and, moreover, a complex thing whose form and organization were stored in the memory of the machine. That icon was preserved intact as it was moved around. It also represented the ability to summon up from the computer's memory a much more complex program – a program moreover that I could 'clone'. I only had to drag my 'live' icon over another inert one and I had two identical versions of the original.

Now Pearson says that the Universe, with its complex nerve-like pathways and its ability to store information, is a great computer. So when something apparently alive appears out of nowhere, exists for a while as a self-mobile entity and then just as mysteriously disappears, we can suggest a scenario which fits most of the facts.

A black dog that runs (or floats) along a stretch of road could be a complex version of my icon on the computer monitor. It has form and it can be summoned up from the memory stored, not on a disk in magnetic form but in the local cosmon grid. Like the icon, it can be made to move at the behest of its manipulator and, again like the icon, it preserves its form as it moves across the grid (the raster) which forms it. That manipulator might, in certain circumstances, be an ET in a flying saucer. Or maybe the memory is left in a certain locality and, for reasons of which we have no inkling, the conditions exist from time to time for the dog to be summoned up out of the memory.

Depending on the energy available, the cosmon grid will be able to create the matter which forms the dog, the Nuetheric memory ensuring that the matter created is woven together in the form of a dog. The eyes of Black Shuck are often said to glow, which may indicate that this is something more than a simple re-creation of the form of an animal entity.

We can postulate the same kind of transitory generation of matter in cases where mediums produce ectoplasm. Because of the law of conservation of energy, whatever energy is needed to generate the material that forms the ectoplasmic image must be lost from somewhere else. In this case, it has been found that the medium loses weight in direct proportion to the extent of the ectoplasm produced. The material of the image is produced from the cosmon grid by the 'spiritual energy' of the medium. When that energy is withdrawn, the material dematerializes and is absorbed back into the grid.

It now becomes possible to believe an abductee who says that he/she was floated out through a closed window, door, or even a solid wall. We may think we are more or less solid but, when we analyze material objects, they are all space.

Take the simplest atom, hydrogen. The atom occupies a space which is roughly a million, million times as big as the space occupied by the electron and the proton that form it. So the hydrogen atom – and likewise all atoms, molecules and cells – is mainly empty space. Only the electrons and the nuclei are 'solid' and, even then, we are not sure whether that statement is true. What looks like solidity is simply the result of very strong electromagnetic and nuclear force fields.

So, for example, a window pane or a brick wall is mainly space and the 'solid' particles of which it is composed are formed out of the Nuether anyway. To those who understand how to manipulate the Nuether it must be child's play to dematerialize part of that pane or wall so that the body can pass through. The memory part of the Cosmon Continuum will enable the pane or wall to be reconstructed just as it was before, blemishes, defects and all. No one could tell the difference.

Likewise, those who know how can construct any kind of entity apparently out of nothing – an owl, a wolf, a dog or a Man in Black. They just need the necessary icon to run the programme for that entity, whose form is stored in the memory of the intelligent Universe. That temporary creation can be absorbed back into the Neuther, from which it sprang, just as instantly.

So here we begin to see evidence of a world which can be transitory. We may not understand the mechanism by which it works but even the realization that it is there can allow us to suggest reasons for some of the bizarre things which happen in the world of UFOs. Therefore, we should not be so surprised when that world seems to spill over into the world of spirits. We indeed have a long way to go before we can unravel the workings of the strange things which people report. Yet, when we look back at the history of conventional science, we see that many of the effects which were once thought to have different causes – heat, light, electricity and even lumps of metal – have all become explicable as different aspects of one all-embracing atomic theory. We now need to work towards an 'atomic theory' of the world below the material, which at present is largely hidden from us but which the UFO visitation has begun to help us tackle.

NINE

INTELLIGENCE FROM ELSEWHERE

IN THE LAST 40 years, something truly remarkable has been happening. We have been getting direct communications from those who oversee the destiny of the Universe. Because of what they have told us and demonstrated to us, we must, before proceeding further, outline how and from where these communications are coming. The entities involved have already been mentioned. They are those who style themselves the Council of Nine.

I first became aware of the Nine, as many others must have done, through Doctor Andrija Puharich's biography of Uri Geller (1974), which described the immensely strange encounters that Puharich (photo 6) came to have with Geller (photo 7). These began in 1971 when Puharich went to meet Geller in Tel Aviv with a view to investigating, on a scientific basis, the amazing reports of the young man's powers to influence inanimate matter by mental processes.

The laboratory reports of the structure of the breaks that Uri induced in samples of metal, simply by rubbing them gently between his fingers, had begun to filter through to an incredulous world and Puharich wanted to know more. He was first alerted to the Geller phenomenon by an article written in 1970 by an Israeli Army officer.

However, Puharich's first close encounter with the Nine had been some 20 years earlier when, on 16 February 1952, he arranged a meeting with a Hindu sage, Dr D.G. Vinod. During this meeting, while Puharich was holding the sage's right ring finger at the middle joint between his own right index finger and thumb, Vinod leaned back and, in the next incredible hour, told Puharich his life story as if he were reading it from a book. As Puharich says in his book: 'His accuracy about the past was extraordinary', and he realized that he was dealing with an intelligence of immense proportions. Vinod was tapping sources of information that Puharich had never imagined could exist.

These sources are most likely to be the same 'Books of Life' that the great clairvoyant, Edgar Cayce, claimed to have 'read' when giving 'readings' to the many people whose lives he assisted. Doris Agee (1989) was still only a child when Cayce passed to another realm, but describes him as a modest humble man who did strange and wonderful things when 'he went to sleep' but who was wont to grow the largest, juiciest, sweetest strawberries she had ever tasted. He was, she says, 'towering tall, laughed often, and had an ability to communicate with children that is given to few men'.

Cayce was himself only a boy of 12 years old when he received his first extraordinary 'help' from elsewhere. In Cayce's biography, *There is a River*, Thomas Sugrue (1942) tells how, in response to his fervent prayers, Bible-crazy Edgar received a vision. He was so preoccupied with this and what it meant that his schoolwork suffered. Yet help was at hand. The voice that he had heard in his vision also told him to 'Sleep and we may help you'. It was late at night and the boy dozed off for some minutes. When he awoke he found that he knew the entire contents of the spelling book on which he was to be questioned next day (Goodman, 1978).

Cayce's readings were largely taken down and stored so that, today, a vast body of his testimonies exists and can be studied by bona fide researchers at the Headquarters of the Association for Research and Enlightenment, at Virginia Beach, Virginia, USA. Visitors can stay at a beachfront motel which is part of a complex that houses, among other facilities, one of the greatest metaphysical and parapsychological libraries in the world. When Doris Agee's book was published in the UK in 1989, it brought the number of books devoted to Cayce's remarkable testimonies to no less than 12. These included *Edgar Cayce on Atlantis* (Cayce, 1968), a book which I personally feel has given us more solid information about the 'Atlantean Land' and its eventual demise than we have ever had before.

Cayce, in attempting to explain how he was able to read the lives of those who came to him for help, guidance and healing, talked of a 'sphere of communication', which was peopled by disembodied entities on various planes of psychic development. He intimated that it was possible to attune mentally with any of these entities and it would appear that Vinod was one of those able to do so.

Cayce described how, in his trance state, he moved upwards along a path of light through various dark and grotesque scenes until the surroundings lightened and he became aware of what appeared as normal cities and towns. Then sounds came, birds sang, and there was music and laughter.

There is more and more light, the colors become very beautiful, and there is only a blending of sound and color. Quite suddenly, I come upon a hall of records. It is a hall without walls, without a ceiling, but I am conscious of seeing an old man who hands me a large book, a record of the individual for whom I seek information.

Thus Cayce explains that:

Each soul, in each experience of assumed bodily form, makes a record. It gains in development; it loses. It exercises its free will, given by God, for good or for evil in each earthly appearance.

So Edgar Cayce firmly believed in reincarnation.

Agee says that a Cayce 'reading' is like thumbing back through a 'soul-diary' dating back not only to the birth of the enquirer but also to previous incarnations, about which Cayce was able to enlighten many of those who consulted him.

It would appear that Vinod was reading from these same Books of Life and was able, through his trance state, to 'travel' and consult, for example, the 'Book of the Life of Andrija Puharich'.

On the last day of 1952, in the laboratory of the Round Table Foundation in Augusta, Georgia, Vinod lay back on a sofa and spoke in English, in a voice which was not his own.

The communication came from an entity calling itself M. According to Puharich, M opened with the words 'We are Nine Principles and Forces, personalities if you will, working in complete mutual implication'. Here M was using the word 'implication' to mean 'entanglement' or 'entwinement'.

The entity M went on to explain that the Nine influenced mankind by 'accentuating certain directions as will fulfil the destiny of creation'. The Nine proposed, M said, to work with Puharich for various reasons, including his great patience. M told him that the Nine did not guide but were the instruments and avenues of some, as yet, undefined purpose.

In *UFO Quest* (Watts, 1994), I explained how, at the outset, M gave the Einstein–Lorentz mass-increase equation in such a way that it indicated a sudden change in the consciousness of any intelligent entity exceeding 99 per cent of the speed of light. This implied that, above this speed, one would cross into the realms of the superconscious, a realm transcending human consciousness. In total, this communication from the Nine occupied $1\frac{1}{2}$ hours and it provided Puharich with a month's work as he and Vinod listened to the tape recordings and tried to come to terms with the deep wisdom of what they were hearing.

In June 1953, a circle of nine people, including Puharich, were treated to a phenomenon well known to psychic researchers but which defies explanation in terms of conventional science.

This time another of the Nine, calling itself R, spoke through Vinod and, in a fully lit room, all nine onlookers saw a pile of cotton threads appear apparently out of the wooden floor about 3 feet in front of Vinod, who was in trance. These threads were not ethereal but a real substance, and there were nine of them. They were loops of finely woven cotten cord and each of the nine onlookers was asked to slip the loop over their right shoulder and under the left arm. The entity R had indicated that, by this process, they were to be created Brahmins. In the USA, where the sitting took place, a Brahmin is defined as a highly intelligent or socially exclusive person and, in Hinduism, the word means 'the ultimate and divine reality of the Universe'.

Those chosen to take part in this demonstration of the powers of the Nine could not all have been mistaken as to the apparent source of this material, nor of its evident production from nothing. Thus, we see an instance of the materialization of matter associated with the Nine. However, we have already said that such materialization is a well-known ability of some of the more powerful psychics. Therefore it is another indication that the same continuum can be used by both human beings and such elevated entities as the Nine appear to be.

The contacts with Puharich continued. On 15 March 1963, he had a form of UFO experience. After a bad day in New York City, he had, to use his own words, 'crashed out' and awoke about 9.40 p.m. Lying on his bed and looking out at the wintry, starry sky, he was suddenly confronted by a bright light. It was stationary and located over a hill about 300 yards from his apartment. The light was a steady blue-green in colour, the shape of a flattened egg and apparently the size of the full moon.

It seems probable that the light was appearing solely to him because he describes feeling that this was a profound moment, that the light was very real, and that in some way it was 'alive'. In keeping with many others who have had similar UFO experiences, he was apparently constrained from attempting to take a movie of the light. It was for him 'a pure experience', unlike anything that had ever happened to him before. Yet, all it seemed to be was a light and it remained where he had first seen it for some 20 minutes before it was suddenly extinguished. He waited for another hour in the hope that it would return, but it did not.

Thus, in many ways, this light was an unnatural phenomenon. It could well have shielded a UFO whose denizens 'spoke' to him, which is why he felt it was alive. It might well be that no one else saw this particular light other than himself. From comparison with other cases in the UFO annals, it is possible that this was the moment when Puharich was programmed to be the companion and mentor of Uri Geller.

Already in this build-up to Puharich's meeting with Geller, we have seen three phenomena which one could well imagine were unconnected. Firstly, there was the original 'channelled' Vinod communication from the Nine; secondly, there was a demonstration of materialization of matter from 'nothing'; and thirdly, there was the UFO experience. Yet were these separate unlinked occurrences or were they all presented to Puharich as a means to establishing an end – the channelling of his life and thought processes towards a future meeting with another? That other, Geller, had already been programmed to ends which included the gaining of a 'scientific' friend from thousands of kilometres away in the USA.

In Tel Aviv in December 1949, the just 4-year-old Geller had an encounter with a UFO while playing in an abandoned garden opposite his home. Looking across a pool in the garden, he became aware of a huge bowl-shaped object settling down out of the sky. It did not resemble any of the aeroplanes his father had shown him. Just as with Puharich in New York, the encounter gave the little boy a feeling of peace and beauty. However, there suddenly appeared what Geller described as a 'shadowy giant' with no arms or legs. From the 'head' of this uncanny entity came a blinding ray of light that struck the boy so forcibly that he was knocked over backwards and fell into a deep sleep (trance?) that lasted several hours.

I am convinced that, during that encounter, Uri Geller's brain was programmed to awaken powers that we may all possess but which we do not have the means to tap at this stage in our psychic development. This is how he was able to influence solid metals to bend and break, watches and clocks to start when they had not run for years, and all the other para-psychic things which he has shown himself capable of doing (Geller, 1975; Puharich, 1974).

One has to read *Uri* (Puharich, 1974) to appreciate fully the development of the astounding things that happened to Puharich and Geller when the 'weld' had finally been made but there are also some events which have a direct bearing on our efforts to put background into the UFO phenomena.

Throughout the time that Andrija and Uri spent together, there were constant, recurring UFO sightings and events, as well as several examples of telekinesis linked to an entity who said its extra-terrestrial base was called Spectra. It delivered this information through Geller while the latter was in trance but all attempts to tape-record the exchanges were thwarted by unseen powers, which either disabled the recorder at the psychological moments, 'dissolved' the tapes while they were still in the machine, or just plainly wiped them.

Possibly among the most remarkable things that plagued Andrija Puharich were the translocation events, if for no other reason than their apparent impossibility. Here is an example.

Puharich did not spend all his time in Israel. He returned to the USA every so often and, during one of these sojourns, he mislaid the earpiece from his Sony ICR-100 radio. He knew that he had lost it in the USA and was pretty certain that it had been in New York City.

Subsequent to this, Puharich returned to Israel and was attempting, with Geller's help, to communicate with Spectra. During one of these sessions, when Geller was in trance, a disembodied voice said: 'Andrija, I have asked Uri to come to me now.' In response Puharich asked if he could use the tape recorder. The voice replied: 'If you do not want to lose the fourth cassette, you will not record. Take this Uri; hand it over to Andrija.'

The incredulous Puharich opened Uri's clenched left hand, only to find his missing earpiece complete inside its case!

After the many apparently impossible things that had occurred to them, Andrija was not as astounded as he might have been, so he went on to ask questions. 'Are you of the Nine Principles that once spoke through Dr Vinod?' 'Are you behind the UFO sightings that started in the United States when Kenneth Arnold saw nine flying saucers on June 24th 1947?'. In both cases, he received unequivocally affirmative answers.

It is highly interesting that, during this session, the communicator told Puharich that, as a means of reaching mankind the Nine can command any communication system that it has devised. 'We will use your tape, phone, radio, television, telegram, letters, computers and so on. Farewell.'

When he tried his tape-recorder – which had not been used for the session – Puharich found that all functions other than 'forward' did not work. When he pressed the forward button, he found on the tape a full recording of the session they had just experienced. To the actual transcript had been added a further message, telling him to hypnotize Uri on a special day and that further messages would be placed on the recorder.

By this time, Andrija Puharich was becoming more aware of the methods used to give him instructions. When a hall light that had not worked for 4 days was suddenly switched on and off by invisible forces, he took that to mean he should wipe the tape, which he did.

This very limited review of aspects of the interaction between Geller, Puharich and the Nine only brushes the surface of the communications and the seemingly impossible demonstrations of the powers of the cosmic entities. In one such demonstration, a ball-point pen, whose three parts had been number-coded by Puharich, was placed in a cigar box. Geller placed his left hand over the box but did not touch it. He kept it there for 9 whole minutes. Eventually, Uri thought that something had happened. They opened the box and found, disappointingly, that the pen appeared intact. But when Puharich lifted it out of the box he realized that it was lighter than before. On opening it up they found that the brass filler cartridge had been removed while it lay in the box.

Such abilities to dematerialize specific objects are amazing to our eyes. We see a metal as a dense array of 'point' objects, namely electrons and nuclei, held together by an impenetrable matrix of strong Electromagnetic fields. How, in the name of the Nine, can one set of those fields/particles be interacted with in such a way as to diffuse through the outer casing of a pen? And how can they be not only removed but also have their spatial relationship preserved so that the same object can be materialized again elsewhere? Even if, as Puharich suggests, the object is taken apart atom by atom, there is still not enough 'room' for the atoms to penetrate the long-chain molecular structure of the surrounding plastic case. Well, we have already seen (page 81) an answer to these questions. They stem from a far too limited view of the way the Universe is constructed. However, from ideas such as the Cosmon Continuum we can see that such dematerializations and rematerializations are indeed possible.

The demonstration of the powers of Spectra was not concluded by the dematerializion of the pen cartridge. At 10.00 p.m. on 7 December 1971, after a set of events that seemed to be directing them towards a specific end, Puharich and Geller, together with Geller's girlfriend Iris, found themselves driving past a dump on a road possibly leading to Lod airport. First they heard a chirruping sound and then they saw the loom of a blue stroboscope-type light over an intervening embankment. It was the light on a UFO.

Geller went over the embankment and into the hollow beyond. He commanded the others to remain where they were. After an anxious wait, which seemed like an eternity but in reality was only about 4 minutes, they saw him returning with something in his hand. It was the brass cartridge with its code number, 367299, scratched on it, just as Puharich had originally marked it.

Now we may say 'Is Andrija Puharich making all this up?' Frankly, I think not because, while the events he describes are bizarre, they are much like many other events that have been vouchsafed to people across the world. Furthermore, his were among the early but not the only communications with the Nine, as you will see in the next chapter.

In addition, we can now, through the theories of R.D. Pearson, understand how dematerializations and rematerializations may be performed.

The particles of Puharich's cartridge (like all material objects) were created by the Cosmon Continuum that underlaid them. Once created, the electrons, protons and neutrons formed themselves into atoms under the influence of the rules that govern the form that material bodies will take. These atoms were, in their turn, welded together by electromagnetic forces into the form of the metals and plastics from which the cartridge was made.

When the cartridge was dematerialized, its whole structure was absorbed back into the Cosmon Continuum. But the Continuum is also a form of computer and therefore has the ability to remember the 'plan' of what it has apparently destroyed. Because of this memory, the cartridge could be reconstructed to appear exactly as before, even to the extent of having its unique number stamped on it.

Going back to the translocation of Puharich's earpiece from New York to Tel Aviv, we can see that transferring the memory of every detail of the device along what we can describe as the Nuether's communications superhighway would be very simple. Because the plan of the earpiece is stored in the Cosmon Continuum, it can be re-activated to form the necessary assemblage of particles that will reproduce the object again. They will not be the same electrons, protons and neutrons that disappeared into the maw of the Continuum in New York but, as no one can tell the difference, the new ones that rematerialize in Israel will definitely reproduce for the owner the lost artefact.

To make this clearer, consider a simple analogy. Assume I live in New York. I have a uniquely-shaped mould which I fill with water and put in the freezer. I show the ice-shape that I have made to a friend. He and I go down to the sea and we both watch the ice-shape melt in it.

Unbeknown to my friend, I then fly to Israel, where I reproduce an exact copy of my ice-shape and invite my friend to come and see it. He cannot tell the difference because, while the water from which I made the ice-shape in New York is different from that in Israel, it is still water and looks identical wherever you may be.

I have dematerialized an object in one place and rematerialized it again in another, and I have managed to do so because I have carried an on-board computer – my brain, which stores the instructions for doing it – between the two places.

In this analogy, the oceans take the place of the cosmon sea and my brain, transported by jet from New York to Israel, parallels the transfer of the instructions for recreating an apparently identical object.

The same kind of explanation applies to the disappearance of tapes from inside tape-recorders, whether or not they are re-materialized. The ideas have wide-ranging consequences for the apparent production of humanoids, as well as strange out of place creatures, such as lake monsters and Big Hairy Men (BHMs), or threads that appear from nowhere and yet are real material (see page 86). Maybe the material world is not as solid as we might like it to be.

TEN

CHANNELLED INFORMATION

ANDRIJA PUHARICH'S account of his experiences with Uri Geller (Puharich, 1974) covered a period that ended around 1972. Following on from this, communication from the Nine was transferred to Phyllis Schlemmer, a deep-trance medium who started to obtain channelled information from them in 1974. It was as if the Nine had decided that a true two-way, question-and-answer dialogue was the way forward and that they could only open up such a channel via a deep-trance medium.

In the remarkable book *The Only Planet of Choice* (Schlemmer, 1994), the results of question-and-answer sessions between certain sitters and Tom, the spokesman for the Council of Nine, using Phyllis Schlemmer as transceiver, are recorded.

Some people might think that 'Tom' is too glib, too common a name for an entity from deep space, yet one has to set that against the earlier communications from the Nine, in which the communicator merely called itself by a single letter, such as M or R.

The communications received through Phyllis Schlemmer continued until 1994, when the book was prepared for publication. I understand, however, that these communications are still being received.

The contacts with Puharich and Geller were, it would appear, something of a hit and miss affair. They may not have been like that as far as the Nine were concerned but the means of communication, and the often arbitrary nature of the way in which the material received was sent or deleted, was probably not considered satisfactory for the Nine's purposes. They seem to have decided that the time had come for real intercommunication with the human race on Earth and I suspect that Puharich was not sufficiently psychic to make this efficiently possible. Meanwhile Geller had his work of disseminating the 'gospel' through his stage, radio and television appearances.

It seems possible that Uri Geller was given the powers that he displayed in order to prepare mankind for what was to come. Thus, we would be more prepared to accept the philosophy of the Nine when they decided to impart it to us. Also, reading *The Only Planet*, one comes to realize that the Nine have a benign, almost fatherly interest in Planet Earth. They see that we are in danger of destroying all that our ancestors have striven for and have suffered so grievously for in the long, long haul to our present level of civilization. A civilization, moreover, which stands tremulously on the threshold of its initial foray into the great expanse of the Universe.

At one stage, in an attempt to explain their, to us, inexplicable nature the Nine said:

> It is as if you would take all that is spiritual within the Universe, and all that was of the intellect within the Universe, and take all of the physicalness that has been refined, and blend it together to make one pureness. It is like a crystal.

I think that, when Tom talked about a 'crystal', he was referring to what we would call a 'single crystal'. This is a theoretical concept whereby the crystalline structure has no imperfections: every atom is in its correct place and its boundaries stretch to infinity. In practice, however perfect, any crystalline structure we can make is bound to have edges, and edges are the biggest imperfections of all.

We come closest to the ideal when we create all-but perfect crystalline layers of silicon in the manufacture of micro-chips. These *epitaxial layers* are buried in a silicon substrate so that they effectively have no boundary. It is this ability to create single crystal layers that has contributed most to the stability and reliability of modern micro-chips. In the early days of transistor manufacture, it was the exposed edges between the various regions of transistors that led to their breakdown and general unreliability.

The channelled sessions with Phyllis Schlemmer have occupied periods between 20 and 90 minutes. In these sessions, Phyllis counts herself down into a deep trance in which she appears to fall asleep in her chair. However, as the trance deepens, she suddenly becomes animated and announces in a new voice that Tom is present and offers greetings and blessings, as is the habit when mediums of other persuasions give readings. Phyllis herself is unconscious and can remember nothing of what has transpired when she regains consciousness. Indeed, Tom is on record as saying that neither 'Our Being's mind nor her soul is in her body' at the time he is communicating. This rather loving term, 'Our Being', is how Tom always refers to Phyllis and, when he leaves, he sends her 'our love'.

There is, by their own admission, only one channel for the Nine and that is through Phyllis. In this way, they maintain the integrity of the messages. Furthermore, it may well be that no other person on Earth has the right combination of psychic make-up. The Nine say they surveyed the whole of the human race before deciding to use Phyllis as their channel. This puts an immense responsibility on this one medium's shoulders and is one which she has shouldered for some 20 years. It demands the complete subjugation of self to the task in hand and carries with it hidden danger. She needs the intervention of an elevated entity who, rather like an anaesthetist during an operation, monitors and maintains her bodily functions while her mind is completely taken over by Tom. This entity comes from the Civilization Altea which, we are told, has overseen the technical progress of mankind.

The voice which issues from Phyllis is that of Tom and it is high-pitched, slow, and often given to speaking in archaic English. However, Tom is not communicating words to Phyllis but ideas, in forms of psychic energy which Phyllis's brain transforms into speech. If Phyllis's mind does not contain the sounds, words or ideas that Tom wishes to communicate, these ideas cannot be communicated. It is rather like having a language on a computer hard disk – only what is already programmed on the disk can be accessed.

Those who frame the questions to be put to Tom are not independent of the psychic presence of their communicator. They sense that their ideas are known before they have ever framed them in words. Issues are elucidated and unspoken questions answered within their own minds but the voice channel is important because, unlike the Geller/Puharich encounters, there is, with Phyllis, no embargo on taped transcripts of the questions and answers.

Thus, we are at last talking directly to those who know both what happened in the past and what we must do to secure the future. It is the most exciting and awe-inspiring development in the whole history of our interaction with the Civilizations of outer space.

The UFOs have made us aware of beings from elsewhere visiting Earth. We see that, despite millions of sorties through the years, no direct harm has come to mankind. In turn, Phyllis' selfless subjugation of her own psyche has led to an understanding of the integration that exists between such apparently unconnected phenomena as UFOs, spirit entities, Biblical patriarchs, etc. At the same time, it has shown mankind the only way forward. Earth is indeed in danger and something must happen in the next decades to reverse the negative trends. We are not alone in the Universe; nor are we a planetary island.

This is a message that is not the prerogative of the Nine and has been re-iterated many times through contactees. Many of these communications and the circumstances surrounding them are brought together in Janet and Colin Bord's *Life Beyond Planet Earth* (1991) and, taken together, they constitute a powerful expression of the fact that, by many means and in many ways, ETs have been trying hard for years to warn us of impending doom that faces us if we do not change our ways.

The channelled information via Phyllis Schlemmer is the most direct and effective means of communication yet used by any of these entities. In comparison, the piecemeal communications with contactees is rather like speaking with the work-force while the communications from the Nine represent pronouncements from the Board of Directors. While the whole organization knows in general the company's policy, only the Directors have their fingers fully on the pulse. Thus, what the Nine say to us is the most important news we have received in modern times and we should listen to it carefully and attempt to understand it as far as we are able.

Reading *The Only Planet* makes one realize, perhaps for the first time, that what happens on Earth has a direct effect on the rest of the Universe. We are important in the great scheme of things and, unless we understand that we are capable of strangling the evolution of an integrated Universe, then we are surely damned. It is not what we do physically that matters. It is what we contribute collectively in love and compassion. This feeds through the spiritual continuum to the Nine. It spiritually feeds them as they feed us. They and we are one and we each need the other. In the psychic 'space' between us, there is room for many other civilizations, some more developed than us but not as developed as the Twenty-four Civilizations which collectively oversee the material, mental and spiritual development of the Universe (fig. 12.5).

It is extremely difficult for us here on Earth to imagine the condition of the beings of the Twenty-four Civilizations. Tom has said:

All beings in them have complete oneness in thought and form. It is not like Planet Earth. Those Twenty-four Civilizations join with us to bring about the plan for Planet Earth that was conceived by all of us in the beginning. In truth, the Council and the Twenty-four developed and created what was necessary on

Planet Earth in order for humanity to live on it, when it was ready.

In his book *Communion*, Whitley Strieber (1987), dwelling on the reality of his 'visitors' and on the way they dealt with him and with others who become the target for Greys, says:

The source of their reticence is not contempt but fear, and well-founded fear, too. They are not afraid of man's savagery or his greed, but of his capacity for independent action.

And a little further on:

I return to the thought that they are a sort of hive. If this were true, then they may be, in effect, a single mind with millions of bodies – a brilliant creature, but lacking the speed of independent, quick-witted mankind. If they think slowly enough, it may be that the human being, fast thinking and autonomous, could be a remarkable threat. It may be that an old, essentially primitive intelligence has encountered a new, advanced form and is frightened of the potential that our completeness as individuals gives us.

Now the Greys originate not directly from one of the Twenty-four Civilizations but from lesser civilizations; yet they may well be modelled on what could be the developed pattern for beings on all planets other than Earth. If the souls within the Civilizations have complete oneness in thought and form, then they are indeed like bees, each member adding his small contribution to the wholeness of the hive. The ant colony has fascinated science-fiction writers for years. Each ant is a microscopic and expendable part of the colony but, together with its fellows, it makes up a mighty force. The organization of civilization on planets other than Earth may be essentially a developed form of the ant-hill or the beehive. 'Can it be,' says Strieber, 'that any one of us has the potential to be at once inferior and superior to their entire species?'

In order to comprehend the message from the Council of Nine, we have to absorb the tenets of reincarnation. Each soul is indestructible and, once created, exists for all time. On release from its Earth body, a human soul may be able to make some choices about where it spends its spiritual life before it either returns to inhabit an Earthly body or occupies another form of being elsewhere in the Universe. Tom complains that Earth souls so enjoy being physical that they do not want to give up the chance of being physical again. Thus they are creating a log-jam in the free trade in souls across the Universe. When we die, we ought to be adventurous and allow our souls to be transported into some other entity in some other civilization, but we do not. We hang on, in a kind of limbo, waiting for a chance to re-inhabit an Earth body again.

However, not all the souls inhabiting Earth bodies are from Earth people of the past. According to Tom:

> Souls from different civilizations of the Twenty-four have come to Planet Earth in your present time for two purposes: to fulfil the purpose of their civilization, and to help Planet Earth in its transformation – otherwise this Planet Earth and the souls that exist upon it will be in bondage, and we shudder to think of the darkness that will take over the Universe. All of the Twenty-four are represented upon this Planet Earth in one form or another.

In *Alien Liaison*, Timothy Good (1992) gives information culled from 'briefing papers' which had been shown to a physicist, Robert Scott Lazar, while he was involved with a Nevada secret test site. Good devotes at least two chapters of his book to Lazar's testimony on many aspects of the alleged possession and flight testing of extra-terrestrial discs. Here I shall pick up on those aspects which help to confirm Tom's testimony.

Lazar confirms that information from Extraterrestrial Biological Entities (EBEs) was recorded in the papers he read to the effect that 'humankind is the product of periodic genetic "corrections" by the aliens'. Tom calls these genetic corrections *accelerations* and they will be covered more fully in chapter 11.

According to Good, Lazar had great difficulty in accepting that our visitors are representatives of those elevated entities that have been the instrument of mankind's development from the very beginning. So may a large number of people but the evidence continues to accumulate. Apparently, the briefing papers said that mankind is regarded by the ETs as physical containers for souls, which is just what Tom has told us through Phyllis Schlemmer. Furthermore, religion was created so that we would have moral rules and principles. However, the main purpose of these rules and principles was to ensure that we 'did not damage the containers'. This throws new light on the Commandment 'Thou shalt not kill'.

Further corroboration has been provided by Bob Oeschler, who, in a radio interview, said that there was, to his knowledge, a deal going on with one species of EBE during the years 1979–82 – and it may still be going on. He confirmed that there are different forms of Grey – some with noses and some without. He was of the opinion that we do not know exactly what these entities want. He said that their genetic engineering programme now covers four generations and the kind of artificial insemination practised on Kathy Davis (see page 166) is more common than is generally realized. He estimated that some three dozen cases were investigated in the USA prior to 1994 and that these were possibly only the tip of the iceberg.

The evidence for Out of Body Experiences (OBEs) is very strong (Currie, 1995). Some are Near Death Experiences (NDEs) but many people have OBEs while they are fully and joyously alive. My wife experienced one when she was 18 years old. She was lying in her bed in the living room (at that time, she was sharing a one-bedroom flat with her parents) when she suddenly became aware that she was up in the corner of the room looking down at her body asleep in the bed below. Many other people have had similar experiences and they help us to come to terms with the 'container' idea, i.e. the body being a physical container for the real person – the soul. Sometimes, and maybe for no apparent reason, the soul will part from the body for short periods. Some people are adept at producing OBEs at will and transporting themselves to other locations. After such a translocation, they return to their own material bodies. This indicates that the soul can exist quite independently of the body and so makes it more acceptable that, when the body dies, the soul does not.

According to Edith Fiore, in her book *Abductions* (1989), the abductors of a lady in her mid-50s were apparently able to induce OBEs in those they abducted. Victoria, as the lady is called, described under regression hypnosis how she had been picked up the previous August and subjected to examination procedures similar to those which she had been experiencing over the ten or more abductions she had suffered since she was young.

In the August abduction, she recalled the presence of many people of different nationalities. She said:

> We're afraid and at the same time, we're calm. They've made the calmness. It's like they got us in a spell. I feel like ...
> I'm not just me. I feel that my body's there but I'm not.
> But I don't know where I am. I feel like I'm looking at my body, lying there.

Fiore asked her where she was in relation to her body. 'I'm above it, looking down at it,' she replied. And in response to the question 'What do you see?' she replied:

> I'm just lying there. I don't feel as if there's any life in my body. Like it's not part of me. I feel like I'm just floating up there, looking down at this row, and everybody else is doing the same thing. We're all up there, looking down at our bodies.

The briefing papers quoted by Lazar stated that the EBEs had informed us that Jesus and two other spiritual leaders were genetically engineered in the sense that 'they were implanted in people on Earth and their births were closely monitored'. This is just what Tom has told us happened and, throughout Biblical history, there have been constant references to what we now see as interactions with space denizens. A good reference for these is *The Bible and Flying Saucers* (Downing, 1968) or *Spacemen in the Ancient West* and *Spacemen in the Ancient East* (Drake, 1968 & 1969).

The mass of information communicated by Tom needs long and careful study because it covers a vast range of humanity's interests. Here we can just pick up some of the matters dealt with that are particularly relevant to this book.

Tom has confirmed that crop designs (chapter 17) are being drawn by entities from outside Earth. Their purpose is apparently to make mankind realize that it is not alone in the Universe. Many UFO manifestations are ethereal in that there is nothing to show for the encounters after they have happened. That is not the case with crop designs. Here we can walk in spaces created by beings from elsewhere. Just being within the envelope of these designs may possibly programme us in a certain way. Those who descend on the designs, either to gawp or to measure and reason, are perhaps being influenced in subtle ways of which they are not aware.

Even if this subtle imprinting does not occur, vast numbers of people who previously wavered between belief and disbelief now say to themselves: 'This has to be real.' They reason that only ETs could draw these complex patterns in our fields with such evident precision and artistry. So the Nine's ongoing commitment to awaken mankind at large to the fact that they are not the only ones in the Universe is given a forward push. The sum total of people who have come to believe in ETs has gone up.

At one stage Tom was quoted as saying:

> The Civilizations are attempting to bring to humankind
> information concerning other beings, other species, other energy

forms, so that humankind may look on this, question it, and then probe into it. You have now been alerted to those energy fields that are in existence.

Is it via 'programmed prophets', such as Uri Geller, and wonderful designs drawn in standing cereal crops that Tom's 'energy fields' are being shown to us?

Tom has admitted that the designs are being drawn via the medium of vehicles which can warp space-time and that their radiations, which have been detected in some designs through unusual forms of radioactivity (Dudley & Chorost, 1992), are outside our experience.

There are many different lesser civilizations visiting Earth and not all are here for our good. According to Tom:

> There are those who would wish to come here because they have begun the destruction of their own home planet and are looking for a place to relocate themselves. Therefore they are experimenting on humankind and animalkind for testing the available possibilities.

We are given the impression of a 'cops and robbers' situation existing between visitors from civilizations doing the good work of the Nine and the ETs from the opposition. The latter do not want mankind to grow in awareness and spirituality and to join the Universal league of space civilizations because, if it does, their chances of one day taking us over for their own ends is diminished.

One of the most fascinating aspects of Schlemmer's book (1994) concerns the acknowledged possibility of an intervention having been spawned by the Nine in 1976. This did not come to pass in an overt way. Instead the super-powers became alerted to a threat – the prospect of invasion by lesser civilizations from space – which led to their cooperation. Thus, the great détente occurred, with all its ramifications, such as the destruction of stock-piled nuclear weapons, the unification of Germany, the liberation of the subject satellites of the former USSR and the overthrow of Communism. Those who thought that all this was too much to be merely coincidence were strengthened in their belief that greater powers than those of mere terrestrial governments were at work.

The above is more than speculation because Mikhail Gorbachev, in a speech delivered at the Kremlin Palace on 16 February 1987, commenting on the 1985 summit between himself and President Reagan, said:

> At our meeting in Geneva, the US President said that, if the Earth faced an invasion by extra-terrestrials, the United States and the Soviet Union would join forces to repel such an invasion. I shall not dispute the hypothesis, though I think it's early yet to worry about such an intrusion.

What a dilemma for the forces of good. Any kind of approach was destined to be taken as an act of war by the major military powers.

Tom has complained that, in the past, mankind has not comprehended the information given to it concerning the Council of Nine and the Civilizations working for the betterment and salvation of Planet Earth. 'Now,' he said, 'it is important to comprehend, and know that what was begun in times past does exist, and continues, and it is time for humankind to know the importance of this information.' However, he then intimated that this cannot happen yet because of certain interference from governments who imagine that vehicles landing from space could pose nothing other than a threat. Well, it might pose a threat to them because they envisage losing their prestige and power but, if they were truly dedicated to the service of mankind, they would welcome such an intervention with open arms. Provided, of course, that the intervention came from the forces for good and not from the opposition.

We have been told that there could once have been a war in the space surrounding Earth between those under the aegis of the Nine (and their executive Twenty-four Civilizations) and the opposition. This had to be averted because it would have had a deleterious effect on Earth's environment. Unfortunately, it appears to be the opposition who are parleying at this moment with the USA and possibly other governments.

While, taken overall, there has been no direct threat from the vehicles keeping Earth under surveillance, making pacts with space denizens, whose modes of thought and possible intentions are not understood, under conditions where we are not permitted to know what is going on, could present us with the biggest threat we have ever had to face.

Luckily Tom has stated:

> The Twenty-four Civilizations, and those that are in conjunction with them, would arrive if Planet Earth were on the brink of destruction from those lesser civilizations. The Twenty-four Civilizations will not permit a take-over but humankind must be aware of the existence of the Twenty-four and those working in conjunction, and of the lesser civilizations.

He intimated that we will then be able to make the correct judgements about the information we get from ETs, but warned that some of the opposition civilizations are just biding their time.

Some of the most basically important revelations contained in *The Only Planet of Choice* concern the soul and the way it is regarded by mankind, and the religions that purport to guard it and give us information about it.

ELEVEN

WHAT HAPPENED
IN HISTORY?

THE SITUATION we now find ourselves in with respect to UFOs can perhaps be better understood if we look back at the history of mankind.

This history will not be quite the same as that recorded in current history books but it is more likely to be true. Once again, we are indebted to Phyllis Schlemmer for knowledge of the sequence of events that shaped us and our world. What follows is based on communications from the Nine and, as it fits very well with other sources of overt and covert knowledge, it is, I believe, what actually happened.

Man as a species first began to emerge 20 million years ago. These early hominids most probably appeared in what is now Africa. They were not alone, however. At the same time, advanced beings, who had come in space vehicles from other civilizations, were also ranging the Earth. They were here, we are told, to further the plan to develop beautiful Planet Earth as a paradise for those lucky souls who would eventually dwell upon it and have the sensibilities to appreciate its natural beauty.

These beings walked the Earth to prepare it for its eventual destiny by sowing specific plants and animals and by giving understanding to the emerging hominids. Their presence is substantiated by the discovery of technological artefacts in circumstances that confirm their extreme antiquity. For example, in 1959, the imprint of the sole of a shoe was found impressed into a rock in the Gobi Desert. The rock was estimated to be 2 million years old (Charroux, 1973). In 1885, a small steel cuboid, $2\frac{1}{2} \times 2$ in approx., fell out of a block of coal in a foundry in Austria. It carried a deep incision around its circumference and it had rounded faces on two edges (Tomas, 1971). Other examples of artefacts whose origins must date back millions of years can be found in the above references. Such objects could not have been created by indigenous Earth people and so must have been left by visitors from elsewhere.

About 1 million years ago, tool-making human beings, Neanderthal Man, emerged and, at the same time, as they began to use their brains and obtain knowledge, so the indestructible part of our being – the soul – began to grow and develop. The palaeontological evidence suggests that the first of the species *Homo erectus* was in existence between 800,000 and 400,000 years ago. There is then a gap of 100,000 years in the fossil record before what could well have been an 'experimental' Modern Man, early *Homo sapiens*, emerged, only to disappear after another 100,000 years, to leave a further 100,000-year gap before Neanderthal Man emerged, about 100,000 years ago. To me, these 100,000-year periods seem to indicate a purpose. They seem to be too regular to be pure chance and could, indeed, indicate the hand of an outside influence performing genetic experiments and allowing this time period for their handiwork to either develop or sink into total barbarism.

In other words, it seems that intelligent societies from space, who were not of the Twenty-four Civilizations, had placed colonies of human-like beings on the planet during the whole period when Man was evolving. They later seeded these 'outcasts from other civilizations' with genes from their own pools and it was these people who were there, waiting in the wings, for the important step forward in Man's development.

There is a conundrum in the evolution of Modern Man that is crying out for an explanation. The type of *Homo sapiens* immediately preceding ourselves was Neanderthal Man. Neanderthals were successful and their remains have been found in relative profusion from southern Britain, throughout southern Europe, into North Africa and eastwards into central Asia. Bones have been dated back 80,000 years and Neanderthals survived and multiplied for the next 45,000 years. Then, about 35,000 years ago, Modern Man (*Homo sapiens sapiens*) suddenly appeared and it becomes increasingly difficult to find solidly dated examples of Neanderthal Man after that time.

So, almost instantaneously, from the point of view of those who maintain that one type slowly developed into the other, our kind replaced the earlier kind of Man. We *are* different but the major differences lie not so much in physical features as in culture. The Neanderthals could make stone tools but never developed their craft. For thousands of years, the archaeological record shows that the Neanderthal stone-workers drudged away, making the same old tools that their forefathers had made. It would seem that they were taught to do this by someone, after which they just went on copying with no creative urge at all. Modern Man was different. From the beginning, he was creating art for art's sake and developing his skills. But no one knows where he could have come from.

Anthropologists say, lamely, that he must have invaded the territory of the Neanderthals and wiped them out. But from where? It is generally accepted that Modern Man developed in central Eurasia and spread out from there. But this immediately poses a question. How can a type of being so far in cultural advance of its predecessor suddenly appear in one spot and develop in sufficient numbers to spread out and very soon dominate the world? Saying this immediately presupposes that something quite other than natural evolution occurred around 35,000 years ago. It indicates a form of 'factory farming' at the horizon of Modern Man. Indeed, everything points to such a conclusion. But where was the 'factory' that produced *Homo sapiens sapiens*? The information that has come via Phyllis Schlemmer gives us precise answers to these questions.

The horizon for Modern Man's advancement is given quite unequivocally by the Nine as 32,400 BC., when a representative from Hoova, one of the Twenty-four Civilizations, arrived with his companions in a spacecraft to establish a breeding colony of hybrids. These developed from interbreeding the indigenous females and the advanced beings from Hoova. The landing of the Hoovids occurred at what is now Aksu, in the west of Sinkiang Province in the far west of China. It was then apparently called Aksiu (fig. 11.1)

These first sky-people came in craft built to resemble birds, as even immense 'birds' would have been more acceptable to the people of an arboreal culture than, say, the flying saucers of today. We saw the same idea still in action in the late nineteenth century, when spacecraft seen over the USA and England were made to resemble airships (photo 8). Similarly, the leader from Hoova came to the Earth people dressed as a bird and therefore became known as the Hawk. We are told unequivocally that he came in a spacecraft but he had with him only a small number of followers.

This small band established the first civilization, which was directly linked to the Nine via the executive intervention of the Hoovids. Thus was established a new breed of human beings: people who were partly of Earth and partly from the stars. Tom has told us that, before the Aksu venture, people with extra-terrestrial origins had been set down on Earth by civilizations of intelligence superior to ours but who were not working in direct cooperation with the Twenty-four. He gave the impression that at least some of these colonies were transported here because they were not wanted on their home planets. This indicates that human beings of some form are indigenous to the planets of the Universe. They may not all look quite alike bodily but the general plan of a human being – upright and walking on two legs, with arms springing from the top of a trunk, the whole topped by a cranium with a form of face – is the working model for most advanced forms of life.

The timing of the real acceleration in the development of our kind is well attested to by anthropologists. It was, they say, some 35,000 years ago that Modern Man suddenly emerged with no apparent antecedents, while Neanderthal Man just as suddenly disappeared. They find this impossible to understand in the context of normal evolutionary pressures. The mystery is compounded when we find the

Fig. 11.1   The position of Aksu in Sinkiang Province of China as well as Urumchi and Uzbekistan.

fossil record shows that, towards the end of the roughly 60,000-year period of his existence, Neanderthal Man became more rather than less primitive. This evolutionary conundrum can be solved if we assume that the degenerating Neanderthals (who were not all of the same rootstock) were being monitored and that it was decided to 'improve' them by cross-breeding with the Hoovids. The cross-breeds, who were partially Neanderthal, were transformed in the space of a thousand or so years into Modern Man. It is also easily possible that the change was, initially at least, not brought about by normal sexual intercourse but by artificial insemination.

Before the arrival of the Hawk and his followers, the average life expectancy of indigenous man was only 20 years and the Hoovids raised it to 120–150 years. This must therefore be the first creation mentioned in the Book of Genesis where God said that He would design man to have an average lifespan of 120 years. Furthermore, the Earth people were small by comparison with the Hoovids and Alteans, who were classed as 'giants' by comparison. The new civilization, with a better diet and advanced methods of healing, increased the projected lifespan to one which was greater than ours today but towards which we may be advancing again.

This first high space being (the Hawk) came to teach the colony about agriculture and animal husbandry, among other things, but, even so, the experiment of colonizing Earth with advanced human beings was not at all successful. It was a civilization that was too advanced for the cross-bred human beings to sustain and, when those of the new breed were allowed to spread out and form their own colonies, they failed to prosper because they needed the constant tutoring of the Hoovids, which they did not get. Thus, while some of their genes must still be flowing in many people's veins, these man–Hoovid crosses were doomed to extinction as a race. However, we are told that the remains of this first civilization are still under the ground of Aksu, waiting to be discovered.

In fact, some evidence of them can be found today. In a cave in the mountains of Uzbekistan, only 600 miles or so west of Aksu, the grave of a young boy associated with six pairs of ibex horns has been discovered. The grave is of extreme antiquity but the cult of the ibex still survives in the region to this day. Such cults are typically European and indicate that the same kind of influences which shaped European cultures still exist in what is extreme western China. This indicates a common source for both.

In 1978, and in the other direction, less than 400 miles from Aksu and not far from the city of Urumchi, an astounded Chinese archaeologist, Wang Binghua, found the graves of a tribe of white people. The bodies had been mummified and preserved in the dry desert air for 4,000 years. Wang excavated over 100 bodies and was struck by their blond hair, long noses and big eyes – all characteristic of northern Europeans and not Chinese (Lowther, 1994).

Recently, Victor Mair, Professor of Chinese at Pennsylvania University, has been able to work on the mummies. He has said: 'There is no doubt that these are Caucasian people from the Bronze Age who thrived in China in communities that lasted at least 1,700 years.'

The wisdom, as preferred by the Chinese until recently, is that China developed independently of any influence from the West. However Tom has told us that offshoots of the Aksu culture were placed in what is now China. As well as this, colonies were established in Atlantean lands and elsewhere. With space capabilities, it would have been quite simple for the visitors to establish such colonies wherever conditions seemed conducive to the development of human beings. The whole world was their oyster and therefore the doctrine of diffusion and gradual development of one form of Man into another is completely negated.

Thus, in cultural backwaters, people who differ very little from their forebears of tens of thousands of years ago can still be found living lives largely untouched by the modern world that swarms about the rest of us.

A good example is afforded by the Ham and Dropa tribes who, even today, occupy caves in the Bayan Khara mountains on the borders between Tibet and China. They are a small frail people quite unrelated to any local ethnic group. In the early 1940s, a Chinese archaeologist found that the Dropas possessed some 25 stone discs, which have since been deciphered. One of them reads:

> The Dropas came down from the sky in their gliders. Our men, women and children hid in the caves ten times before sunrise. When at last they understood the sign language of the Dropas they realized that the newcomers had peaceful intentions.

To back this up, there are ancient Chinese legends of men who came down from the clouds.

Thus the Dropas are still today living the same life, and preserving the same culture, that was bequeathed to them by their space visitors who knows how long ago. The Bayan Khan mountains lie some 900 miles southeast of Aksu but the whole of this great cradle of original civilization, lying lost between Europe and Asia, is a region where little has changed for many millennia.

TWELVE

THE LEGACY OF ATLANTIS

IT IS NOT GENERALLY realized that all the land which made up Atlantis did not founder in 'one terrible day and night' but sank in stages over a period of many tens of thousands of years. This sudden cataclysmic end to what appears to have been a great civilization occurred in about 10,000 BC but, before then, there had been other periods of disturbance. We do not know the date of the first period but the second is given, both by the Nine (Schlemmer, 1994) and by the readings of Edgar Cayce (Cayce, 1968) as about 28,000 BC. The inhabitants of Atlantis (fig. 12.1) may have been of Hoovid origin, being an offshoot of the Aksu culture. However, the Hoovids were not the only one of the Twenty-four Civilizations to be involved in the evolution of Man. When it came to the practical, scientific and technological side of the new human nature, the Civilization Altea was involved and Altea (as well as the Civilization Ashan, which oversaw the artistic) had most to do with the development of the higher civilization in Atlantis which followed the 28,000-BC disturbances. These appear to have produced some sinking of the previous Atlantean continent so that the land became broken into islands.

Before the first Aksu experiment, it appears that the indigenous peoples were only able to communicate by animal-like noises. It was one of Altea's important contributions to teach them language so that they could verbalize to one another. Thus members of early *Homo sapiens* spoke a single language and, as they spread out, they took this language with them. Here we see the answer to another conundrum that taxes the philologists. Why do so many of today's languages appear to stem from one universal language? The answer can only be the one which many unfettered thinkers have suspected, that it was taught to a nucleus of accelerated human beings who spread or were sown across the world. We are told that this early language was consonantal, i.e. the vowels were inferred, just as Hebrew is today. As

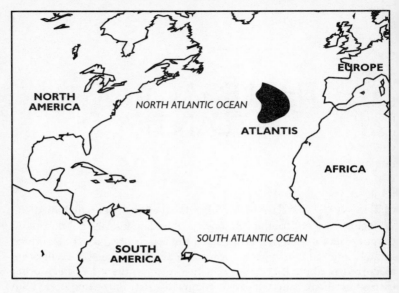

Fig. 12.1   How Otto Muck imagined Atlantis to look in the days
before its final demise.

the Hebrews are the only Hoovid race to survive largely unchanged,
so Hebrew is possibly the nearest we have to the original universal
language. It is also of great interest to learn that Ancient Egyptian was
also consonantal and so no one now knows exactly how the Egyptians
phrased their words.

Both Cayce's readings and communications from the Nine confirm that the technological civilization of Atlantis was, at its peak,
ahead of our present-day civilization. The Atlanteans, according to the
Cayce readings, used electricity, aircraft, photography, television and
radio, etc., as well as telepathy. The readings also indicate that they
had space travel, anti-gravity devices and advanced forms of nuclear
power. In addition, Cayce constantly refers to 'the crystal' (in one
reading 'the terrible mighty crystal'), which, in some unexplained
way, eventually set in motion the train of events that led to the final
destruction of their highly technological civilization in about 10,000 BC
and the loss of the last of the Atlantean lands, leaving only the tops of
the highest mountains to form, e.g. the Azores and Canaries islands.
The Nine have inferred that experiments with heavy water were also
involved and that these somehow set off a chain reaction that was

sufficiently powerful to lead to an entrainment of the Earth's own seismic forces. It was this entrainment that enabled the final destruction of Atlantis to take place in what seems an impossibly short time, measured in days.

We glimpse how this could have happened in the work of the Serbian genius, Nikola Tesla. Around 1900, Tesla, having already laid the foundation for the generation of the alternating current we enjoy today, was working on a literally earth-shattering theory. It concerned what he called *terrestrial stationary waves*. He saw that the Earth was a huge resonator and produced an oscillator, which he put in contact with an iron pillar. He adjusted the frequency of the oscillator until he found the frequency which resonated with the natural vibrations of the Earth.

The result was terrifying. He produced an effect like an earthquake as the vibrations set first the column, then the building housing it, into resonant motion. By the time the effect had begun to spread to adjoining buildings, producing panic in their occupants, Tesla decided enough was enough, smashed the oscillator and abandoned the research.

What the final outcome would have been, had Tesla been a scientist mad enough to allow his brainchild to have its head, no one knows. What we do know is that the US Government impounded certain of Tesla's laboratory notes on his death in 1943 and still withholds them. The rest of the notes are housed in the Nikola Tesla Museum in Belgrade.

Perhaps the 'terrible mighty crystal' in Atlantis was also capable of setting the Earth into resonant vibration. A tuning fork, when placed on a sounding box whose natural frequency matches that of the fork, sets the box vibrating and amplifies the tuning fork's note. In Tesla's experiment, the oscillator was the tuning fork and the Earth the box. In the case of the scientists of Atlantis did such a device get out of hand, setting in motion a train of events that no one could control?

In about 11,000 BC, the Hawk returned but this time to one of the far-eastern outposts of Atlantis, namely Crete. It should be realized that the Atlantean sphere of influence extended from Greece right through the Mediterranean, via the Atlantean lands, to the Americas. In the years prior to and surrounding 11,000 BC, Hoovids intermingled with colonizing emigrés from the doomed Atlantis and so spawned the Hebrew race.

The Hebrew's, therefore, have a double dose of Hoovid genes within them, leavened by Altean and Ashan influences. Their leader now became known as Yahoova or Jehovah. At roughly the same time,

Son of Hawk became leader of unspecified lands, situated off South America but undoubtedly under the sway of the main Atlantean influences and culture.

It appears that Abraham was a Hoovid, and a product of the second Hoovid intervention in the development of Planet Earth. This is where the longevity of the outer space races and their ability to reappear after the passage of millennia taxes our credulity. Yet the Nine's statement of facts is so sure-footed that we would be unwise to dismiss it. After all, when their chronology squares with our own preferred wisdom, as it does, for example, with the abrupt change from Neanderthal to Modern Man, then why should we believe one set of dates and dismiss the others?

The Biblical Abraham was, according to historians, born in Ur of the Chaldees and lived some 4,000 years ago. Yet the Nine's testimony states that Abraham was first manifested on Earth around 10,000 BC. Nevertheless, that would not, on the present evidence of Hoovid longevity, prevent him being in Ur in a new guise some 8,000 years later. When it comes to our contacts with the civilizations of outer space, we need to abandon many of our preconceived ideas of what is and what is not possible.

Probably because of the benign nature of its surroundings, the Atlantean civilization prospered and became one of high technology, a technology that was exported to their colonies. As well as developing aircraft and spacecraft, they eventually mastered the techniques of astral travel and so could transport themselves across their vast empire at will without the need for any technological device.

It seems that the last 1,000 years in the history of Atlantis constituted what the Nine have called the 'problem period'. This was when the Atlanteans used their knowledge of genetics to produce composite creatures. This suggests that monsters such as the Minotaur actually may have existed, especially as the Labyrinth was in Crete. The Atlanteans also experimented on themselves, attempting to increase their physical pleasures by artificially enlarging their sex organs. Their abilities with transplant techniques led to lifespans being extended to several thousand years.

Edgar Cayce's readings confirm in many details the image of Atlantis given by the Nine but they also portray a constant 'war' between the forces of good and evil. The former were, according to Cayce, called the Sons of the Law of One and they were opposed by the Sons of Belial. The latter, it seems, believed in making life easier for themselves by employing a subclass of labourers who were held in such low regard that they were termed 'things' and not considered to have souls at all. The Sons of the Law of One, on the other hand, were the spiritual brethren but, unfortunately for Atlantis, just as is threatened today, the material eclipsed the spiritual.

Apparently it was in about 11,000 BC that the Hawk and his people came directly to Atlantis and remained until its demise. The final, awful end of Atlantis was an explosive cataclysm of such immense proportions that relatively few escaped. Yet many colonies of refugees from Atlantis spread themselves around the periphery of the new Atlantic Ocean and the geo-cataclysm that sank Atlantis spawned the folk memories of the Flood. There are some very convincing books on Atlantis, including the original one by Ignatius Donnelly (1882) and later ones, such as '*Quest for Atlantis*' (Leonard, 1979). It was not simply a natural disaster but was triggered by scientific knowledge that, when put into practice, proved uncontrollable.

It would be useful here to get some other psychic testimony on Atlantis. Dr David Zink, in *The Stones of Atlantis* (1978), describes his efforts to unravel the secrets of the megalithic works which lie under the sea at Bimini in the Bahamas. Like us, when faced with an impenetrable past, he has resorted to what he describes as 'psychic archaeology'. He encountered a young psychic, Carol Huffstickler, who gave him independent readings about the site and some important extra-terrestrial information. Huffstickler's chronology in many ways paralleled that of Edgar Cayce and the Nine.

I have no room to draw all the parallels between Carol's testimony and those of the other psychic sources which I have quoted but, all the time, connecting threads appear. For example, the Bimini and Minoan cultures were related, although the Minoan was the later. So, were the Minoans refugees from Bimini when the latter's base eventually became untenable? That would make sense and dovetail the Minoan culture into that of the late Atlantean. The Bimini culture was contemporaneous with the Magdalenian culture in Europe, which is currently dared from 15,000 BC, a date which Carol described as 'much too recent'.

Among other communications, Carol Huffstickler kept receiving the name 'Pleiades'. She became aware that this site was connected with the cosmic races that had seeded this planet. They were peripatetic races travelling from planet to planet as the need arose. Their brief was to teach the inhabitants a religion suitable to their situation and state of development. They established colonies for this purpose in several different places. However, the resistance of Earth people to such intervention resulted in very little progress towards higher advancement.

The Pleiades intervention, by highly developed and benevolent beings, is dated at 28,000 BC – a date which coincides with the first of the upheavals in the Atlantean lands. There is another intriguing tie-up here. The connection of the name Atlas with Atlantis has been noted by many writers and the Pleiades were traditionally the seven daughters of Atlas and Pleione.

While Carol Huffstickler was giving this testimony, she also made references to the state of development of the Pleiadeans. They were not material as we are but could change shape and form through their own mental processes. They came to assist in a further acceleration to the upward advance of mankind and that, she says, was their 'life's work'. Ours was 'to build and become conscious of who we are'.

However, in the beginning, the Pleiadeans came to a capital city and main religious centre which one assumes was the capital of Atlantis. As described by Edgar Cayce, the Earth people occupying Atlantis at that time were still very much in the 'thought-form' and did everything by telepathy. The role of the Pleiadeans was to stimulate physical action as part of the ongoing programme of developing physicality in Earth people. This was later (in our time?) to revert to mental action so that we could achieve our goals without the need for physical strength.

In ages previous to our own, physical strength was the only means by which anything could be accomplished. More recently, men have used their minds to develop the crane and the earthmover to replace muscle and sinew. When presented with a task which involves physical effort, we now sit down and design a machine to relieve ourselves of the task. We have moved on from a time of 'magic', when certain beings on this planet could manipulate natural forces and achieve greater works than anything we can now produce, through a physical interlude, to a modern world where we are still very, very physical but our physicality is overlaid with a veneer of mental sophistication.

It is generally agreed that the greatest edifice in the world is the Great Pyramid at El Gîza near Cairo (hereafter referred to simply as the Pyramid) and the information from the Nine is that the Pyramid was started 150 years before the final demise of Atlantis. This makes sense when we realize that Charles Piazzi Smyth (1867) and others were right when their careful measurements showed the Pyramid to be a time capsule. It was, I am sure, built as a repository for the constants of Earth's size and rate of rotation, plus the basic system of weights and measures, as well as many other fundamental measurements. Its incredible stability on a rock surface that was artificially levelled over many acres speaks of an attempt to place something

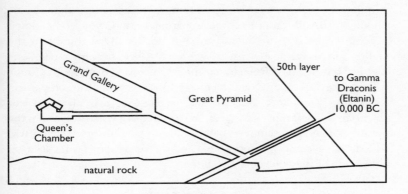

Fig. 12.2   How Richard Proctor envisaged that the Grand Gallery would have emerged from the flat top of the half-completed Great Pyramid. The Descending Passage is shown oriented to the position of Gamma Draconis (Eltanin) as it would have been in 10,000 BC.

on the Earth that was virtually indestructable by water, fire or earthquake. An early date of 10,500 BC for the building of this structure was quoted by Edgar Cayce in his readings.

We have been so brain-washed by Egyptologists' insistence that the building of the Pyramid from start to finish was achieved in the reign of Khufu (or Cheops), the second Pharaoh of the 4th Dynasty (whose dates are given as 2590–2567 BC) that no other ideas have been entertained. Yet there is an ocean of doubt over much of what happened in Ancient Egypt, including the dates of its Pharaohs.

So the Nine's assertion that a new reincarnation of the Hawk – one called Khufu – was only given the understanding of the secrets of the Pyramid some 3,000 years after its inception, i.e. in 6257 BC, could contain a measure of truth. There is very good evidence that the Pyramid was built in at least two stages, a theory proposed 100 years ago by British astronomer, Richard Anthony Proctor (fig. 12.2).

Just before the turn of the nineteenth century, Proctor (1883) advanced the idea that the Grand Gallery of the Pyramid only made sense as a 'meridian slot' oriented towards the southern sky and facilitating the observation of the transit of the heavenly bodies, even in broad daylight, from deep within its cavernous interior. For this astronomical device to operate, the Great Pyramid could only have been built up to the fiftieth course of masonry, out of which the upper end of the Grand Gallery would have emerged. When you contemplate the inanity of carefully building a great slot-like edifice in the middle of the Pyramid, for no apparent reason, you come down heavily on the side of Richard Proctor. Personally, I think that the Gallery also only makes sense if it were a platform for a great telescope (fig. 12.3). If we compare a similar modern device – the Transit Circle, which once operated in the Greenwich Observatory – the comparison is obvious (Tompkins, 1973). If such a telescope existed in Ancient Egyptian times, it must have been constructed elsewhere, placed in the Grand Gallery and removed before the top part of the Pyramid was added. What could be slots to anchor the telescope can be seen on either side of the floor of the Gallery.

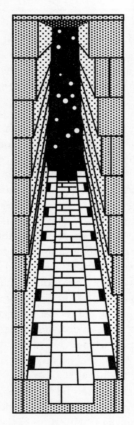

Fig. 12.3 The Grand Gallery as it would have appeared before the Great Pyramid was completed, with the stars visible in broad daylight. (After Proctor, 1883)

The Nine have told us that additions were made to the Pyramid in about 5000 BC but that it was not finally completed until 3000 BC, which is some hundreds of years before the time usually assigned to Khufu (Cheops) by Egyptologists.

The horizon for advanced civilization in Egypt is given as 6000 BC, when the Hawk returned for the third time. Again he came as a bird but this time as Horus. As in the past when the space-people came to Earth, his retinue became worshipped as gods by the primitive people with whom they had to work. This was a situation which the Nine did not particularly like. They were quite prepared to take mankind into partnership but were forced to allow the free will of the native population to have its head, however unpredictable the outcome.

Many people in Egypt at this time were refugees from Atlantis but, for some 2,000 years, the overall civilization of Egypt apparently made no progress. Then, in about 4000 BC, a breakthrough occurred and, in a generation or two, most of the skills evidenced by archaeological findings came suddenly to fruition. For example, in a matter of 100 years, Egyptian carpenters had progressed from the simplest of skills to the use of mortice and tenon joints, drills, etc. Such a transformation could only have occurred under the tutelage of very adept teachers.

This 'overnight' flowering of the arts and sciences of Egypt has been attributed by Egyptologists to the arrival of a 'Master Race' from elsewhere (Edwards, 1949). This race has also been called, more accurately, 'The Followers of Horus'. Can we interpret them as being representatives from Altea and Ashan, the former providing the technology and the latter the artistic creativeness? The Egyptian civilization, with all its formal grandeur, then flourished before declining into chaos, as happened to all the tutored ancient civilizations that were eventually left to their own devices.

We can understand the sudden flowering of the Uruk culture if we accept that Ur was founded as a colony of Atlantis. We are told that the civilizations of Mesopotamia, Egypt and China (fig. 12.4) were all founded by the same basic Hoovid/Altean hybrid peoples. The fish god, Ioannes (or Joannes), appeared with the appendages of a fish in order to provide something earthly to which the people could relate. However, just like all the other civilizations that were spawned by those from space, Ur grew to prominence and splendour and was then destroyed.

The Hawk symbolism is still with us today. It plagued Andrija Puharich during his time in Israel. Associated with UFO phenomena – mainly red lights in the sky – Puharich observed hawk-like creatures with a 2-ft wingspan in broad daylight. On one occasion, while he was

Fig. 12.4   Positions of places in the Middle East mentioned in the text together with other well-known places and areas for reference.

in his hotel room, one of these 'hawks' floated in from the direction of the sea and hovered close to his balcony while looking him directly in the eyes. He sensed then that this was no earthly hawk. Uri Geller was with him and Puharich allowed his eyes to follow a 'feather' that floated upward from the hawk, thus directing Geller's attention to a dark spacecraft hovering over the hotel. In line with other, similar sightings the spacecraft was visible only to Geller, and Puharich saw nothing. How this trick was performed I do not know but it has been reported often enough in the UFO literature to make one realize that, when one person sees a UFO and another does not, the former is not necessarily seeing things, nor is the other blind.

Eventually, in this potted history of mankind as revealed to us by the Council of Nine, I come to the third manifestation of Hoova as the Nazarene – the one we call Jesus the Christ. He was sent, we are told, to expand compassion – a concern of many of his teachings. His was a virgin birth by artificial insemination during the 'dream' which the Bible says Mary had. I cannot accept unsubstantiated miracles but this single fact helps me to believe in the essential truths in the Gospels. A form of artificial insemination is being practised by space beings at this very time on some Earth women, although the results are not 'Sons of God' but rather poor examples of human-like children. However, the abductions seem like dreams to the girls involved, although the embryo is not allowed to come to full term. Yet the technique is there and obviously has been there for millennia.

It follows that Jesus and Jehovah are one and the same, both being reincarnations of the Head of Hoova, and so is Allah, and this is what makes the bloody wranglings between Gentiles, Jews and Arabs over their religious differences so meaningless. This is perhaps why the Nine have decided to tell us all this, in the fervent hope that those with sufficient power will put an end to internecine strife so that mankind can move forward as one.

Before we leave this Earth history, as elucidated by our space communicators, I will summarize what we have been told about the organization of the 'management' of the Universe. Human beings have asked the questions and Tom has tried to answer them. However, many of the concepts are beyond our understanding. Yet, despite this, a new light has been shone on matters about which we previously had only the vaguest of notions. This is what Tom has told us.

The Nine occupy a god-like position in the psychic 'chain of command' – they are a kind of buffer between God and the rest of the souls of the Universe (fig. 12.5). It is confirmed that the wonderful phrase 'God is love' is literally true. God is the ineffable and unknowable result of love-energy fed from the souls of the beings of the Universe through the intermediation of the Nine. As love grows among the beings with souls, so God is enriched and 'enlarged'. This is not a one-way process, however, because, as God is enriched, so 'He' is able to feed more love back to those at the bottom of the spiritual food-chain – us!

I am not a religious person in the orthodox sense. Yet when I read Christ's words 'Even as you do it to the least of my brethren you do it unto me', I now understand what he meant. It is one of the tragedies for this era's mankind that the established religions, which have been given all the basic answers to how man can advance spiritually, have so besmirched the message that the majority of thinking people no longer seek their solace and understanding in church.

The executive branch of the Nine comprises the so-called Twenty-four Civilizations. These are spread throughout the Universe and actually perform physical, mental and spiritual tasks on the inhabited planets. One of their tasks is to prepare uninhabited planets – such as Earth once was – for the emergence of humanoid types into which souls can eventually be introduced.

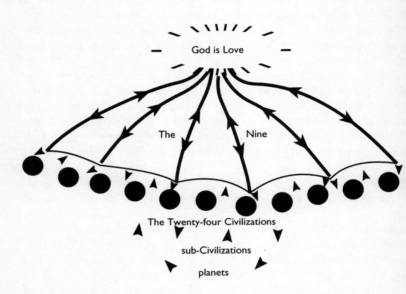

Fig. 12.5   An 'umbrella' interpretation of the 'command structure' of the Universe from the information communicated through Phyllis Schlemmer. Planets like Earth are in contact with sub-Civilizations whose vehicles (UFOs) we see continually. Both these are in contact with the 'managerial' branch of the structure – the so-called Twenty-four Civilizations, who oversee the day-to-day running of the Universe. Acting as a 'buffer' between material, semi-material and spirit-like entities on all these levels are those who choose to identify themselves to us as the Nine Principles and Forces. They are one step down from God, and the spiritual energy that makes the Universe function, namely love, feeds to and from the godhead who is fount of love in its broadest sense. This flow is shown by arrows on the ribs of the umbrella.

1 The prototype de Havilland Venom nightfighter of the type involved in the UFO encounter over southeast England.

2 An impression of aerial phenomena seen over Nuremburg, Germany, on 14 April 1561. The cylindrical objects are likely to be Leviathans with light patches down their sides. They are evolving saucers which may be seen landing lower right. Other saucers, rod-shaped objects and flying crosses are also depicted. The central crescent-shaped object with a sun's face indicates a very large saucer which was as bright as the sun.

3 *Left* A typical 'daylight disc' over Barra de Tijuca, Brazil, 7 May 1952. (*Fortean Picture Library*)

4 *Right* The metal cube that Alan Hilton's friends found in their car after their abduction event. (*Alan Hilton*)

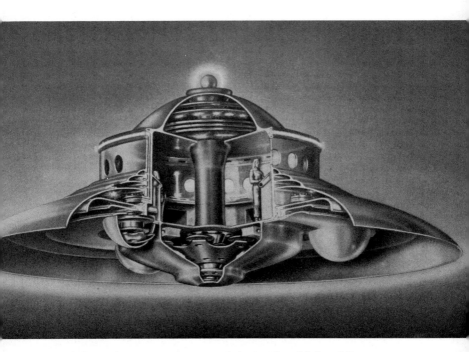

5 Leonard Cramp's intuitive drawing of the inside of Adamski's saucer, showing the prominent central column very like the gravity wave-guide set-up shown in Fig. 5.1. (*Leonard Cramp*)

6 *Above* Andrija Puharich. *(Dennis Stacy/Fortean Picture Library)*

7 *Below left* Uri Geller performing a psychokinesis experiment on a Luxembourg television show in 1988. (*Dr Elmar R. Gruber/Fortean Picture Library*)

8 *Right* The Peterborough 'airship' of 23 March 1909 depicted over the Cathedral. It resembles in many ways the craft seen over the USA. (*Fortean Picture Library*)

9 *Below* The fallen Obelisk at Avebury, as William Stukeley saw it in the eighteenth century.

10 *Below top* A 'scorpion' crop design drawn in a wheatfield near Devizes, Wiltshire, UK, during the summer of 1994. (*Steve Alexander*)

11 *Below bottom* The 'spider's web' crop design drawn in two stages during the nights of 9/10 and 10/11 August 1994, close to Avebury Ring. (*Steve Patterson*)

12 *Top right* The Mandelbrot crop formation drawn 11/12 August 1991 at Ickleton, near Cambridge, UK. (*Cambridge Newspapers*)

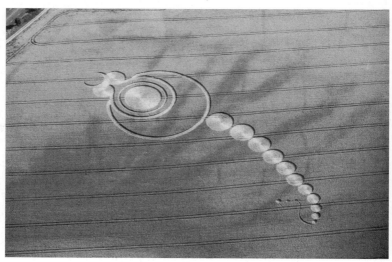

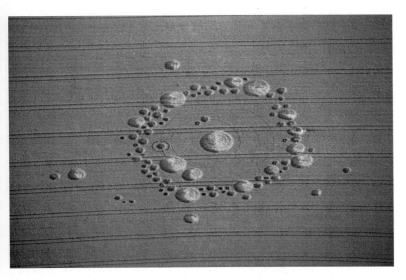

13 No less than 92 circles plus a ring were made in this design at Bishops Sutton, Hampshire, UK, during one night in 1995. Do these signify the nuclei of the 92 atoms which are natural to Earth and does the circle with a ring represent an atom? There may be another message underlying this. Does the central circle represent the Sun, the first faint circle the orbit of Earth/Moon, and the larger one the orbit of Mars with the (emphasized) parking orbit of a spacecraft around it? This incredible device was just one of a whole series of complex and beautiful designs produced this one summer, each one intricate enough to puzzle fully those who still cling to the hoax hypothesis. (*Steve Alexander*)

14 *Above left* A big cat, thought to be the so-called 'Surrey Puma', photographed in 1966 at Worplesdon, Surrey, UK, by two ex-police photographers. (*Fortean Picture Library*)

15 *Above right* A close-up of a 'Bigfoot' humanoid creature taken from a frame of a movie film shot by Roger Patterson at Bluff Creek, northern California, on 20 October 1967. (*René Dahinden/Fortean Picture Library*)

16 *Below* A photograph of Polish medium Franek Kluski materializing a bird in 1919. (*Fortean Picture Library*)

Edgar Cayce has, through his readings which touch on previous incarnations in Atlantis (Cayce, 1968), pulled aside the curtain on this aspect when he described the origins of humanity as 'thought-forms' which came to and entered material bodies, much as we might put on a coat. This was, according to Cayce, 'before Adam was in the Earth'. We can now equate Adam with the Aksu creation, so it was in remote antiquity. Cayce also said that, at first, these souls 'had the union of sex in the one body' and only later did they differentiate into male and female. Here we may see why we all seek for the perfect soul-mate. We are perhaps looking for the other half of ourselves. Sometimes we find that soul-mate and then life is bliss – but much too often life forces many people to take second best.

To help our understanding, I will liken the Universe's chain of command to an umbrella (fig. 12.5). It is an umbrella with nine spokes, each of which is one aspect of the Nine Principles and Forces. At the hub of the umbrella is God, that reservoir of spiritual energy which we call love, to which the results of our unselfish acts of compassion for our fellow beings, be they human or animal, flow. The greatest of these acts, we have been told, is when a person lays down their life for a friend. But there are many less dramatic but no less significant acts, such as rescuing and nursing back to health an injured or maltreated animal.

Clustered around the spokes of the umbrella, we can imagine the planets of the Twenty-four Civilizations. They are very far away from Earth in the Universe but that is no drawback with the communicational abilities which they possess.

The Civilizations are in 12 complementary pairs. The Twenty-four are, in some ways, in the position of managers under a board of directors – the Council of Nine – and they exist on physical planets but their lifestyle is very different from that of Earth people. For example, unlike us, Alteans are all the same size and are limited to a total population of 144,000. They have an iridescent appearance but lack hair and cannot vocalize. However, they share some features with us and we are told that the physical human seed came from Altea. There are people here on Earth today who are of Altean descent.

Only a certain number of the Twenty-four have any continuing involvement with Earth, although all have, at some time, contributed to the Earth's development. The ones most involved with us are Hoova and Altea. Both Hoovids and Alteans can manifest in physical form on this planet, and when they do so, it is often impossible to tell them from indigenous humans. Hoovids are small and dark and have straight hair while Alteans are fair. The Ashans, on the other hand, have different facial features from us. However, as all the denizens of these advanced Civilizations are capable of revealing themselves in ordinary human form, it is ultimately their minds and souls which are different.

Below the 'managerial' Civilizations there are the sub-Civilizations and these may often have their own agendas. Thus, if we receive visitors from other planets, we must treat them with caution because they may not be here for our good. However, many of them are doing the positive work of the Civilizations in attempting to help us on the path of spiritual advancement.

At the bottom of the pile come planets like ours, although it would be wrong to assume that this is a heirarchy of the kind we experience on Earth. Earth is as important in the Universe as any Civilization because, if it were not, the constant reincarnations of the Heads of Hoova and Altea, as well as many others, would not have taken place. We are loved and cared for but only in the way that a teenager is cared for by intelligent and understanding parents. The Council of Nine cannot prevent us going our own way. They may wish to sway us by reasoned argument – to make us see the light – but they are powerless to prevent our going downhill if we so choose.

Some of the Civilizations and their special responsibilities are summed up in fig. 12.6. The communications that were delivered through Dr Vinod originated from Spectra, which we have learned is an adjunct to Hoova. In a similar way, the Civilization Ancore is linked with Aragon – a Civilization dedicated to healing and the healing arts. Zeneel is, to me, rather hazy, being described as the 'Alchemist of the Universe'.

Thus, for the first time, we can begin to see that Earth is not an abandoned island alone in space. We are cared for and we are also here for a purpose. There are higher minds who do not wish us to negate that purpose by our stupidly arrogant ways. We have learned these facts – whose importance cannot be overestimated – through the gradual unrolling of our understanding of what space visitors have contributed in the past, and are still contributing. It would not be too much to say that our study of UFOs over the last 50 years has awoken us sufficiently for many now to be able to accept the messages which are coming to us from space.

Just after World War 2, only a very few people were prepared to acknowledge that flying saucers were real and to draw the obvious conclusions as to their origins. Since then the acceptance level of a vast phalanx of mankind has gone up considerably. We have moved from a situation where most people laughed at the idea of spacecraft coming here from outer space to one where the majority are prepared to accept that UFOs are extra-terrestrial spacecraft. Furthermore, a substantial number are ready to concede that we owe our position of being creatures that lie somewhere between god and animal not so much to gradual evolution – although that has played its part – but to intervention from elsewhere. And the revolution in our collective thinking is going further. We are gradually learning not to be fazed by the unnerving abilities which our space visitors show with mind control. Only in this way can we prepare ourselves for an overt intervention, if it should come.

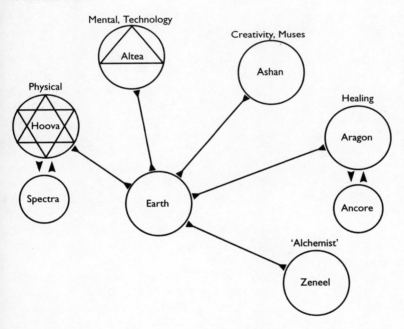

Fig. 12.6 Some of the more important Civilizations servicing Earth. Hoova (population 5 million), Altea (population 144,000) and Ashan have had most to do with the shaping of Earth's destiny. However, Aragon and its attendant Civilization, Ancore, assist those who are healing the sick. The role of Zeneel is not very clear from Phyllis Schlemmer's testimony. Spectra, an attendant of Hoova, was the Civilization which apparently programmed the Geller/Puharich episode. It seems likely that the sign of Hoova is the Star of David and that of Altea is the pyramidal triangle (the meridian cross-section of the Great Pyramid).

THIRTEEN

GREAT MYSTERIES OF THE WORLD

A TELEVISION PROGRAMME put out by the British Broadcasting Corporation in 1993, in their *Horizon* series, described an attempt to reconstruct a pyramid. It was a very small pyramid and the unholy mess that the project eventually became demonstrated better than any words that the Great Pyramid was not purely the work of human hands.

The Nine have told us that the design of the Great Pyramid, and the overseeing of its initial construction, was carried out by representatives of Altea but that much of the the labour was human. However, Hoova, Ashan and Myrex all played a part. This explanation immediately makes sense of the conflicting evidence that, although the Egyptians built the pyramids, the construction methods and wonderful abilities with dressing and laying heavy stones up to a height which tops the dome of St Paul's Cathedral, were quite beyond the unaided competence of the indigenous Egyptians of the time.

The preamble to this same television programme told us in awestruck tones that the Ancient Egyptians built the pyramids without the help of the wheel or several other important items of fundamental technology. Thus, judged against our knowledge of how a technological civilization develops naturally, this must mean that, if the Egyptian civilization developed naturally in the same way, then all the allied technologies should have been present. Yet manifestly they were not. To most thinking people, such statements only serve to confirm that the Egyptian civilization did not develop naturally. In particular, the Great Pyramid does not make sense in the context of what some Egyptologists would have you believe.

The information we have via Phyllis Schlemmer is that the Great Pyramid was built some 150 years before the final destruction of Atlantis, i.e. in about 10,000 BC. In about 5000 BC, additions were made and eventually, after a span of 6,000 years, it was completed. This is backed up by the Ancient Arab historian, Ibrahim ben Ebn Wasuff Shah, who said that an antediluvian king, whom he calls Surid (or Saurid), started the Pyramid in response to a dream that a huge planet would fall to Earth. Furthermore, a famous traveller, ibn-Batuta, said that Enoch of the Hebrews ascertained, from the position of the stars, that the Flood would come and so built the Pyramid 'to contain books of science and knowledge and other matters worth preserving from oblivion and ruin' (Tompkins, 1973). As we now know that the Pyramid is itself an indestructible 'book', whose dimensions give us information on the size of the Earth and its rotation rate, as well as storing ancient measures and incommensurate numbers, such as *pi*, these traditions are strengthened.

There is, moreover, nothing organic in the Great Pyramid by which it can be radiocarbon-dated. The only reason for its building being attributed to the Pharaoh Cheops (or Khufu) is a cartouche, coinciding with one known to be that of Cheops, which was found in one of the so-called chambers above the remarkably constructed King's Chamber in the centre of the Pyramid.

These chambers are actually just spaces between 'floors' of stone, each of which consists of eight or nine monolithic slabs, laid parallel to one another and each weighing 50 tonnes or more (fig. 13.1). There are five floors and five chambers because, over the uppermost floor, there is a massive gabled roof made of dressed limestone slabs. A good reason for this construction was first put forward by its discoverer, Colonel Howard-Vyse, and has been substantiated by others who have followed him. As the Pyramid was being completed, the builders had to relieve the vast weight of masonry above the King's Chamber and this was how they achieved it (Tompkins, 1973).

It was in the upper spaces that some masons' marks were discovered, daubed in red paint. One of them was recognized as similar to that of Khufu, who is currently considered to have reigned in the third millenium BC. However, some doubt still exists, even among Egyptologists, as to whether there might not have been a much earlier king with a similar cartouche (who we shall call Khufu I). Tom has told us that this is true. The Khufu involved in the additions (Khufu I) lived in 6257 BC and was a reincarnation of the Hawk. The Pyramid was not completed before the second Khufu (who we shall call Khufu II). Thus the cartouche of Khufu II postdates the start of the Pyramid by some 6,000 years, having been daubed in the spaces between the masonry as the vast blocks of stone were placed over the King's Chamber during the final phase of construction. This could have been done in the reign of Khufu II because there is considerable doubt

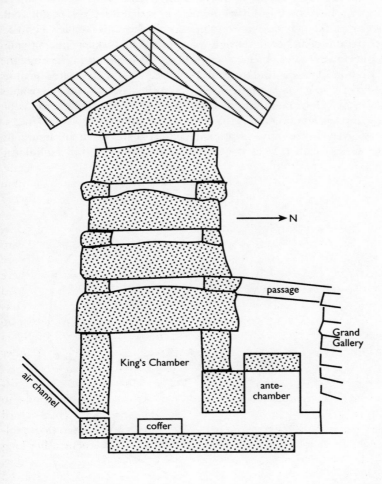

Fig. 13.1   The massive blocks and 'roof' placed over the King's Chamber when the Pyramid was finally completed. The latter was carefully placed on the top surface of the truncated Pyramid before it and the Grand Gallery were lost in the piling-up masonry. It was a cartouche of Cheops, in one of the upper spaces between the blocks, which led Egyptologists to date the Pyramid to Cheops' reign.

about the relative antiquity of the Pharaohs. Tom has said that the 'understanding came to him' (i.e. to Khufu II) as to how the Pyramid was to be completed.

On page 117, I drew attention to the Grand Gallery buried in the heart of the Pyramid. What I did not say is that it has removable roof stones as if it were once open to the sky. In this, it is paralleled by the remarkable chamber at Mais Howe on mainland Orkney, in Scotland. Mais Howe is a curiously erratic edifice and the abilities of its builders with stone dressing, and the care taken in its construction, are equalled only by the great Pyramid itself. Its corbelled roof has removable slabs, like the Pyramid, which indicates that it also was originally designed as an observatory. When its observatory work was done, it was covered over with a great mound of earth, just as we are assuming the Grand Gallery was covered in stone (Rider, 1975; Tompkins, 1973).

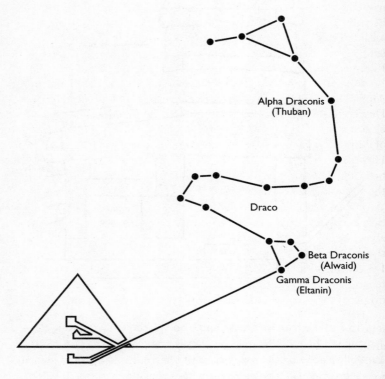

Fig. 13.2 How the Descending Passage would have been aligned with the pole star Gamma Draconis (Eltanin) in around 10,000 BC.

In the Great Pyramid, the Grand Gallery's upper end is aligned very accurately with the southern wall of the Queen's Chamber (fig. 12.2) while its lower end is on the level of the floor of the Chamber. The Gallery, therefore, is not some strange whim of the builders but was designed as an integral part of the structure. Proctor (1883) recognized that, even with no astronomical instruments being involved, a close approximation to true sidereal time could have been obtained by stationing observers at points along the Gallery and the stars could have been seen even in broad daylight from its cavernous depths.

How the Gallery emerged above the fiftieth course of masonry, and its relationship with the Ascending and Descending Passages as well as the Queen's Chamber, is shown in fig. 12.2. It is important to realize that the King's Chamber is so-called because it has a horizontal ceiling whereas the Queen's Chamber has a gabled roof. They were named by the Arabs who, by brute force, opened the sealed Pyramid in AD 820; it was the custom of the Arabs to bury their kings in tombs with flat roofs and their queens in ones with gabled roofs. There is no evidence that any body, king or otherwise, was ever interred in the Pyramid.

In an attempt to date the Pyramid, Proctor was able to find that Alpha Draconis, the pole star of several millennia ago, aligned with the Descending Passage at the same time as Alpha Centauri (one of the closest stars) aligned with the Grand Gallery. He thus obtained a date of 3400 BC, which would now appear to be out by over 6,000 years. However, there is evidence to show that these features could have been angled to another significant star of this same constellation when the Pyramid was first designed.

For a very long period of time, different stars of Draco (the Serpent) were close enough to the pole to be used as pole stars. In about 10,000 BC it was Eltanin (Gamma Draconis), one of the stars in the head of Draco (fig. 13.2), that would have aligned with the Descending Passage (Fix, 1978). Thus, there is nothing in Tom's testimony which need conflict with other evidence about the date of origin of the first stage of the Pyramid.

Every aspect of the Great Pyramid produces amazement in those who study it with an open mind. Its base covers 13 acres but the artificially levelled rock plateau on which it stands is possibly a greater wonder than the Pyramid itself. By what means was this rock levelled to within a fraction of a centimetre over such a vast area? Certainly not by hordes of native Egyptians chipping away with copper chisels. We are told that the Egyptians knew no metals other than copper and gold.

Yet we find that, even in the archaic period which preceded the Pharaonic dynasties, the teeth of saws and the eyelets of needles were punched out by a material harder than the hardened copper of which they were made. So, if unaided human beings were unable to perform these tasks, we must look to extra-terrestrial agencies for the means.

The same goes for the 2.5 million or more blocks that had to be accurately placed. The lightest weighed no less than 2 tonnes and the most massive 70 tonnes. How such blocks were lifted to the height of a 40-storey building is beyond explanation in normal terms. The idea that ramps could have been used produces vastly more problems than it solves. It makes for a feat of civil engineering greater in magnitude than the building of the Pyramid itself. In any case there is no sign of such ramps ever having been employed during the Pyramid's construction.

When faced with an impossibility, one has to seek another solution. It may seem bizarre to many but there is evidence for the lifting of massive stones by the application of sound. The *Drona Parva*, one of the Sanskrit books which shows (among other things) the technical abilities of the Ancients in India, describes how one of their aerial ships, a vimana, was powered (Leslie and Adamski, 1953). In one place, the books mention the use of the syllable 'OM' which, when uttered in sufficient volume, gave the great 'car' propulsion and lift. Among the folk memories of the Caribs, we find: 'People did not walk up and down stairs in the very old days. They hit a plate and made a song and the song said where they wanted to go – and so they went' (Leslie & Adamski, 1953). Similarly, in Irish folklore, we find: 'In the old days everybody danced in the air like leaves in the autumn wind – people made a song to a plate'.

Thus the idea that suitably tuned sound could overcome gravity has been a part of human tradition for millenia. So, when a questioner asked Tom how the great blocks of stone were lifted and placed in the Great Pyramid, he was told: 'It was with the benefit of crystal, with the benefit of vocal sound tuned to crystal, with the sound of OM – there were many voices'. It appears that, in relatively modern times, the Tibetans had mastered the art of moving stones through the application of sound and it has been reported (Schlemmer, 1994) that Sven Hedin, a Swedish traveller, captured this feat on film early in the twentieth century but that the film is under lock and key in a Swedish museum.

In 1880, William Flinders Petrie, a largely self-taught surveyor, took instruments which his father had designed to try to establish, once and for all, the true dimensions of the Pyramid. Peter Tompkins' *Secrets of the Great Pyramid* (1973) gives a good resumé of what he accomplished but here I can only give a few of his more astounding conclusions.

Petrie found that the original casing stones, some weighing over 15 tonnes, had been placed, together with a film of mortar no thicker than a fingernail, over an area of 35 sq. ft. He found that the edges of the casing stones were made so straight that they only varied by $\frac{1}{100}$ in, in lengths of over 6 ft. Petrie said: 'Merely to place such stones in exact contact would be careful work, but to do so with cement in the joint seems almost impossible: it is to be compared to the finest optician's work on a scale of acres.' Herodotus, the Greek historian, who saw the Pyramid in about 440 BC, said that it was still covered in its full mantle of polished Tura limestone and that the joints were so fine that one could hardly see them.

Another place where optical accuracy is in evidence is in the Descending and Ascending Passages. Petrie found that the Descending Passage differed from the vertical by only $\frac{1}{10}$ in over its entire length of 350 ft. Near where it emerged into the light, it was even more accurate – to within $\frac{1}{50}$ in. There has to be an explanation for such accuracy.

It has been suggested that, as the Ascending Passage is equally accurate, and slopes at exactly the same angle to the horizontal as the Descending Passage, each was designed to act as a very accurate telescope to determine an exact moment in time when a certain heavenly body was precisely aligned with the Descending Passage. A pool of mercury could have been used as a mirror to reflect the light from the body to an observer in the Grand Gallery, whose floor is canted at the same angle. However, as the passages are inhuman in their dimensions, being 3 ft 9 in high and only 3 ft 5 in wide, it would appear that they could not have been cut by human beings, nor were they designed for the ingress and egress of human beings. If the Pyramid had been a purely human structure, its artefacts would have been of human proportions and they are not. The Grand Gallery is for giants and the Passages are for dwarfs.

The only artefact that exists in the Pyramid is the coffer in the King's Chamber. This great granite chest was luckily intact when Petrie came to measure it and to consider the methods that might have been used in its construction. It has since been badly vandalized by tourists, who have chipped a large portion of one corner away. Petrie calculated that the volume of grain it contained was 4 quarters – an Imperial measure of volume. Thus it appears that the British quarter is one quarter of the grain that would just fill the coffer in the King's Chamber. Just as with the British inch and foot, which are only fractionally different from their Ancient Egyptian equivalents, Petrie showed that many of the standards of the Imperial system of weights and measures went back some 5,000 years. We now realize that they are much, much older.

Also, from his mechanical knowledge, Petrie concluded that the only way such a carefully crafted chest could have been cut from a single block of hard granite was with saws at least 9 ft long with diamond-studded teeth. Equally, to hollow out the inside would have required drills with diamond cutting edges on which a force of at least 2 tonnes would have had to be exerted. This seemed to Petrie, as it must to most other people, to be asking the impossible of the Ancient Egyptians.

However, according to tradition, the coffer originated in Atlantis and was brought to Egypt and placed in the King's Chamber before it was roofed over. If this were true we have no way of knowing how this remarkable artefact was made. Yet, looking at Petrie's drawings, one is led to the conclusion that maybe it was not cut out of a block at all; perhaps the Atlanteans had perfected a means of softening and casting stone. Comparing the other evidence of their technical prowess, this is worth consideration.

I could continue to list many impossible things that were achieved in the construction of the Great Pyramid, things which make us realize that there is no way in which the untutored Egyptians could have designed and built it. And there are other considerations which suggest that the designers saw things from the same global point of view as we do today with our satellites and manned spacecraft.

For example, whoever positioned the Pyramid did so on the thirtieth parallel, showing that they were fully aware of the Earth as a sphere with imaginary lines of latitude and longitude across it. The Egyptians expressed the idea of stretching parallels and meridians by two birds, usually doves, and the Greeks used the idea of shooting an arrow to express the same idea of drawing imaginary lines on the Earth's surface. There is no doubt that latitude and longitude were fully understood by the ruling élite in Egypt and that they used the same system that we do today, with 360 degrees in a circle. We know this because their basic measure of length – the geographic foot – was obtained by dividing 1 degree of arc at the equator into 360,000 parts. Basing their number systems on six may stem from Hoova, whose symbol, the six-pointed Star of David, was adopted by the State of Israel.

Britain was not, in the eyes of the Civilizations, in any way inferior to Egypt. Indeed, it may have been more favoured. One reason for this contention lies in the placing of geodetic markers at Avebury Ring as well as at Thebes.

In the main room of the Temple of Amon Ra at Thebes there existed a thimble-shaped carved stone, called an *omphalos* (navel). Thebes and our word 'thimble' may both be derived from the Phoenician word *thibbûn*, meaning 'navel'. This stone was placed with very great accuracy on the parallel of latitude 25° 42′ 51″ N, which is two-sevenths of the distance between the equator and the pole. The longitude was the meridian forming the official eastern boundary of Ancient Egypt (Tompkins, 1973).

In the centre of the South Circle within Avebury Ring there was once an immense upright stone, which William Stukeley called 'The Obelisk' (photo 9). It had fallen even in Stukeley's day but its position is known with some accuracy and it was placed on the latitude that was twice that of the omphalos at Thebes, i.e. four-sevenths of the distance from equator to pole or one-seventh of the circumference of the Earth (fig. 13.3). This dwelling on the magic number 7 could indicate that Avebury was a primary position on the Earth if not *the* primary position. It would have been fixed by representatives of the Civilizations in who knows what antiquity.

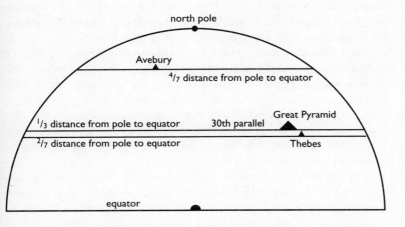

Fig. 13.3 The exact placing on Earth of the omphalos in the Temple of Amon Ra at Thebes and the Obelisk in the centre of the South Circle at Avebury Ring, as well as the Great Pyramid on the thirtieth parallel, indicates the space capability of those who placed them.

Through Phyllis Schlemmer, we are told that Stonehenge was designed by representatives of Altea, so it follows that Avebury must have been their dreamchild as well. Using the Earth's rotation as a clock, it is significant that the Avebury Obelisk lies exactly on a meridian that is 7 seconds of time west of that on which Stonehenge was established.

Thus, whatever may have happened to draw a veil over Britain's glorious past, we can see here the hand of the Civilizations sojourning in the region which is now Wiltshire and, by inference, many other of our ancient places as well. It seems likely to me that, if the Star of David is the sign of Hoova, then the pyramidal triangle on whose proportions the Great Pyramid was designed must be the sign of Altea; these logos have been used in fig. 12.6.

Therefore, it is not too great a leap of imagination to envisage these space beings descending in their spacecraft at Avebury after carefully fixing the position for the major stone and supervising the work of erecting it. Around this stone, the rest of the edifice eventually grew, but it was the 'gods' who first decided where it should be.

So it appears that, whenever we find a culture explosion in a time when archaeology indicates that the people were primitive, we have to look for a teacher or set of teachers from one or more of the Civilizations. Thus, when we find the most amazing cities being built in 6000–8000 BC, as we do in Southern Mesopotamia, at Jericho in southern Palestine, and Catal Hüyük in Turkey, as well as later at Susa and Harappa, and Mohenjo-Daro in the Indus Valley, we have to ask: Who came from above to give the culture its boost?

Catal Hüyük was a strange city with a population of possibly several thousand but it had no city gates because the windowless and doorless walls of its perimeter houses formed a completely blank wall around the complex. Even stranger, there were no streets to service the clusters of adjoining rooms that were separated by courtyards; the rooms had to be entered via their roofs. In Jericho as well there were no streets as such, which makes these very ancient cities look strangely inhuman places (Hamblin, 1973).

Yet amazing things were done. Jericho's defences (although against what or whom is difficult to detect) consisted of massive walls surrounded by a ditch over 25 ft wide and 8 ft deep, which was excavated out of solid rock. The settlement covered some 10 acres, which means that approaching half a million cubic feet of rock had to be extracted. By what means did those who oversaw the building of Jericho perform this amazing feat? The total population of Jericho was, we are told on the best authority, a mere 3,000 people. And also why did they go to such immense trouble when it would appear from the archaelogical evidence that they had very primitive tools? There must have been beings involved to whom such feats of civil engineering were child's play.

Tom has told us that the one called Ioannes came from the Civilizations and taught the people of Mesopotamia so that the Uruk culture sprang into being. However, while Ioannes appears as a man dressed as a fish, a representation of which was excavated at Nineveh by Layard in the mid-nineteenth century, he did not, according to Tom, actually come from the sea, as we are otherwise led to believe.

Now a word about Mohenjo-Daro, the greatest city of the Indus Valley culture. Here we have another somewhat inhuman city, dated to around 2000–3000 BC, consisting of a well-appointed Citadel with, among other civic buildings, a Great Bath and sumptuous houses for a ruling élite. This in contrast to the lower city area, which was built on a grid-iron plan running north–south and east–west. Here the main streets were 30 ft wide and cut up the down-town area into some 12 blocks, each covering about 22 acres. Servicing the blocks were narrow lanes, which were well supplied with efficient drains, even to the extent of having manhole covers to clear them if they became blocked. There were many wells and it seems that hygiene was a major consideration. Yet the rooms had no windows, even though they were often the equivalent of two storeys high.

Like all these bold examples of civil engineering that lie buried beneath the debris of millennia, these cities foundered. Often they foundered so quickly that those who study them are at a loss to explain how such obvious cultural excellence could have disappeared so rapidly. Yet, if we assume that they only sprang into being because those from the Civilizations came and oversaw their construction and subsequent development, then we must expect that, when the Civilizations' interest was withdrawn, they rapidly declined into barbarism and decay.

In the thousands of years following the destruction of Atlantis, the Civilizations tried to repair some of the damage to the upward progress of mankind. Yet they were doomed to failure because they could not continue to intervene directly and also leave mankind with free will. They stretched the human race far beyond what it could itself sustain and so, when they withdrew, their wonderful constructions fell into chaos.

Only in the last 2,000 years have they hit on what we hope is the right plan for the furtherance of mankind. They have planted religious faiths, such as Christianity, Islam and Buddhism, in the hope that, under their moral guidance, we will struggle, however imperfectly, up to a situation where the lot of common man can be improved without their direct help. They have had to withdraw from overt intervention and rely on keeping us under surveillance with spacecraft and their denizens. They have fed us with knowledge and ideas through the minds and actions of great men and women. Some of these ideas have been benign while others may have been contrary to the great plan for *Homo sapiens*. But eventually we have won through to a position where, if we have the sense to grasp the opportunity, we can make Earth the paradise it was originally designed to be.

Looking at the plans of these ancient cities, I am reminded of the cells of a beehive and prompted to speculate. At Mohenjo-Daro, for example, could the little windowless houses have been confinement cells for the nurturing of women who had been artificially inseminated? This would make sense of the good drainage. The resulting babies would have continued the programme of human/Civilizations cross-breeding which started at Aksu some 30,000 years earlier. Those who were overseeing this programme could have lived in the proper houses that have been discovered and the grand facilities of the Citadel would have catered for their needs.

When the necessary number of cross-bred individuals had been produced and released into the community then the representatives of the Civilizations could have withdrawn, allowing their experiment to proceed in whatever way free will dictated. However, that would have meant that their cohesive presence was no longer there to weld together those left behind and so the great cities fell into decay.

This notion has to have some measure of truth in it because the more mundane explanations do not provide any meaningful answers. Suffice it to say that there were many great cities and civilizations that flowered suddenly from apparently nothing and just as quickly decayed. Such behaviour goes against the accepted ideas of the gradual development which has led to our present civilization. For that reason, because we have had to do it on our own (or appear to), there is a better chance that, despite its imperfections, the world civilization of today may be lasting. That is, if we do not ruin it by overpopulation and greed.

FOURTEEN

INFILTRATORS

THE ADVANCED HUMAN experiment which started at Aksu nearly 35,000 years ago had one previous great chance to succeed. That was the Atlantean culture which progressed technologically further up the scientific tree of knowledge than we have yet done. Yet, just as seems likely with our developing subatomic and biological sciences, some Atlanteans used their knowledge for ulterior motives.

Today, things are not that much different. We pour billions of dollars into state of the art research into the fundamental particles of nature and their laws, not so much in the pursuit of knowledge for its own sake but because there is potentially a big matter–anti-matter bomb to be made and one or other of the super-powers is determined to get it first. The Atlanteans found a secret such as this and managed to create such a world-shattering explosion that they foundered with their knowledge, taking a large slice of humanity with them.

At the same time, because in a technological civilization science tends to develop on a broad front, the Atlanteans carried out experiments in molecular biology which, while enriching their lives and increasing their lifespan, were also used to create monstrous hybrid creatures. They also worked to heighten their physical pleasures.

We are only in the infancy of molecular biological techniques, but have a somewhat similar scenario today. There is a great deal of money to be made from the results of molecular biology and, where money talks, sense and reason fly out of humanity's window.

One example that will strike a chord with most people is Steven Spielberg's film of Michael Crichton's novel *Jurassic Park* (Crichton, 1991). The basic idea that extinct species such as dinosaurs can be recreated from their DNA is not so far-fetched that we cannot consider it feasible. Yet, as this cautionary tale so horrifically explains, when you play with nature in such a way you literally have a velociraptor by the tail.

The situation with regard to our space visitors is not quite the same. Certain of them, in antiquity, have, I am sure, created monsters – perhaps even the dinosaurs – *and* destroyed them! Yet today, even though these visitors are interacting with us in certain ways, the intervention seems to be muted. Earth is not such a cosmic playground as it once was.

Even the so-called 'opposition' seems to have more basic sense than we do. For, up to now, no one has seriously suggested that we are being contaminated by diseases introduced by visitors from outer space. Perhaps this is due to the way the visitors usually blow away like leaves before the wind whenever curious human beings come too close. People who are abducted usually suffer only mental problems afterwards and not many physiological ones other than nose bleeds.

However, sometimes the close encounters are very close and, just as with our own astronauts, the visiting entities must, one imagines, be clinically clean before they visit our alien world. Certain events described by otherwise highly stable and intelligent people seem to indicate that overcleanliness on our part does not matter to the denizens of flying saucers. Yet we may be able to contaminate them!

Daniel W. Fry was, in 1950, employed at the White Sands proving ground near Las Cruces in New Mexico. He had a highly responsible job in charge of the instrumentation of the missile control systems. It was at White Sands that the Americans, after World War 2, initiated their intercontinental ballistic missile and space programme, using German scientists and engineers plus captured V2 rockets. It was a place in which the UFOs took a very special interest (Buttlar, 1979).

In the late evening of 4 July 1950, Fry was at the old static V2 test site when he detected a dark object above him, blotting out the stars. This object proved to be a 30-ft diameter flying saucer when it landed only some 25 ft from him. It was apparently seamless with no ports of any kind. Being curious, he went to touch it, and later described its surface as an unbelievably smooth silvery metal over which was a faint violet aura. I explained in my previous book, *UFO Quest* (Watts, 1994), how this aura might arise. As his fingers came into contact with the craft, he experienced a tingling sensation and a disembodied voice warned him, in colloquial American, not to touch – a warning that was reinforced when Fry found himself thrown backwards onto the ground.

The voice, which indicated that it was the occupant of the device, continued to speak to him and the following points in the transcription are of particular interest.

The voice told Fry that it could not actually appear on this planet for another 4 years because it would take it that long to acclimatize to our atmosphere and gravity, and to become immune to our germs. Its mission was to discover how far humans were along the road to adjusting their ways of thinking so that they could accept the fact that space was not theirs but populated by many space races. For centuries the expeditions to this planet had met with little success. They needed to find more fertile minds and more intelligent people who could accept the new ideas. Fry, with his technical knowledge, was certainly one of those. 'We would like to help the inhabitants of Earth with their further development,' said the voice and told him that the craft was remotely controlled from a mother-ship some 900 miles above the Earth.

Fry was astounded when the entity invited him on board for 'a little trip'. He was even more amazed when the UFO whirled him into space at an unbelievable speed. Yet Fry did not at first believe the craft had moved because he experienced no effects of inertia at all. This is in accordance with the idea that UFOs can draw space into themselves and, on release, travel with it (see page 61).

The craft took him over New York, dropping from an unknown height to a mere 100,000 ft. He only had a brief chance to see the diamond-like lights of the city before the UFO whisked him back to White Sands. He emerged in confusion and, as the craft took off, was 'sucked forward' several metres by its force field. However, he could still watch its orange-red glow, which turned to a deep violet as it disappeared.

Fry immediately prepared a written report with all the technical details but nothing about the case emerged until 1962. It is not surprising that the space denizens, who are on our side and want to help, are frustrated by our overall resistance to their message. They seem to have tried all kinds of tricks in their desire to talk to us, possibly even going as far as to infiltrate our most secret centres.

It was in 1947, a mere 8 days after Kenneth Arnold had opened the modern UFO era by sighting spacecraft in California, that a shining disc was seen flying over Roswell, New Mexico, in a northwesterly direction (Berlitz & Moore, 1980). The next day, William Brazel, who managed an old ranch near Corona, some 75 miles northwest of Roswell, discovered some curious wreckage spread over a large area. In a swathe that was about 300 yd wide and $\frac{3}{4}$ mile long, there was debris that included beams $\frac{1}{2}$ sq. in with indecipherable hieroglyphics on them. Although they looked like balsa wood they were not and, while flexible, they were very, very tough and would not burn. There was also some material that resembled tinfoil and some brown parchment-like stuff. All this was extraordinarily tough and very light. The 'foil' could not be dented by a sledgehammer, nor was it affected in any way by a cutting torch.

On that same evening, at around 11.30 p.m., certain witnesses say they saw a UFO going down in a trajectory somewhere north of Roswell.

The next day (5 July), an actual 'crashed' disc-shaped UFO was discovered near Magdalena in an area west of Socorro (fig. 14.1), which is some 150 miles west of Corona. More sensationally, there were alien bodies lying around this craft.

Apparently first on the scene were members of the Anderson family (Good, 1992), who happened to stumble on the disc when out looking for moss agate stones. Although he was only 5 years old at the time, Gerald Anderson, the only one of the party who is still alive, and now a retired police chief and deputy sheriff, has vivid memories of the event, enhanced by regression hypnosis.

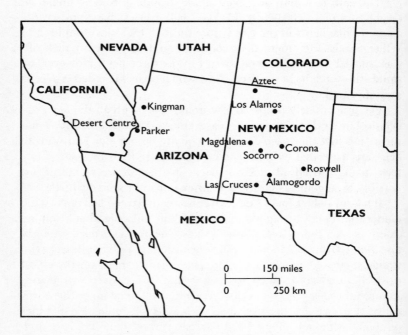

Fig. 14.1 Sites of UFO activity in the southern USA.

The disc was, according to Anderson, stuck into the side of a hill and, when they went up to it, they saw 'three creatures – three bodies – lying on the ground underneath this thing, in the shade'. However, not all these bodies were dead. Two seemed to be, but one appeared to be alive, even if badly damaged, and and there was a fourth, apparently unharmed. From his 5-year-old viewpoint, Anderson thought that the undamaged one had been giving first aid to the others but, he said, it 'recoiled in fear like it thought we were going to attack it' when the five of them came up.

Soon afterwards, five students and their professor from the University of Pennsylvania, out on an archaeological dig in the area, arrived. The final civilian to appear was Grady Barnett. Attempts at communicating with the undamaged ET in several languages failed but Gerald Anderson gives some interesting details. Despite the desert heat, the craft was unexpectedly cold to the touch, as were the bodies. He experienced what others have done in the presence of ETs. The undamaged one looked at him and seemed to Gerald to be reading his thoughts – 'it was as if his thoughts were in my head'.

This episode was rudely interrupted by the arrival of armed soldiers, who immediately began to terrorize the adults, threatening to take away their children and not return them should they dare to say a single word about what they had witnessed.

Meanwhile, the debris near Brazel's ranch had been recovered by two officers from Roswell Field and a statement was released to the press that the remains of an extra-terrestrial craft had been recovered. Despite some limited exposure in the media, a rapid programme of damage limitation was set in motion. The remains were, according to the official statement, just those of a weather balloon and its tinfoil radar target. The officers who had recovered the debris, and everyone else who had any involvement, were sworn to secrecy and Brazel himself was locked in jail for about a week while the ranch site was scavenged for any signs of the remaining debris.

There is a mass of evidence in Good (1989 & 1992) for the essential truths behind all this, including details of the recovery of the disc and the ETs who were apparently first taken to Roswell Army airfield. It is said that the damaged alien died soon after arrival at the airfield but that the undamaged one survived for 2 or more years in captivity at Los Alamos. This was, however, just one of a series of 'crashes' of UFOs in the great desert areas of New Mexico and Arizona (fig. 14.1). Following the Roswell incident there were others: at Paradise Valley, Arizona, in the same year; Aztec, New Mexico, in 1948; Kingman, Arizona, in 1953 and New Mexico in 1962.

There are some strange aspects of these cases. While there have been cases where UFOs appear to have blown up in mid-air and others have been recovered on the ground in various parts of the world, the numbers are very small compared with the number of UFOs reported. In other words, the UFOs seem to be very reliable craft so I am convinced that, while UFOs may develop problems, they do not crash unless there is some good reason for them doing so.

Maybe the event occurred at Roswell rather than anywhere else because, stationed at an airfield to the south, with the most awesome weaponry in the world, was the first American atomic bomber force. Also, in this same desert area, were White Sands and the atomic weapon establishments of Los Alamos and Alamogordo.

I am not alone in thinking that so many crashes in one highly sensitive area are meaningful. In his novel *Majestic* – based very solidly on fact, including the real names of many of the people involved – Whitley Strieber (1990) makes it quite evident that he considers this crash to be an artifice on the part of the space denizens. He thinks that the 'bodies' were expendable, as was the craft itself, and that it was a wonderful way of infiltrating the innermost sanctum of the then most secret airbase in the USA. It was, indeed, a 'Trojan horse' but what I am personally not aware of is how far the infiltration went. Maybe nobody knows because we are never, it seems, on the same wavelength as those who control the UFOs.

Whatever dialogue with the UFOnauts might have occurred subsequently, it is doubtful whether military interrogators were the right people to conduct it. It would have required people of humility with very open minds, people able to show love to entities which did not really resemble themselves either physically or mentally. Such attributes are not normally found in the higher echelons of military organizations. The then current thinking of the US High Command was that, somehow, one or more of the visitors' spacecraft was to be shot down so that its technology could be assessed and, if possible, duplicated. Similar thinking must have pervaded the Kremlin at the time, while the British Government adopted a wait and see policy.

An Atomic Energy Commission engineer (name withheld) says that he and other specialists were taken in blacked-out buses to a desert site near Kingman, Arizona, where they saw a disc, 30 ft in diameter, embedded in the sand. The engineer said he saw one of the 'dead' occupants, a humanoid 3 feet tall. I write the word 'dead' in inverted commas because I do not believe that we really know what death means in the context of advanced robotic creatures that hover somewhere between solid humanity and psychic manifestation, seemingly able to shift from one state to the other. The term used by the US authorities for such creatures is Extra-terrestrial Biological Entities (EBEs).

According to Gerald Anderson, the Magdalena EBEs were about 4 feet tall, with oversized heads and jet-black, almond-shaped eyes. In this they were typical Greys and we have already seen the strange hypnotic effects that these entities can command in the case of Gerald Anderson. Young as he was, Gerald remembers a sensation of falling and tumbling. From his description, the EBE had somehow transferred his own emotions to the boy, who later confessed that he felt the entity's emotions as if they were his own.

Now, so much later, Gerald Anderson has sized up, to his satisfaction, the connection between the debris found at Corona and the crashed craft at Magdalena. There was, apparently, a gash in the side of the crashed UFO which they saw and Anderson thinks that it was caused by a mid-air collision between two such craft, one of which exploded – there was apparently a mid-air explosion that rocked the Brazel ranch – while the other crashlanded at Magdalena. The only problem is – what causes a UFO to explode? It is more likely that it was purposely destroyed because only debris was found near the ranch and nobody has ever hinted that there were bits of alien bodies among it. In any case, from the description of the debris, it does not seem to have come from a gash in the side of a disc-shaped UFO. One wonders if the debris was nothing whatever to do with the downed UFO at Magdalena but was scattered as a diversion for reasons unknown. Maybe the visible gash in the Magdalena disc was also contrived to make this acceptable to us as a 'crash' for surely any damage to the disc would have been hidden in the hillside.

So, whether Anderson's appraisal is correct or not I do not know. Suffice it to say that an EBE capable of getting inside the head of a 5-year-old – and so capable of infiltrating the mind of anybody else – was, as far as my information goes, held for 2 years within the confines of one of America's top-security establishments Los Alamos. Perhaps only one entity was destined to survive this event and perhaps one was enough.

FIFTEEN

FROM THE STARS

IN HIS REMARKABLY well researched and well argued book *The Sirius Mystery*, Robert Temple (1976) showed that an otherwise obscure African tribe, the Dogon, possesses knowledge that must have originated from space visitors from the star system of Sirius. Sirius is the seventh closest star to Earth and is 8.7 light years away. Also it is the brightest star in the sky, being outshone only by the brighter planets.

As far as the Dogon are concerned, the origin of creation lies not here on Earth but with the white dwarf star, Sirius B, which revolves around Sirius A – the brightest star in the sky. Temple calls Sirius B by a botanical name 'Digitaria', but the Dogons call it *po tolo*, *po* being the word for the smallest of their cereal grains. This usage is similar to the 'grain of mustard seed' mentioned in the Bible and is assumed to represent an atom. It is highly significant that, although Sirius B is totally invisible from Earth without powerful telescopes, its motion determines the Dogon calendar.

However, to have a very active mainstream star like Sirius A accompanied by a star that is the end product of stellar evolution is curious in itself; white dwarfs have been mainstream stars, like the Sun. These have, with age, expanded into red giants and then collapsed into superdense dwarf stars which may not shine sufficiently brightly to be detectable in telescopes.

Before the middle of the last century, none of our astronomers suspected that Sirius A had a superheavy companion but slight wobbles in the former's motion showed that one had to exist. So how could the Dogon have known this? How could they have known that the orbital period of Sirius B around Sirius A was 50 years?

They also possess very advanced mathematical concepts, for their traditions specifically say that Sirius A lies at one focus of the elliptical orbit of Sirius B and they draw diagrams to show that they know what this means (fig. 15.1). Furthermore, say the Dogon initiates, *Po tolo* (Sirius B) rotates on its axis. Modern astronomy shows that stars do rotate and maybe it is possible for tribesmen to equate the Sun with a star and to obtain the idea of rotation by the observation of prominent sunspots at sunrise or sunset. But how did the Dogon know this about an invisible white dwarf? In any case, modern astronomers cannot yet measure the rotation rate of Sirius B, which the Dogon say 'revolves upon itself over a period of one year'. This rate is considered by astronomers to be quite within the bounds of possibility.

The region of the Dogon lies south of Timbuktu, now in the Mali Republic, and mainly south of the great northward bulge of the River Niger. Temple suggests that the Dogon, in some way, were originally from Libya and that they interbred with the indigenous tribes of the area where they are now found. Because of this, he theorizes, they

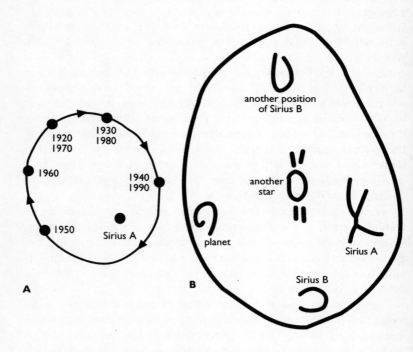

Fig. 15.1   (a) The orbit of Sirius B about Sirius A and the former's positions at various dates in its 50-year cycle. (b) The equivalent diagram as drawn by the Dogon. The planet is likely to be the one from which the amphibious Nommo came. (After Temple, 1976)

could have been privy to knowledge and traditions that stretch back through Ancient Egypt to Sumeria. However, if Temple is trying to prove that knowledge of the Sirius system could only have come from visitors from that system, then it would be mere child's play for them to have set down wherever they thought fit. Thus we do not need to postulate an overland route for the spread of this knowledge. It could have, literally, come out of the air.

Temple, like everyone else who has studied the matter, is convinced that the Sumerian and Egyptian high civilizations sprang suddenly into being. However, Tom has told us that this came about because of the setting down of reincarnated representatives of the Twenty-four Civilizations who were, with their own retinues, able to instruct the local people in arts and crafts.

The place in Palestine to which space people regularly came was Megiddo. This is an extremely ancient and strategically placed city in Caanan, in the north of Palestine, and according to Tom, was established in 9228 BC, which makes it some 3,000 years older than acknowledged by modern archaeology. Close by is the hill, har Megiddo, a name that has been corrupted into 'Armageddon'. Tom is quoted as saying:

> It was a stronghold for those who maintained a contact and communication with us, and it was a stronghold of truth. Those that opposed in their thinking or in their reverie had decided, by destroying truth, they would be able to control Planet Earth.

It is from the idea of the struggle between good and evil that the modern idea of Armageddon stems.

Megiddo was founded, according to Tom, by a group who, although not from Atlantis, migrated to the site at the time of the final destruction of Atlantis. They were, however, no ordinary migrants as they remained in constant contact with the Civilizations. Here, we are told, was an entry port for those from the Civilizations, including the Hawk in one of his later reincarnations. It was here that the first 'energy nodule' was established, so that those from dimensions beyond the physical could enter and exit at will from Planet Earth. Tom has described it as a place for holding 'summit meetings'. Other nodules were established around the Earth in following millennia.

The written history of Megiddo starts with the annals of Thutmosis III (see page 11) who, in 1468 BC, defeated a Canaanite army near there. However, the archaeological record stems from the excavations carried out in the large mound, Tell el-Muteselim, which revealed no less than 25 occupation levels. The oldest was a small cave in the bedrock dated to the pre-Pottery Neolithic period (7500–6000 BC). The site was abandoned in about 600 BC but Tom says that the remains of Megiddo in its earliest phases still remain to be uncovered.

However, what the known record shows (Negev, 1972) is the constant contact with Egypt. It was an Egyptian stronghold after Thutmosis's conquest and, as late as 942 BC, was taken by Pharaoh Sheshonq I.

So space contact with the area existed here and was spread to Egypt, as well as to Mesopotamia. It is claimed by some that the civilizations of Ancient Sumeria and Ancient Egypt developed separately but this cannot be the case. Those who founded the proto-civilizations, with all their manifest abilities, were from the same fount of knowledge and expertise that was not of this world.

Temple (1976), in *The Sirius Mystery*, shows that the esoteric priesthoods of the Sumerian civilizations, the pre-dynastic Egyptian civilization and the pre-Hellenic civilization of Greece also knew these facts about the Sirius system. They dressed up their knowledge in myths and puns but *The Epic of Gilgamesh* (Sandan, 1970) contains hidden but nevertheless recognizable allusions to the number 50, as well as other references that point to the same basic knowledge of the system.

Anubis, the dog-headed god of the Egyptians, represents Sirius and, in the writings of Plutarch, we find:

> By Anubis they understand the horizontal circle, which divides the invisible part of the world, which they call Nephthys, from the visible, to which they give the name of Isis; and as this circle equally touches upon the confines of both light and darkness, it may be looked upon as common to them both – and from this circumstance arose that resemblance, which they imagine between Anubis and the Dog, it being observed of this animal, that he is equally watchful as well by day as night.

Actually I am led to think that we call Sirius by the name 'Dog Star' for deeper reasons than this, and not merely because Sirius dogs the heels of Orion the Hunter. Why, for example, do those who say they sprang from Sirius call themselves the Dogon?

Isis is identifiable with Sirius A while her sister Nephthys is described as 'the invisible' and corresponds to Sirius B. Such correspondences, and many, many more that Temple has brought together, make it quite evident that the features of the Sirius system were well known to the Egyptians. Furthermore, *an* meant 'heaven' in Sumerian and one is struck by the fact that the same syllable starts the word Anubis, while *neph* means 'heaven' in Greek.

There must be, at least, a third component of the Sirius system because it seems inconceivable that beings are able to exist on a white dwarf star. This third component must be a planet – maybe a watery planet – for Isis is connected with water and Temple makes connection with the fish-god, Ioannes, who came out of the water and returned to it. It was Ioannes and his entourage, the Annedoti, who taught the primitive Sumerians how to develop an advanced civilization. However, Tom has gone further and has said that Ioannes was a reincarnation of Joseph, the Head of the Civilization Aragon.

Plutarch, in his *Moralia*, wrote that: 'Isis was born in the regions that are ever moist'. In his comments on this and related matters, Temple wonders whether a planet, Sirius C, could support intelligent amphibious beings, perhaps like mermaids and mermen. He even makes the unusual comment that they might resemble 'our intelligent friends the dolphins'.

It was therefore of great interest to find that Tom has said that the dolphins 'that nurse your youth, were citizens of Atlantis'. That souls of Atlanteans could happily transfer to sea creatures is perhaps a revolutionary idea to many but, when you realize what (apart from the slaughter undertaken by certain nations) an idyllic life a dolphin must lead, perhaps some of us might consider it as an avenue of escape from an increasingly crazy world. Anyway, Tom has said that 'by choosing the sea they could do no harm, and they enjoy mating joyfully'.

The Dogon are quite adamant that the founders of their special knowledge were amphibious creatures from the sky. They call their leaders the Nommo and they are the 'Instructors' or 'Monitors'. They say that the Nommos must live in water. They came in an ark which landed somewhere to the northeast of Dogon country and the Dogon say that their ancestors came from a country which could conceivably be Egypt or a neighbouring country, such as Libya.

They describe the landing of the ark in terms that we have come to associate with our own soft-landers, such as *Snoopy* used in the Moon landings. 'The ark landed on the Fox's dry land and displaced a pile of dust raised by the whirlwind it caused.' (The reference to 'the Fox' cannot be gone into here and interested readers should consult Temple's book directly. They will then be led to the exemplary work of two French anthropologists, Griaule and Dieterlen, who spent 9 years with the Dogon and whose report on the associations of the tribe with

Sirius formed the basis for Temple's researches.)

This spacecraft, or ark, was apparently primitive compared with the ones we see today. It made a thunderous vibrating noise when landing, created gouges in the ground and skidded. There was flame that went out when the craft landed, which indicates that some form of rocket propulsion was involved. Temple's book contains Dogon drawings of what they call *sirigi*. These are are representations of the Nommo's spacecraft and look just like rockets (fig. 15.2). There was also a mother-ship, which the Dogon describe as a new star hovering in the sky and in which the Nommos eventually left Earth.

Having discussed the possible position of the suspected planet Sirius C in the Sirius system and made suggestions as to how highly intelligent amphibious ETs might have evolved, Temple comes down to the crunch of contact with space people. There is, he concludes, no way we can speak of a 'Sirian God' because, by definition, God is the same for all the Universe. Earth people and ETs may, in their spiritual evolutions, define and worship many gods but eventually, as we do now, they will have to come to understand the spiritual system under which the Universe operates. The Council of Nine, through their spokesman Tom, has given us the information but we are not yet fully able to comprehend it. Temple wrote:

> There is no doubt that it is at the level of our deepest concerns –
> our religious and philosophical ones – that contact with an extra-
> terrestrial civilisation will make its deepest impact on us. And it
> is at this friable level of our preconceptions that we are most
> vulnerable. Here the foundations of our beliefs can crumble with
> the first shock wave. Here the entire edifice of our civilisation
> can give way. Only by being prepared can we safeguard our own
> cultural integrity.

Although, at the time he wrote his book, Temple could not entertain the idea that the contact had already started, many of his suppositions are now, in the light of what we have since learned from ETs, very valid. It is not surprising that the Establishment does all in its power to reject the idea of modern Nommos coming to visit us and give us information. Information, indeed, that is too important to be generally accepted. However, like the Dogon initiates, we must set down and pass on what we have been told by our space visitors so that, eventually, our whole 'tribe' will come to believe it and will be able to reorient its narrow, greedy, materialistic way of life a long the way which leads to our planet's salvation.

I have described the Sirius contact in detail because it is one of the most difficult for the sceptics to refute. They can either accept that we have been visited and infiltrated in the past or they can merely ignore it. Either way the truth will not be gainsaid. However much the political correctness of our time seeks to suppress the truth, eventually it will out. There is some light at the end of this tunnel through the US Freedom of Information Acts which, although they still cannot cut through the full veil of secrecy that surrounds many of the issues most

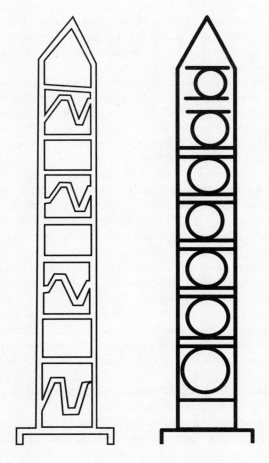

Fig. 15.2   The rocket-like *sirigi* designs of the Dogon. (After Temple, 1976)

important to the future lives of ordinary men, women and children have at least paid lip service to the idea that information on sensitive issues should be available to the public at large.

There is now a large body of literature concerning the claims of others who have been visited, sometimes abducted or otherwise 'talked to' by beings from stars of our galaxy. A good resumé of these will be found in *Life Beyond Planet Earth?* (Bord & Bord, 1991). There is, of course the Zeta Reticuli encounter of Betty and Barney Hill described on page 157. There is also the case of Lonnie Duggan, an Idaho farmer, who surprised a hairy extra-terrestrial extracting blood from his horse and who was told in a mechanical voice that the ET came from a planet of Tau Ceti (11.8 light years away). Duggan was also told that, when we 'learn to live in peace with one another and to banish wars', then contact will be made and they will share their knowledge with us.

Olaf Nielsen, while walking near Halmstad, Sweden, on 25 April 1960, was taken into a hovering spacecraft. He eventually found himself in a 'large brightly lit cavern', which was a kind of sub-terranean hangar for Earth-based UFOs and contained a device said to be used to form a magnetic force field to repel some 'opposition' ETs from the vicinity of Orion. They were described as the 'Dark Ones' and, unlike his 'captors', wished to take over Earth for their own purposes. The intriguing idea is that we have extra-terrestrial defenders actually occupying bases on Earth. Certainly there are many eyewitness accounts of UFOs entering the oceans and so maybe visiting underwater bases of which not even our spy satellites would be aware.

Other contactees, such as Mario Restier, who was taken from Volta Redonda, Brazil, in 1949, were told that their hosts were from Orion. This makes the source star difficult to pinpoint because the constellation of Orion consists of several bright stars which are at different distances from Earth. For example, Beta Orion (the star Rigel) is some 880 light years away and, while most of the prominent stars are considered to be at roughly this distance, some are somewhat further away.

Three Venezuelans (two businessmen and a gynaecologist) also encountered entities claiming to be from Orion. This occurred on 7 August 1965, when they were contacted by two very tall (7–8 ft) men with long yellow hair and the oft-reported large eyes, dressed in shining metallic one-piece suits. These came down a 'beam of light' from a large UFO, which hovered 30 feet away. Among the information imparted telepathically to the gynaecologist, who asked the questions, the entities said they came in peace to study the psyche of humanity. According to them, there were seven inhabited planets other than Earth and they gave the name *gravitelides* to their craft, which operated by means of 'a nucleus of concentrated solar energy which produces an enormous magnetic force'.

This technical information is well in line with the other sources of information on UFO propulsion (see page 45). The 'nucleus of concentrated solar energy' presumably refers to a nuclear reaction similar to that which occurs in the intense temperature and pressure of the sun's interior. The magnetic force is well known and well documented as a by-product of UFO propulsion systems and is connected with the warping of space in order to project from one point to another across its great depths.

One very interesting comment which the ETs made was that each planet investigating Earth sends its expedition in a vast mother-ship, half as big as the moon, which is parked behind Mars. Certainly the UFO waves of 1950, 1952, 1954 and 1956 correlate well with the closest approach of Mars to Earth but the Vallées (1967) point out that, after this, the correlation is not so good. As the Venezuelan encounter occurred in 1965, the Vallées would be of the opinion that, at this time, and taken over all, the 'Mars effect' was not proven.

This case was investigated by a competent UFOlogist and the men themselves were adamant that their experience be kept from the media. One of their number suffered for some time from the shock of the encounter and was afraid of a return of the entities.

For some reason it is very hard for humanity to accept the idea that space denizens may be interested in our welfare. It laughs at the idea that the communications received by the contactees are given for the purpose of sowing the seeds of the reform of its destructive ways. This seems to be the viewpoint of the overseeing Nine but other, more parochial visitors may be worried more about their own welfare than ours.

During the Cold War period, the message given so often to contactees was that the space peoples were worried that, should we manage to blow ourselves into oblivion, then other planets on nearby systems would also be affected. The communications via Phyllis Schlemmer have told us in no uncertain terms that humanity cannot be allowed largely to obliterate itself because we are already a drag on the plan for the Universe and to start the human experiment again might prove impossible. Looked at from the Council of Nine's viewpoint, the sudden liberation of untold millions of souls with no bodies to reinhabit would be a spiritual disaster of unknown magnitude.

Behind the apparently random contacts and the disparate information, this is the recurrent theme. For all our sakes, stop the ongoing and accelerating destruction of Earth's resources. It is a green message that is luckily beginning to be taken seriously. It will hurt our narrow interests. Unthinking and greedy people will pursue the god of money and profit, despite any warnings that they are given but maybe, just maybe, the tide of ordinary humanity's opinion can tip the scales. I have been told by a trance medium that it will be the youth who come to adulthood and positions of influence by 2025 that will start the real fight back. It is a pity that we have to wait so long and that the message from the planets is not being more closely listened to now.

SIXTEEN

THE CHOSEN

IT WAS A CLEAR night and the moon was so bright that the husband and wife driving along US Highway 3 hardly seemed to need their headlights. They were in a hurry because they had heard that a hurricane was forecast and they needed to get to their coastal home in Portsmouth, New Hampshire, before it should strike. This is why they were travelling through the night, in the hope of being home by 2.30 a.m.

However, it was past 10.00 p.m. before they were south of Lancashire, New Hampshire. Then they saw what they at first thought was a bright star. That impression was soon replaced by apprehension when the 'star' moved first across the face of the moon and then came down and seemed to be following them.

The two people were Barney and Betty Hill, whose abduction case is possibly the best known of many that have been reported. It has been as 'scientifically' investigated as any such incident can be. One of those involved was Allen Hynek and some of the replies of Barney and Betty when under regression hypnosis are given in detail in *The UFO Experience* (Hynek, 1972). However, Hynek stopped short of giving the whole story, which was fully recounted in *The Interrupted Journey* (Fuller, 1966).

From their testimony under hypnosis it appears that the Hills were first put into a partial trance state so that Barney was perfectly capable of driving the car but was 'forced' off the main highway and onto a side track. The track led towards a waiting UFO that was, according to the Hills, orange in colour but seemed as bright as the Moon. There were several 'men' on this track ahead of them when the car was brought to a standstill.

Some of these men approached the car and, after opening the doors, escorted Betty and Barney down the road. Betty felt that she was asleep but then she woke up to find herself being escorted through the woods. She was aware of Barney behind her and that he was 'sleep-walking' so she shouted angrily to him to wake up, but to no avail.

One of the men, described as short and wearing a kind of uniform, was walking beside her. He spoke to her in colloquial English, reassuring her that they only wanted to do some tests and that, when they were over, the Hills would be returned to their car. 'You'll be on your way back home in no time,' he said.

Colloquial communication that comes via the medium of telepathy is, for many people, one of the most difficult things with which to come to terms. Taken on their own, 'spoken' words such as described by the Hills could be explained away as some form of psychological wish to normalize the situation by making the ETs seem more like human beings.

However, there are many of these abduction events, now independently recorded, where similar 'talking' occurs. Apart from the independent corroboration which their testimonies under hypnosis afforded, the Hills' account is backed up by the accounts of many people who have also had abduction experiences. We may not understand how it is done but speaking through the mind is a technique normally used by ETs and one which they find very easy and natural.

Barney independently recalled, under hypnosis, that he was forcibly taken up a ramp and felt that his feet were not fully in contact with the ground. He was angry but impotent to stop the men doing this. He then described how he found that parts of his body, e.g. his fingers and legs, were numb. Eventually he found himself on an examination table.

The Hills' description of the ETs is interesting as it is in some ways the same as, and in other ways different from, the testimony of others who have experienced similar events. Barney described the 'leader' as wearing a shining black coat, overlaid by a black sash and wearing a cap that made him look like a 'naval captain'. Betty described the men as having skins with a greyish tinge and no ears, but it was their deep black eyes that most impressed her.

We have seen that Greys are the ETs most often involved in these abduction events and they have been described by one of the more naturally human-like forms of space persons as 'our soldiers'. This indicates that Greys are used to perform possibly unsavoury tasks under higher command and, therefore, may not necessarily be ultimately responsible for their actions. It also indicates that, just as with any military personnel on Earth, we must expect to find a spectrum of abilities and concerns for the task in hand.

In the craft, the Hills were separated. Betty was kept in one room while Barney was taken into another. Betty described her room as being the shape of a slice of cake with the tip cut off. This would, of course, be the shape if, in a circular craft, rooms were arranged radially around some central core. The walls, she said, gleamed with a bluish light.

It is often assumed that these extra-terrestrial beings have no feelings but what happened to Betty Hill (and has happened to others in similar circumstances) indicates otherwise. The 'captain' and a 'doctor' made her sit on a white chair for a form of medical examination of her eyes, neck, nose, ears and teeth. This proved to be painless. However, they then laid her on an examination table and, having removed her shoes and dress, tried to introduce a needle-like instrument into her navel to carry out what she divined was a pregnancy test. Betty tried hard to prevent this but the doctor persisted and the pain caused her to burst into tears. This reaction astonished the two ETs and the captain laid his hand over her eyes, which stopped the pain momentarily. Thus Betty concluded that they did not mean to hurt her.

The doctor went into the next room to attend to Barney while Betty 'talked' to the captain. The means of communication between Greys and human beings appears to be one by which the ET introduces a thought pattern into the human mind which is transformed into, in this case, English. The brain has a stored vocabulary which, in some unexplained way, is triggered by a thought pattern to create the English equivalent of the ideas which the ET wishes to convey. It is, apparently, usually very accurate so that recipients can believe what they are being told. However, sometimes the mode of speech is somewhat archaic. Something similar must occur in reverse because, often, there is no verbalization on either side.

However it is done there is no doubt, from the wide testimony of contactees and abductees, that this form of telepathic communication is a reality. Thus, when the Hills say that the ETs 'spoke' to them, or that they 'spoke' to the ETs, there is a seemingly normal conversation except that no vocal cords are involved.

That the ETs are often not fully aware of our physical qualities was evidenced when the doctor suddenly entered from the other room with Barney's false teeth in his hand. There was consternation when he found that Betty's teeth could not be taken out and, even though Betty tried to explain how human beings often lose their teeth with age, apparently the ETs could not understand how one human being could have removable teeth and another fixed teeth. Barney was also stripped naked and laid on an examination table where an appliance was placed over his genitalia, presumably to test them in some way.

There is a remarkable twist to this story. Betty asked the captain where they came from and, in reply, he showed her a three-dimensional star-map which 'somehow opened from the wall'. Thick lines on this map indicated prominent trade routes, thin ones occasionally used routes and dashed ones expeditionary routes. Obviously Betty could not recognize anything from this map, even though the captain said that the Sun was somewhere on it. The presentation resembled a holographic projection in that the 'stars' floated as spheres of light, apparently in the air, and there were 12 prominent ones.

Under regression hypnosis, Betty was able to recall the relative positions of the 12 stars. Using a model reconstructed by an astronomer, Marjorie Fish, Dr Mitchell of Ohio State University searched for a similar pattern in the immediate Universe using a computer. He found the configuration and was astonished to discover that it represented a section of the local Galaxy as it would appear from Zeta Reticuli, which is 36 light years away! (fig. 16.1)

Back on Earth, and in their own car again, the Hills were amazed to find that they were 35 miles further down the road than when the incident first occurred and they had apparently lost $2\frac{1}{2}$ hours of their lives, with little or no recollection of what had happened. Only under hypnosis did the details of their ordeal come to light.

There is, to my mind, no valid reason why this saucer-shaped spacecraft with red 'fins' on either side and winking lights around its periphery (as described by the Hills) should not have come from somewhere as far as 36 light years away. We are only in the infancy of our knowledge of how to achieve speeds beyond (or even close to) the speed of light. The idea that UFOs cannot be extra-terrestrial because they cannot travel faster than light is an overly simplistic approach based on our present knowledge. Einstein allowed us to understand and work out the consequences of travelling at speeds below the speed of light 300 million m/second (18,640 miles/second) but his formulae say nothing about what happens above that speed. It seems obvious that one of the first lessons we must learn from the space visitors is that we still do not know it all – or even a small part of it.

When the Hills had their abduction experience in September 1961, investigations into UFO phenomena were in their infancy. It was thought that the Hills had had a one-off experience but further investigation, by open-minded people with the necessary experience and techniques, has shown beyond doubt that the Hills' ordeal is not at all rare. Indeed, the number of people who may have been abducted

A

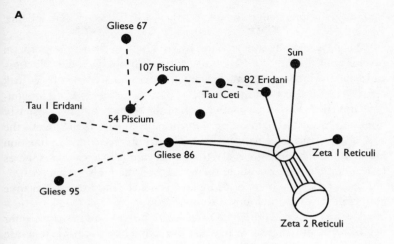

B

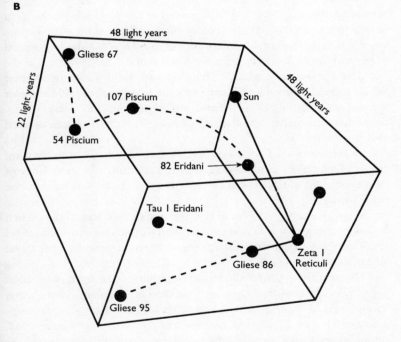

Fig. 16.1 (a) The holographic star map as recalled by Betty Hill under hypnotic regression. (b) The equivalent three-dimensional star map as elucidated by Marjorie Fish. Solid lines are trade routes regularly used by the Zeta Reticulans while dashed lines are exploratory routes.

without their knowledge and against their will is greater than anyone knows.

We have already referred to Budd Hopkins, who has written several books (1988 & 1991) on his in-depth probings into abduction cases and has arrived at some disturbing conclusions. Many people just refuse to entertain the implications of what researchers like Hopkins have unveiled. Yet, just as with much of the rest of the UFO saga, the unpalatable facts have to be faced eventually. We *are* being visited on a regular and intrusive basis by beings from outer space and hiding our heads in the sand will not make them go away. All we can do is try to learn as much as we can about them and their methods so that we lose our fear of the unknown. But Hopkins is not the only researcher into abduction cases as the following story shows.

A woman called Gloria was in bed with her husband asleep beside her. She was sure that she was awake but found herself unable to move a muscle and thinks that this was due to several hideous grey figures who were standing by the bed. It seemed like a very vivid dream and, on waking, she recalls saying to these entities: 'I'm not going to let you control me'. Less than a fortnight before this incident she had seen a UFO and the experience had really shaken her.

Gloria had gone to a lady hypnotherapist, Edith Fiore, because of psychological problems that were affecting her health, but Dr Fiore suspected something deeply disturbing lay skulking in Gloria's subconscious and that it was this which was at the root of her trouble (Fiore, 1989).

Under hypnosis, Gloria recalled the face of a weird entity with a big head which she described as looking something like that of a frog or a toad. This entity was apparently angry because Gloria was not cooperating.

She was staggered to recall that she apparently floated out of her bedroom *through the wall* and ended up on the pavement outside. The theories of R.D. Pearson (see page 65) show us, in some measure, how this may be possible.

The next thing she recalled was undergoing some form of medical tests and examination in a room that smelled peculiar. There were three kinds of 'people' in the room, including some 6-ft ones that attended to her. She could not see exactly what they looked like because they were covered in shroud-like garments but they had long, yellowish hands. As well as these there were short ones who gave directions. She says that the third group were just like human beings. The short ones had wrinkly skin and no hair. They had nasal openings but no noses. Their mouths were rudimentary and did not move. Yet they were 'talking' but, again, the communication was telepathic. The human-like entities had almost transparent skin through which she could see the veins. Apparently there were both males and females.

All kinds of medical equipment were used on her. There were tubes going to her body, including her nose, and she was on a table with her legs up. One tube was in her stomach and she had a feeling in her hip as if she had been kicked. Some form of radiant light was brought to these two areas and it felt warm and a tingling sensation swept from her stomach and down to her hip. At one stage they checked her eyes with what she described as a little tube which made a buzzing noise.

There were two apparently identical blond-headed 'just average' people who brought her to the room. So several different entities were involved.

She was told that they only chose people who they knew would help. She didn't know what she could do to help but they told her it would come in due course.

There was a 'very good' human-like personage who 'talked' to her during her examination. She described him as being entirely human with light brown hair and 'absolutely beautiful' blue eyes, which had a hint of brown about them. Interestingly, she said, 'He seemed familiar' and then, when asked to recall any previous experiences, she described a situation which made it evident that the first time she was infiltrated was as a developing foetus!

Despite reading many cases of abduction this is the first case I have come across where an abductee has recalled being infiltrated before birth. Yet the description of the colours that surrounded her, and the foetal position she was in, as well as her saying that she had 'no age', make it quite obvious that she was recalling a pre-natal condition. When asked by Dr Fiore to go further into this recollection, Gloria told her in so many words that the ETs are capable of creating life; changing life as it develops as well as terminating it. Yet they can then recreate it because they do not like terminating a life and so can apparently put it into a temporary state of suspended animation.

When phantom miscarriages occur, doctors, unversed in the ways of ETs, shake their heads and wonder what happened to make them think a foetus was dead when in fact it was later born naturally. Such babies may well one day grow into very special people and one of the important tasks of the investigators into the abduction phenomenon is to learn as much as possible about the details of what is often a fairly routine and now well-understood sequence of events. Not every foetus that is, medically speaking, dead and then regains life is necessarily an infiltrated baby but, once something is known to be possible, then the event can be looked for. When these infiltrated babies are born, they may already be seeded with special powers. They can be directed from elsewhere but they still retain their free will. If, in their future lives, they do not wish to cooperate with the infiltrators then they do not have to do so. It is their choice, if they know what they are being asked to choose between.

Before the regression session was over, Gloria told of a later abduction when she was in a white 'egg-shaped' room that was illuminated with an all-pervading light. She was reading a book with the aid of a device which, she was told, was a 'learning tool'. This helped her absorb the knowledge in the book. The book was not written in English but looked somewhat like Arabic or Hebrew and parts resembled Greek.

This time there were three entities, who she described as 'instructors', but while they were of normal height they had the same white, thin transparent skins, through which their blue veins could be seen, as some of the entities previously described. They had big almond-shaped yellow/brown eyes and very large foreheads.

The knowledge Gloria was acquiring, she said, concerned learning the truth and shunning false beliefs. There seemed to be a memory of a previous intervention because she felt she had seen these pages of writing before. She was particularly struck by the feeling that these instructors seemed to have for one another – a mutual sharing of their knowledge and, as she put it, 'a kind of happy excitement' and enthusiasm for their task.

And what was their task? She was told that, as mankind as a whole was not ready to accept the wisdom from without, so some chosen ones, such as her, would have the knowledge forced on them. There is, in what she is told, a decided criticism of the belief systems that currently mould mankind's religious institutions.

Tom, the spokesman for the Nine, has given us the same message. In his testimony, only Buddhism is going the right way and Christianity, Judaism, Mohammedanism, etc. have been given the answers but have besmirched the message by overlaying it with dogma and ritual. They have followed the path of aggrandisement for their priests and control of their followers at the expense of modestly conveying the message of truth and humility that their 'prophets' were sent to teach.

The instructors told Gloria that their abduction method was the only way in which they could pass on the message. They were unable to arrive on Earth overtly and teach directly because of the attitude of a majority of the human race which would not welcome a message of love and understanding. In particular, those who aspired to high places in society would see such intervention as a threat to their power and would immediately move to ridicule the message, or even use military or other force in an attempt to destroy the instructors.

Again Tom is on record as saying that such an intervention might be attempted in the future but, if representatives of the Civilizations came down and were threatened, they would have the means of dealing with it. When we see how easily ETs can control the minds and bodies of their chosen abductees, it is apparent that there would be no bloodshed. It is difficult to imagine but, should such a 'landing' occur, to be met by a group of politicians and military top brass, the latter could well be programmed by the ETs to remain passive and cooperative before they could try any tricks.

Gloria was also told of the 'opposition', who are based on other planets or working through people in high places in an attempt to cause disruption and wars. They may well be behind certain means of mankind's eventual destruction. Yet, she was told, the most destructive of all is Man himself. Something most people have divined for themselves!

Because of their greater exposure and the more open awareness policy in the USA, the American experiences are much better known than those elsewhere, but this is a worldwide phenomenon. Similar events in the UK are reported in *Without Consent. A comprehensive Survey of Missing Time and Abduction Phenomena in the UK*, by Carl Nagaitis and Philip Mantle (1994).

The cases investigated by these two researchers contain the same general run of events that featured in most of the American ones. It is the constant reiteration of the feelings engendered in the abductees, the examinations they have to undergo, their descriptions of their surroundings when abducted, etc., plus their insistence that they were talked to without verbalization that make one realize that this is not some kind of massive psychological hoax. There are many people who would have you believe that abduction experiences are a form of psychosis because they cannot bring themselves to imagine what, to them, is unthinkable. People really are being taken against their will into ET spacecraft and being subjected to medical examinations and given ideas and thoughts by alien beings.

Whitley Strieber, like Gloria, Phyllis Schlemmer, Andrija Puharich and Uri Geller, is another of the 'chosen'. He is one of the people who have been repeatedly abducted from childhood and it would seem that his contribution to our gathering acquaintance with the ETs is to be a wonderfully erudite communicator through the written word. His books, *Communion* (1987) and *Transformation* (1988), express in a unique way how he first came to recognize the powers which were intervening in – or even controlling – his life, and how he met and overcame his dread and fear. He describes, in *Transformation*, how he became another person through the intervention of those who he calls his 'visitors'.

In *Intruders*, Budd Hopkins (1988) describes, in considerable detail, how 'Kathy Davis' (real name now known but not used here) was used as the surrogate mother for an ET/human hybrid which she called Emily. Undoubtedly, Kathy was one of the chosen because this deeply disturbing event, which struck to the bottom of her psyche, was just the most dramatic in a long series of encounters which had gone on for most of her life.

One of these contact events occurred when she was 16 years old and involved experiences akin to those which others have had.

It was the Fourth of July weekend and Kathy had gone with her friend Nan, Nan's parents, younger brother and boyfriend Sam to a cabin in a remote part of the Rough River Park in Kentucky.

At one stage, late in the day, the girls had been talking to some boys on the CB radio which was installed in Nan's father's Chevrolet truck. It was such a friendly conversation that the girls had invited these boys over for a party at the cabin. One of them seemed to take a particular shine to Kathy and she wanted to meet him.

Despite the remoteness of the cabin, and the girls being sure that they had never mentioned its location, the boys, who said they were camping nearby, seemed to have no difficulty in locating it.

There were three boys and they arrived down the dirt road in a 'chunky old car with hardly any lights'. This car did not bounce on the bumpy road like a real car would have done. It only had one headlight and no tail lights. It was indeed a very curious 'car'.

It was nearly midnight and the others had gone indoors, leaving Kathy in the Chevrolet to meet her visitors. She was more struck than ever with one boy, who was blond and seemed to be the leader of the party. She felt that she was already in love with him.

When Kathy took the three boys into the cabin, things were very strange. Everyone was up but the television was not on. Even Nan's little brother, who ought to have been in bed long ago, was there and it was unusual for Nan's parents to be up at that late hour. They seemed to be frozen in fixed positions and did not move during the 'party'. Only at the end, when the three strange boys left, did all the participants come back to life.

It seemed to Kathy that they had a good party but only the blond boy (BB) spoke. His two companions did not utter a word during the apparently long time they were there. However, conversation was struck up when the BB said that the boys were part of a band. Interestingly enough, the BB only made conversation on topics he had already been prompted about. For example, he asked Kathy which music she liked and, lo and behold, that was the music which the band played. They drank only what Kathy said was available.

The BB's two companions were clones of one another. They were tall and thin, in contrast to the BB, who was short and stocky and wore casual but different clothes. They never uttered a word but just stood, apparently immobile, one near the door. In this they appear to be somewhat like Men in Black (see page 37).

When they left, the BB kissed Kathy on the cheek but the kiss did not produce the feelings that a young girl would normally have when kissed by a boy she adored – she just felt odd. Yet, when he smiled at her, she said it made her feel 'warm and good'.

It took Kathy a whole week to get over her feelings of infatuation with the blonde visitor. He seemed to have cast a spell over her. What Budd Hopkins finds odd is that, as described, the BB could have been Kathy's twin brother so closely did they resemble one another.

To complete the 'impossibilities' in this event, when the girls went to look for the place where the 'boys' were supposed to be camping, they found it was in an area completely devoid of campsites.

What we do not know is the purpose of this strange encounter but Hopkins draws attention to a similar scenario featured in *The Betty Andreason Affair* by Raymond Fowler. There are many other abduction-related cases where some of a group are switched off so that others can be abducted. In this connection, Kathy recalled a recurrent dream in which she is sitting in a truck at night, talking over a CB radio. The lights go out and the radio goes dead. She is confronted by four spinning lights descending in front of the truck. She is terrified by this and hides down behind the dashboard. She hears herself saying: 'Who are you?' and 'What's happening?'

So whether this party actually took place or whether Kathy was 'programmed' to believe it happened is difficult to judge. Yet it seems an very elaborate way of conducting an abduction – if such a thing took place. However, it is the kind of weird happening that those who have been chosen have to contend with.

The constant factor in most abduction cases seems to be the involvement of Greys. Like human beings, they are not all of the same temperament. Some appear friendly and others not so friendly but, unfortunately, we cannot be sure that their disposition is not one assumed for the moment. After all we have to remember that only human beings have free will.

Greys are very active on this planet and we have to ask: Why? Why do they continually tag and abduct certain people? There is unfortunately no complete answer at present but certainly they are always subjecting their victims to medical examinations, which indicates some form of in-depth surveillance of the human race. Their methods of mind control are very subtle and we have seen that they can even take people out of double beds, perform their examinations, etc. and then return them to bed without the partner being aware that anything untoward has happened. However, sometimes they do make mistakes, as described by Hopkins (1988), where a young woman was abducted from her bed and woke up with her wet feet on the pillow and her head at the foot of the bed. In another case, several children and their mother were abducted but the children were later returned to beds other than their own.

In *Communion*, Whitley Strieber (1987) gives the transcript of a regression hypnosis session he had with a psychiatrist, Donald Klein. Strieber was in bed with his wife and, after an unspecified period of sleep or near sleep, he became aware of a number of Greys entering the bedroom. They were bald and wearing blue coveralls, except for the leader who had what he described as 'cards' on his uniform.

Strieber had to get out of bed and, when he had taken off his pyjamas, he was moved downstairs onto the front porch to a waiting 'black iron cot'. He lay down on the cot which he knew was no such thing and was 'flown' off with his captors all around him. He could see the sky and the clouds but, despite being naked, was not cold. He 'awoke' in the woods but was then lifted up more than 100 ft. The next thing he knew there was a floor beneath him although he could not comprehend how it had got there.

He found himself sitting on a bench in a small room which had a nasty odour about it. An entity, who he thought was an old female, talked to him. (There was some doubt as to whether this inhuman-looking being had a gender but we will assume it was female.) She wore a tan suit and was 'a little person made out of leather'. She sat right in front of him and examined his face. She then gave him to understand that an operation would be performed on him. He was now very scared and screaming. However, the operation seemed to consist of a 'bang' at the back of his head so he calmed down.

While some of Strieber's recollections are garbled in the transcription, it appears that the female entity induced an erection in him but, although no form of intercourse occurred, it is not evident whether a sperm sample was taken. This, however, seems likely as it has happened to other men in similar circumstances. The ETs also took a blood sample from his finger, tried to put something in his mouth and inserted a form of probe into his rectum.

When this was all over, he was rapidly transferred back to his living room, cold and tired. He was aware of two entities in the room. He then went upstairs, put on his pyjamas and got back into bed with his wife, who had apparently not stirred, and went to sleep.

There is also in this transcription a recollection of a former abduction when he was 12 years old. At that time, he apparently had contact with this same female entity but, again, the recollections are garbled and it is this which, to me, brings the ring of truth to these deeply disturbing memories. If someone was going to make this up they would have a much more coherent story to tell than the one which emerged under hypnosis.

The above cases of abduction have enough similarities and differences to make it clear that the ETs involved are, in many ways, of a similar kind. The psychological methods they employ, their control of gravity and the medical examinations suggest a planned series of interventions for a purpose we do not yet understand. Suffice it to say that abductions are far more frequent than we once thought. In fact, in the early days of the modern flying saucer saga, they were not even recognized as part of the phenomenon.

As we saw in the case of John and his family (see page 35), whole vehicles and their occupants can be abducted and, in one case, reported in *Alien Liaison* (Good, 1992), aircraft have been seen to be apparently abducted.

A great deal of UFO activity has been occurring in Puerto Rico in the last few years and one of the centres for this activity is the region around Laguna Cartagena (see page 31). On the evening of 16 November 1988, a Puerto Rican family witnessed an incident in which two jet fighters were chasing a UFO. The UFO stopped and the fighters flew manoeuvres all around it until they both suddenly disappeared into the bottom of the UFO and the incredulous witnesses could not hear their engines any more. The UFO had apparently 'swallowed' the fighters, which did not reappear. Instead, two balls of light came out of the UFO and shot away at great speed, whereupon the large UFO also disappeared at great speed.

This is not an isolated incident because, in *Alien Update*, Timothy Good (1993) records another similar incident in the same area just over a month later. In this case, there were over 100 witnesses to the disappearance of two US Navy fighters into the maw of a huge triangular-shaped UFO. While there can obviously be no official confirmation of these events, other interventions by the US authorities in the area (reported by Good) suggest that there is perhaps a two-way interaction between the UFO denizens and the US authorities. Were the two small UFOs that left the bigger one on 16 November perhaps an exchange for the fighters? Obviously, we do not know but the evidence that something immensely significant is occurring, and that it involves liaison between extra-terrestrials and terrestrials, is being considered by some researchers as a genuine possibility.

The work that people like Budd Hopkins and others are doing is of immense value. Those who have been abducted are often frightened people who are living with half-recalled memories of things that have happened to them in what they tell themselves are dreams and yet which they know deep down are no such thing. Often, as their experiences involve very private events, they cannot talk to anyone about what has been done to them. This is particularly true of the men who have been subjected to the forcible donation of sperm. In some cases (Hopkins, 1988), highly unwilling men have been forced to couple with alien females, although, in the much publicized case of Antonio Villas Boas (Buttlar, 1979), this may not have been entirely the case. In one of Hopkins' cases, the abductors made an error in that they took what they thought was sperm from a man who had had a vasectomy and so only obtained seminal fluid – which apparently made them very angry.

What abductees need more than anything is a sympathetic and knowledgeable ear to pour their suppressed emotions into. They need to know that they are not alone and that many, many others have been 'raped' in the way they have. The uncovering of evidence of an ET/ human hybrid breeding programme explains how some young adolescent girls can find themselves pregnant when they have never had any form of sexual intercourse. They may still have intact hymens and yet they have all the signs of early pregnancy.

Regression hypnosis – and sometimes conscious recall – has found that these girls have had abduction experiences. In some cases, early abortion thwarts the ETs' intention of later abducting the girls again and removing the developing embryo. The embryo must then be cultured in some 'test-tube baby' laboratory elsewhere but sometimes, in cases investigated by Hopkins and others, the developed child is brought back and shown to the surrogate mother.

Knowledge like this, if more widely disseminated, would help prevent the awful family scenes there must be when parents – partic ularly fathers – are confronted by tearful and terrified daughters who cannot understand how they can be pregnant and cannot convince anyone that they have never known a man. Here is a case where knowledge of the abduction phenomenon is of vital importance if innocent girls are to be saved from untold agonies.

We have to break through the deplorable conspiracy of silence that surrounds this phenomenon and it is good to see that, at last, the abduction syndrome is being recognized by certain people in the media. However, there is still a tendency to include psychiatrists on such programmes. Invariably, these psychiatrists have not studied the subject which they are discussing and produce barren hypotheses which have little or no bearing on the abduction scene. The abductees, already deeply affected by rejection and ridicule, are made out to be liars, who are inventing the stories for their publicity value. In fact, the exact opposite is the case. The last thing true abductees want is publicity and the only reason they pluck up the courage to appear on television or radio is the altruistic one of helping others to realize that they are not alone in their ordeals.

One final example (Hopkins, 1991) will help corroborate the car abduction experience given. It was April 1961 and a young second lieutenant was driving from New Jersey to Fort Jackson, South Carolina. While he was still in North Carolina, he realized that his fuel tank was only one quarter full so he resolved to fill up at the next town. However, he never reached it because someone, he assumed it was a policeman, waved him down and directed him onto a dirt road. As he drove down the narrow lane, his lights and engine died on him but the car continued to move forward while, at the same time, it was wafted into the air.

After what seemed an instant, it was morning and he found himself in the room of a motel, lying fully clothed on the bed. In disbelief, he went to the front desk, where he found that the motel was just outside Fort Jackson. When he located his car in the car park, he found that the tank was still a quarter full and that the mileage was about the same as when he had last looked.

Such 'impossible' events are bread and butter to those who investigate the abduction phenomenon and, time and again, their bizarre details corroborate one another. The more evidence that can be accumulated, the sooner these disturbing events will lose their sensation value and then we will be making progress towards understanding them better.

SEVENTEEN

CYPHERS IN THE CROPS

MYSTERIOUS FORMATIONS have appeared for many, many years in fields of growing crops across the world. However, over the last 10 years or so, each summer has yielded, particularly in the fields of standing cereals in southern England, the most amazing designs, furtively drawn during the night, when no one was looking. Photo 13 is one of the 1995 season's offerings while photos 10 and 11 show two of the 1994 crop. All these are very remarkable and just the latest in a long series of such manifestations that first came to the attention of the media at large in 1982 (Delgado & Andrews, 1989).

The early examples of crop circles were just that – circles, but, since then, those ETs who are using our fields as canvases for their art have had, if you will pardon the pun, a field day. Each season's group of designs seems to be more beautiful and complex than the last, as if those who are drawing them are saying 'try hoaxing that one!'

For some reason, it is the area of Hampshire/Wiltshire that is most visited by the phenomenon at present, perhaps because it contains a high density of prehistoric remains. For there is no doubt that the circle makers have a predilection towards placing their designs close to, and often oriented with respect to ancient monuments (photo 11). For example, in the past 10 years, there have been vastly more designs laid in the area of Avebury Ring than chance would warrant (fig. 17.1).

Avebury is the nucleus of a galaxy of important and unique monuments that includes Silbury Hill and the nearby massive long barrow of West Kennet. All these, in their own way, are unique. Avebury Ring is the largest and most complex henge monument in England, Silbury is the largest manmade mound in Europe, and West Kennet is the finest example anywhere of the art of long-barrow building.

Crop designs have been laid by the stone avenue that stretches south from Avebury towards Overton Hill (where there was once a

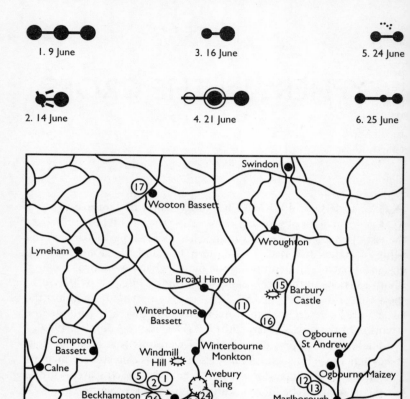

1. 9 June

2. 14 June

3. 16 June

4. 21 June

5. 24 June

6. 25 June

Fig. 17.1   The positions of 30 crop designs drawn during the summer of 1991 in the region of Avebury Ring. Note the concentration of designs near to Avebury and its satellite sites. (Based on an illustration by Richard Adams in *Cerealogist*, 1991)

stone circle) and near to Beckhampton, which once marked the end of another stone avenue stretching out westwards from Avebury.

However, Avebury is not alone. Designs have, for example, appeared regularly near Stonehenge. On 17 July 1991, a wonderful design, based on circles encompassing and embellishing an equilateral triangle, appeared near Barbury Castle, an Iron-Age hillfort at Wroughton, near Swindon. For sheer area and complexity, it is recognized as perhaps, to date, the most intricate of them all (Bartholomew, 1991).

Then there was the design generally accepted to have the deepest significance of any yet found. On 12 August 1991, in a field of wheat at Ickleton, near Cambridge, a representation of the figure which is called the 'Mandelbrot Set pattern' or just the 'Mandelbrot Set' (photo 12) appeared overnight.

The majority of this design is almost heart-shaped with satellite circles sprouting from it and it was discovered by a private pilot, Mr Cherry-Downes, who flew regularly over the site and was thus able to confirm that it had not been there the previous evening. According to Bartholomew (1991), a local lady-farmer, Mrs Wombwell, said:

> It was incredibly precise. Each circle was perfect – at the base of the heart-shape it tapered down to a single stalk of wheat. Every stalk had been flattened one quarter of an inch above the soil. There were no footmarks, and no sign of machinery. It was beautifully done – how, I can't even begin to speculate.

The reason why the Mandelbrot was so significant was that here, drawn in a field and spanning some 180 ft, was the most complex design in mathematics, and one that could not be interpreted as anything else.

When you see a crop design that resembles, for example, a whale (of which there have been several), then it may look like a whale to you but what did it mean to those who produced it? With the Mandelbrot there was no such uncertainty. Those who engineered its drawing knew that they were producing something which we would im mediatelyrecognize. They also realized that the ramifications would lead to certain unequivocal conclusions. Thus, they were speaking directly to us and saying, among other more esoteric things, that they know the same mathematics as we do. They know of Benoit Mandelbrot's work on fractal geometry, which is wide ranging in its implications and has things to say about how living organisms grow, as well as being connected to the modern chaos theory. Those who drew it probably trod the same path long ago and are maybe glad to see that, now, after the ages when mathematics was developed mainly as a tool for the furtherance of science and engineering, thinkers are using mathematical method to produce the embryonic stirrings of a disciplined approach to living organisms.

It might also be significant that this design appeared near to the grey-stone University of Cambridge – the most ancient university in the country. For, when the geometric results of the method of 'iterations' that Mandelbrot devised appear in a wheatfield, an intellectual statement is being made.

So the placing of this design so close to an ancient seat of learning might conceivably be significant. Yet it was largely a one-off and very few crop designs have appeared in Cambridgeshire. For, although the designs have appeared all over the UK and the world, there is no doubt that it is Hampshire/Wiltshire which commands the deepest attention from whatever, or whoever, is producing this remarkable modern phenomenon.

Fewer designs have been drawn in the fields of the Essex–Suffolk borders where I live but I have been privileged to investigate some of them. I well remember the first time I found myself in a crop design. It was at Fordham Place, not far northwest of Colchester, and the design was in the form of a dumb-bell (Watts, 1994).

When you see for yourself the gentle and yet purposeful way in which the stalks of corn are bent as they emerge from the earth you cannot, like Mrs Wombwell, help being amazed by the artistry of it. The circles of the Fordham dumb-bell were so carefully drawn that I had no difficulty in calculating to the centimetre what their diameters were – and they were identical. At the centre of each was a hole which a probe proved in both cases to be $9\frac{1}{2}$ in deep and almost full of loose earth. Around these holes the laid stalks had been bent in two or three places to follow the tightness of the bend. Yet the connecting 'handle' of the dumb-bell was in many ways the most remarkable feature. It was exactly 6 ft wide throughout its length. This dimension proves to me that those who are drawing these designs are working in ancient measures, which would again tie in with their affinity for ancient monuments. They could well be using the geographical foot which the Ancient Egyptians inherited from somewhere else and which is the result of dividing one degree of arc at the equator into 360,000 parts. This measurement is considered to be among the most basic and the Imperial foot differs from it by only a fraction of an inch. In wheat, drilled a matter of centimetres apart, it is impossible to tell the difference. There is reason to believe that the unit that we call a foot was not devised by some erudite Earth person at all but was bequeathed to us by the predecessors of those whose vehicles we still see in our skies today.

The Fordham dumb-bell appeared in 1990 and, the following summer, an almost identical one was drawn in the same place, but with a slightly different orientation. This ability to duplicate designs is well known and often the same design is drawn in various places in the same locality. For example a 350-ft long formation was drawn in wheat at Alton Priors on 19 July 1991. It was dubbed a *keygram* because of the key-like device at one end. An all-but identical keygram to this one was drawn near Avebury just 1 week later. The dimensions were exactly the same, 'within the limits of experimental error' as they say (Bartholomew, 1991).

Such ability to duplicate complex shapes indicates a kind of programmed computer-like intelligence lying behind the execution of the designs. The designs, however complex, appear to be drawn in a very short time – maybe in seconds. It is rare to see any manifestation of it being done and, in some cases, the design is mysteriously added to after the main part has been drawn.

While some people are still doubtful, everything I have read on this subject indicates an extra-terrestrial origin for the crop designs. The observation of a disc sweeping a circle at Butleigh, in Somerset, in 1991 (Watts, 1994) is a rare event because the UFOs involved know how to keep themselves hidden from view but, in June 1994, a UFO was seen by several witnesses near Arad, in Romania, in the act of making a crop design (*Cerealogist*, 1994).

Several of the eye-witnesses were too terrified to speak or, if they did make statements, they were somewhat incoherent. However, a shepherd, who was sleeping out with his sheep and only 150 yards away from the field involved, said that it happened 4.00 a.m. on Monday 20 June. He went to check his sheep and was confronted by a 'light like the moon only much bigger'. The light appeared again a few minutes later, when the shepherd was preparing to eat in his hut. The corrugated roof and the walls of the hut shook and, when he went outside, he was thrown to the ground by what he described as a powerful 'blast of wind'.

The UFO was of the typical saucer shape and had a transparent dome, from inside which shone a powerful white light. Incredibly, the shepherd could see two bearded entities standing at an open door. He estimated they were some 5 ft 6 in tall and one had a thin face and slanting eyes. He heard them talking in an unknown language and observed some form of instruments in their hands.

The UFO hovered about 10 ft above the wheatfield for some 2 minutes before a bluish flame-like emanation came from the centre. The shepherd described it as like a thick rod about 5 ft long. Immediately afterwards the object shot up into the air and vanished making a noise like 'a cannon being fired'.

The shepherd's most telling statement was that the resultant crop circles were only made as the UFO began to rise. Investigators say that the design consisted of a ring about 140 ft in diameter and some 13 ft wide over most of its length, although there was a considerably wider section covering an arc of some 70 degrees. In the centre was a small circle about 20 ft across.

The wheat stalks were described as being heavily pressed down and were swirled anti-clockwise but I have to be careful here. Only the most basic of crop designs was made in this case and perhaps this is not at all typical of the way the phenomenon usually manifests itself. Could this UFO have drawn, say, the scorpion design shown in photo 10? I doubt it. That would have entailed much greater artistry. Personally, I envisage a computer-control beam of complex electro-magnetic radiation painting the designs from a UFO hovering much higher up than the 10 ft or so of this Romanian example.

All we can say is that the Romanian observation shows us that some simple crop circles may be created by UFOs that hover low over cornfields. The complex designs of recent years may not be made in the same way.

After this event, the sheep refused to sleep in their old pasture and the dog ran away whenever it heard the sound of an approaching vehicle.

Many typical UFO events are associated with the crop formations. On 26 July 1991, a 4-minute videotape was taken of a pulsating light which moved purposefully over a wheatfield near Milk Hill (Good, 1993). On the video, this light is seen to hover occasionally and, at one stage, goes down into the crop itself, re-emerging along a tractor lane in the crop. It finally flew up into the sky but, as it did so, it passed closely over a tractor driven by Leon (surname suppressed), who was able to confirm that a small disc had indeed buzzed over his tractor.

A report on the crop-circle phenomenon in North America in 1990 (Good, 1993) attempted to classify what Americans call UGMs (Unusual Ground Markings) but it appears that, out of the 80 or so examples from the USA and Canada, quite a large proportion were not of the pictogram kind found in the UK. In a few cases, lights, etc. were seen in the vicinity prior to the discovery of the markings, which were usually circular in shape. However, one of the important aspects of the

British pictograms is the complete absence of any burning. Once burning of vegetation is seen we are not looking at the same effect shown in photos 10–13.

Similar low-grade circles, etc. have been reported from the former USSR, Italy and Holland, but very few from France. However, there was a sudden eruption of circle making in Germany during 1991, including a true pictogram at Gransdorf, near Hildesheim. This formation consisted of 13 almost identical circles, plus a ring with a cross within it.

Investigators of the phenomenon report that, at times, humming noises are heard, vague lights float closely above the heads of the corn and, sometimes, mysterious cracklings are heard while luminous streamers appear. All these manifestations could be associated with strong electromagnetic radiation and all of them can be reproduced using high-voltage terminals. They add substance to my contention that the most likely explanation for the manner in which the stalks are laid is via the establishment of a high potential difference between the heads of the stalks and the earth. This would entrain a current of ions in the stalks, which could then be bent by a transverse magnetic field using the *motor force* (the rotation of an electric motor induced when current in the armature flows across the lines of a magnetic field generated by the field coils).

In the case of crop laying, both the high potential difference and the magnetic field are possibly broadcast from the UFO responsible but only become manifest where they are required, i.e. at crop level. This ability to project EM effects to a point without affecting the space between is something which we do not yet possess.

However it is achieved, there is no doubt that the crop-circle phenomenon is having a great impact on those who come into contact with it. It is on the philosophical level that the pictogram artists are having the strongest effect. The book *Crop Circles – Harbingers of World Change* (Bartholomew, 1991) is typical of this approach because it is based largely on the intellectual impact of crop designs rather than descriptions of them. The hunt for hidden meaning is just what the crop artists are looking for; they want us to think; to rise out of our Earth-centred shells and embrace the Universe.

With most UFO-related phenomena, no such calling-cards are left. Vague indentations where landing legs have rested, scorched vegetation, even a few fuzzy photographs or video shots lack the impact of a crop design. It is there for people to see and to experience. Even after it has been harvested, the crop has yielded an unequivocal statement that no one can wish away. Those who do not believe in an extra-terrestrial origin for a wonderful design such as the Ickleton Mandel-brot must fall back on the hoax alternative, even when that alternative is so obviously wrong.

There is no doubt in my mind that crop designs are being created from outside Earth. The impact of the pictograms lies in the conversion of so many to a belief in life outside of Earth. Even if that were the only message, it would still be a great one. We are being forced to confront the fact that we are not alone in the Universe. Also we see the effects of energy fields which we do not fully comprehend but which are in use by other more intellectually advanced civilizations.

However, there is evidence (Schlemmer, 1994) that more than one group of space entities is getting in on the crop-design act. Some of these mean to distort the message that the higher-minded groups wish to convey. They might even be helping a few human hoaxers to corrupt the tidings. However, those circles in which the stalks are unbroken and bent just above the ground and those where the stalks are kinked in several places to follow the very small radii near the centre of circles, etc. are the genuine ones. The dowsers can also tell genuine circles from bogus ones. However, not all the bogus ones need necessarily have been made by human hoaxers. They may have been produced by the 'opposition' in order to confuse us as much as possible.

Some interesting responses have been obtained from the ET intelligences responsible for the crop designs. It was early in August 1991 that a line apparently of script appeared in a wheatfield near Milk Hill, Alton Barnes, Wiltshire. This formation was different from any other that has appeared before or since.

It seemed to be in reply to an American mystery hunter, John Eric Beckjord, who, a week earlier, had tramped out the message 'Speak to us' in a field a few miles away. Beckjord thought, for various good reasons, that the Milk Hill script was a response to his own plea.

Together with other scholars, Professor Gerald Hawkins, famous for *Stonehenge Decoded* (1966), produced a translation of the rune-like script (*Cerealogist*, 1993). The message was interpreted as 'Oppono astos', which is Latin for 'I oppose acts of craft and cunning' or, more colloquially, 'I am against hoaxes' (fig. 17.2).

It certainly seems odd that, on the only occasion when someone used a cornfield to write a message to the crop artists, it was followed in the same area, and within a week, by a coded message which those who investigated it were convinced was not the work of hoaxers.

Undoubtedly there have been hoax designs and the impact they have had on those who investigate the phenomenon is out of all

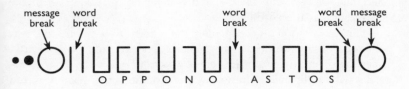

Fig. 17.2 The Milk Hill glyphs and their interpretation according to Gerald Hawkins.

proportion to their numbers. Yet, leaving aside the artistry and precision of most of the designs, we only have to contemplate the armies of hoaxers that would have to be deployed throughout fields in Wiltshire and Hampshire in order to create a small fraction of the number of designs that appear to realize that hoaxing is not the answer. We would also have to take on board the idea that, if hoaxing is rife, then there have to be many groups of people across the world who wish to spend their summer nights demolishing farmers' crops.

For example, in the summer of 1991, there were no less than 30 more or less complex designs drawn in the fields in an area of diameter 15 miles centred on Avebury Ring (*Cerealogist*, 1991). This was just a dense conglomeration in a sea of further designs throughout the area (fig. 17.1). If this does not convince the doubters, one only has to compare the careful work of the real circle makers with the tangled mess that is produced by the hoaxers. It is easy, in almost all cases, to distinguish at once between designs which are the work of those who, for their own ends, wish to confuse and provide ammunition for an already sceptical media and the thoughtful and intricate work of the real thing.

It has been found from soil analysis that odd radioactive isotopes are to be found in the soil in certain crop designs. They tend to be isotopes whose resultant radioactivity would be commensurate with bombardment by low-energy subatomic particles. They certainly exist and are not found in control samples taken from outside the designs (Dudley & Chorost, 1992). Since then a group of cerealogists have considered the work of Dudley and Chorost and have had to conclude that, while unusual isotopes may be found in crop designs, the case for them was not fully proven by the original workers. However, the isotopes found by Dudley and Chorost were of the types I would have expected were the designs being swept by ET forces. So as far as I am concerned the matter is still open and we cannot lose sight of the fact, so often demonstrated to those who study this phenomenon, that maybe someone powerful was afraid of the results and acted accordingly.

The information on the phenomenon given by the Nine confirms that the designs are drawn by agencies from outside Planet Earth. They are given to us to make people question and think about extra-terrestrial intelligences. Until now, the visitations that have occurred across the millennia have had no significant impact on the thinking of the human race but, by drawing these complex patterns in the cereals, no one can say they have not happened. From that point of view, they are a means of opening up humankind's awareness. As Tom has so quaintly put it, 'Let the personalities of humans move their own hair out of their own eyes'.

As so often happens with things that are of vital importance to the future of the human race, the media are virtually ignoring the phenomenon and are leaving it to the cerealogist buffs and the growing numbers of people who are opening their minds to the Universe at large. It may not be the quickest way to disseminate the message but then maybe humanity as a whole is not ready for the message. However, the sales of books on the subject of mysteries, and on crop designs in particular, indicate otherwise. Once again, it is only the powers that be who are suppressing the glad tidings with which we are being presented.

EIGHTEEN

ANIMAL ACTION

IF, AS WE SAW in Chapter 16, human beings are prey to beings from space then animals are even more so. The space denizens appear to consider it important not to damage us unduly but they certainly do not have the same regard for animals. In this, they thinking seems to be very close to our own because, like us, they seem to consider that, while the life of a human being may be considered sacrosanct, this is not the case with animals.

In April 1897, at Le Roy, Kansas, there was a case of cattle rustling. One of the principal witnesses was Alexander Hamilton, who at one time was a member of the House of Representatives. In his testimony, which was backed up by an affidavit with ten signatures of worthy members of the local community who knew him, he states that he was woken up by a noise amongst his cattle (Vallée, 1966). To his utter astonishment he saw an 'airship' slowly descending onto his cow lot. By the time he, his son and a tenant had arrived at the corral, armed with axes, the craft was just 30 ft up. They were within 50 yd of it and it was a 300-ft long, cigar-shaped object with a transparent carriage underneath. Inside, they could see six very strange beings who were jabbering in some unknown language.

The craft was, in general, dark reddish in colour and, when something made its occupants aware of the three men, a bright light was turned on them. A great 30-ft diameter turbine wheel below the craft, which had been slowly rotating, suddenly increased the speed of its revolutions with a buzzing noise and the vessel rose 'lightly as a bird'.

It rose to some 300 ft and hovered directly over a 2-year-old heifer, which was caught in the wire of the fence. The men went over to free her but found she was secured by her neck to the craft above by a red rope. They wrestled vainly to get it off and so, to ease the poor beast's frantic struggles, they cut the fence wire, whereupon the craft, heifer and all, slowly rose and disappeared towards the northwest.

That was not the last that Hamilton saw of his heifer because, next day, a neighbouring rancher, who lived 3–4 miles west of Le Roy, discovered the hide, legs and head in his field. The rancher was highly mystified that an animal could be butchered in that way and yet there were no tracks and no blood.

Twenty-three years earlier, between January and April 1874, something unknown slew as many as 30 sheep a night in Cavan, Ireland (Keel, 1975). Incisions were made in their throats and the blood was extracted but no flesh was eaten or removed. Because of elongated dog-like tracks, many stray dogs were shot but the prints were much larger and of a more powerful creature than a dog. A similar incident in 1905 at Badminton, England, was reported in the 1 November issue of the *Daily Mail*. Again, sheep were slaughtered by having their blood removed but their flesh was left untouched. Once again, inoffensive dogs were blasted by posses of trigger-happy farmers who shot at anything that moved near their fields. The killing also spread to other parts of the UK. By December of that year, 30 sheep had been killed in the same way near Gravesend, Kent. In the following year, the phenomenon moved to the vicinity of Windsor, and also to Guildford, where no less than 51 sheep were slaughtered in a single night. The killings stopped as suddenly as they had started, an important fact to bear in mind when considering what might be the cause of these incidents.

Such killings share a number of common features. Invariably the predator escapes detection; no remains of any animal are found and the matter becomes forgotten when the danger has passed. This is not how ordinary terrestrial predators work. There would be droppings, or the remains of the victims would be dragged away to some den or other, eventually to be found by someone. One predatory animal must mean two and more of the same species or how did the animal get there in the first place? These creatures leave no evidence of their presence. If they did not have the ability to kill, most people would consign them to the category of spectres. In view of the cow and horse mutilations of recent years, it could well be that the 'animal' involved did not actually exist and that tracks, etc. were laid to make the local populace think that an animal was involved. The real work was meanwhile being undertaken by ETs under the cover of the 'animal' artifice.

Another aspect is the quite inhuman ability to butcher an animal and not to leave the place covered in blood. This, and the incredible surgical abilities with which vital organs, etc. are removed leaving the rest of the carcase untouched, place these cases firmly in the space visitor's camp. Sometimes these organs, as well as the brain, are removed through impossibly small holes. In *The Invisible Predators* (Dodd, 1995), there is a photograph of the minute hole through which the brain of a fox has been removed. This animal was found on a moor at Staintondale, North Yorkshire, in 1993.

In many instances where mutilations of animals have occurred there have also been the usual signs of UFO activity, i.e. lights, or more formed shapes, such as discs, flying very low, often in restricted air space. There was an horrific case near Eagle, Alaska, in which one of five backpackers rose before dawn, left his tent and went to the stream to wash (Duplantier, 1979). He was astounded to see some 20 saucer-shaped craft hovering nearby but, by the time he had roused his friends, the craft had gone. There was, however, a large burned circle where the grass was brushed out clockwise from the centre, in, one imagines, a manner akin to the way crop circles were created in the Romanian case (see page 177). There were four triangular indentations 2–3 in deep in the ground just inside the edge of the circle. However, even this evidence of UFO activity did not prepare them for what they then discovered. Literally hundreds of animals had been slaughtered. The legs and antlers of moose had been removed and put in separate piles. The organs of elk had been removed, while eyes and claws were missing from grizzly bears. In the case of caribou, the skeletons had been removed. Yet the most amazing thing was that, despite Eagle being about as far inland in Alaska as you can get, close by was the body of a 15-ft whale and this, in its turn, had been gutted. The latter discovery to me authenticates this otherwise bizarre report because no one making up a story would have conceived of a butchered whale being found so far from the sea.

There was a great wave of these kinds of events across the USA in the second half of the 1970s (fig. 18.1). It is estimated that, during this time, there were some 7,000 cases and the circumstances of these mutilations do show certain common characteristics. The lack of any spilled blood has already been mentioned but one puzzling feature, which intrigues anyone who deals with cattle or horses, is how the animals were first of all approached. There were never any signs of of a tranquilizer gun or anything similar being used to quieten the victims before slaughter.

Reports of mutilations date back to the nineteenth century when, for instance, North American Indians reported buffalo butchered in strange circumstances, but the matter came to headline attention in the USA in the 1960s.

Fig. 18.1 The distribution of sites of cattle mutilations in the USA in the 1970s.

In early September 1967, Mrs Berle Lewis who kept her 3-year-old Appaloosa horse, Skippy, at a ranch in San Louis Valley, near Alamosa, Colorado, was deeply shocked to find him dead in horrific circumstances. His head had been severed from his otherwise intact body. Blood, brains and spinal fluid had been drained and vital organs, such as the heart and kidneys, removed.

Another typical horse case occurred in October 1985, near Fairfield, Great Falls, Montana. The mare was first observed lying in a strange position on the top of a hill. Close inspection revealed that the face was stripped of flesh right back to the bone, so that the jaw and the skull were revealed. This surgical removal was uncanny in that it was complete but showed no sign of cutting to separate flesh from the underlying bone. The sexual organs had been cut out in a circular pattern and the mammaries removed. An ear and an eyeball were missing while the windpipe had been exposed by the removal of neck muscles.

However, the greatest number of these cases in the USA concern cows. One occurred at Griffen Valley, Arkansas, around 19 August 1990 (*Daily World*, 1990). The farmer, Huron Griffin, discovered that one of his registered herd of Swiss Brown cows had been mutilated. Udders, anus and genitals had all been removed, as well as the left ear, with surgical precision. Even more sinister than this was the fact that another three of his herd had disappeared without trace in the previous 3 months.

Another example occurred in March 1977, when a steer was mutilated at Everett, Washington State. The veterinary surgeon who inspected the carcass was sure that predators had not been responsible because he could not have duplicated the incisions with any of his own instruments or expertise. Recent research has shown that high heat – sufficiently high to boil the animal's blood – is part of the effect of whatever cutting technique is used by the ETs. It has therefore been suggested that a form of laser cutting device was used.

Not only cattle and horses have been involved, although these make up the greatest percentage of the total. There have been cases of dogs and cats, as well as rabbits, and, in one case at Newquay Zoo in March 1979, eight animals were mutilated, including wallabies. Again the animals were drained of blood and they were all beheaded. Tests showed that the carcases were radiaoactively contaminated. The investigators were convinced that this could in no way be the work of human beings. One wallaby was lifted out of its enclosure and over several 5-ft fences with no sign of any disturbance of the ground or the fences.

These few examples illustrate the general tenor of these visitations. The most obvious reason for not attributing them to the work of predators or Satanic cults (as has been suggested) is that no terrestrial mutilators could excise these organs and other parts of the bodies without leaving bloodstains. Further, as one who personally has been around domestic animals, particularly horses, for many years, one of the most unnatural things is the way in which the animals must be in some way mentally tranquillized before being drained of blood and mutilated. I imagine trying to approach a horse or a cow, especially when in a herd situation, and realize that the animals would be very wary, even if they did not turn and flee. Furthermore, there would be the noise of the animals themselves, as well as that of those who were trying to catch them. The silence in which all this is done is one of the most uncanny aspects of these cases. The mutilations are also performed at great speed, vastly faster than any veterinary surgeon could perform such operations, especially during the hours of darkness. Lights are seen in association with these events but they are usually in the air. Also there often seems to be a pattern to the interventions. This has been detected in the USA, starting in 1973, at the same time as a wave of UFO sightings occurred. Kansas was first affected, then Nebraska, followed through 1975 by Colorado, New Mexico, Texas, Montana, Utah, Oklahoma and Missouri (for map, see fig. 14.1)

When, in response to these attacks, cowhands and others have set watch overnight in places which were likely to be visited, they have occasionally seen humanoid figures which appeared to glide over the ground and did not walk or climb fences in any way that could be likened to human beings.

Linda Howe produces documentaries for film and television companies in the USA. Her 1980 documentary *Strange Harvest*, about the animal mutilations in the USA, gained an Emmy award. She has since written a book, *An Alien Harvest: Further Evidence Linking Animal Mutilations and Human Abductions to Alien Life Forms* (Howe, 1989), and some of her extensive research has thrown a little light on this mysterious issue.

For example, she describes the ordeal of Myrna Hanson and her small son, who attempted to interfere with the mutilation of a cow in New Mexico. Myrna discovered two white-suited ETs working on the cow but, before she could interfere, both she and her son were abducted into a brilliantly lit disc that took them to an underground facility which she thought was in the Las Cruces region of New Mexico. This lies to the southwest of Alamogordo in the San Andrés Mountains (for map, see fig. 14.1).

There, she was made aware of a humanoid figure which was undergoing 'treatment' in a vat of reddish liquid and that the liquid was related to blood fluids and tissues removed from animals.

So here is a possible reason for the carnage which continues to be reported from Europe, the former USSR, Canada and Australia, as well as the countries already mentioned. Linda Howe (Good, 1993), has described how, during midwinter 1991/2, Oklahoma, Kansas, Arkansas and Missouri experienced a wave of mutilations. There was another unwanted visitation in Alberta between April and July 1992, when six cows or calves were butchered on one farm.

It is possible that none of these butcherings was actually carried out on the ground, which could account for the virgin nature of the dead animals' surroundings. Linda Howe has recorded a 1973 case in which Judy Doraty and her daughter Cindy were abducted after seeing a calf floated up into a UFO in a pale beam of yellow light. Judy found herself in the same UFO, observing two Greys excising tissue from the calf's eye, tongue and testicles. She was left with the feeling (recalled under regression) that all this had to do with the survival of the extra-terrestrial race and also the human race.

Further credence is given to this view by a report drawn up by Officer Gabriel Valdez of the New Mexico State Police (Good, 1992) about an incident at Manuel Gomez's ranch near Dulce, New Mexico, on 24 April 1978. An 11-month-old bull had apparently been 'dropped by some kind of aircraft north of Mr Gomez's ranch house'. Valdez stated that the rectum and sex organs had been surgically removed but that the bull had bruising around the brisket, indicating that a strap had been used to lift and lower the animal 'to and from the aircraft'. There were also 4-in diameter footprints which, it was conjectured, came from and returned to a hovering aircraft. This carcase was fairly intensively investigated with some interesting results, which can be consulted in Good's book.

Because I have dwelt on cases in the USA, it may seem that animal mutilations and abductions are confined to the Western world but there are reports (ICUFON, 1985) of similar events in Japan. In the 9 November issue of *English Yomiuri Weekly* (1989) there was a typical report of cattle mutilation. Wahei Farm lies some 9 miles southwest of Takko town, in Aomori Prefecture, in the very north of the island of Honshu. The farm had a herd of some 100 head of cattle and, one day in early October, the cattleman discovered a 4-year-old black cow which had been killed overnight and whose udders, half an ear and the tip of the tongue had been surgically removed. Again, there was no sign of blood and no evidence of any struggle. The farmer, Mr Sadar Kine, remarked that to separate a single cow from the herd and overpower it usually required the services of about ten men. Mr Kine suffered from depression and bouts of inexplicable fear for as long as 3 months after the cow's death. At the end of October, a similar incident occurred at another farm in the same area, when an udder was removed with no blood-letting. As in other countries, there was a spate of sightings of lights in the sky during the period when these multilations occurred. There may have been other mutilations but Japanese farmers are very careful about becoming involved in strange goings-on and tend to remain silent. Indeed, silence and failure to report the true nature of these kinds of event is not confined to Japan.

There was a spate of horse mutilations in the UK in 1992–93. Once again, they started suddenly and ended suddenly and no one was ever caught. The majority of incidents occurred in Hampshire and its surrounding counties but some spread northwards into Hertfordshire and eastwards as far as Essex and Suffolk. There have not, to my knowledge, been any cases reported in 1994 or 1995 (the time of writing). The usual speculations about the perpetrators of these horrors included Satanic cults and a group of highly mobile horse-haters (or even just one person) but, as in the cases cited so far, the problem has been to explain how nervous and excitable animals such as horses could be tranquillized so that the surgical procedures could be undertaken.

Despite the difficulties, we must try to suggest some scenarios which might be behind the large number of animal mutilations. It has been suggested that the UFOnauts are collecting animal matter for use in the construction of solid physical entities. Proponents of this theory believe that, as many of the UFOnauts so far encountered seem to lie somewhere between physical and psychic entities, they need physical material to clothe their attempts to appear as similar to human beings as possible. In this way they may make themselves more acceptable to us. Also they need to be physical in order to operate in an otherwise physical world.

According to Tom (Schlemmer, 1994) Earth is unique in its physicality. No other planet in the Universe is as physically dense as Earth and the souls of entities from other worlds are reincarnated here in order to learn what it is like to be a fully physical person. Earth is the 'college' where the souls of the Universe are sent to learn hard lessons in being human so that, later, if they should appear on other planets in entities that are nearer to 'thought forms', they will have experienced full physicality.

In the next chapter we will look at some of the weird and wonderful 'animals' and monsters of various kinds which have been reported, often to be laughed off as the products of diseased minds. Many of these seem to be associated with the appearance of UFOs and to lie in that same 'impossible' world where beings can appear and act physically apparently out of nowhere and, after a sojourn on this planet, disappear as mysteriously as they came. It may be that the UFOnauts need animal protein and organs to flesh out these entities.

NINETEEN

STRANGE CREATURES

WHEN 6-YEAR-OLD Charlotte and 4-year-old Francesca Hutchinson ran in and told their mother that there was a lion in their garden, they were met with disbelief but, when Mrs Hutchinson looked out, she found that they were telling the truth. They watched the lioness for 10 minutes, during which time she sniffed the ground and urinated before loping off across a neighbouring field. Their next-door neighbour reported crushed grass as if a large animal had spent the night in their garden (*Daily Mail*, 18 August 1994).

The date was Wednesday 17 August 1994 and the sighting sparked a major alert in the hamlet of Rudston Parva, near Bridlington, Humberside, where the Hutchinsons lived, involving armed police, animal experts and a helicopter. Nothing whatever was found and no zoo or wildlife park in the area had lost a lioness.

Just over a month later, there was another report in the same newspaper but this time a lioness had turned up in a rural area north of Basingstoke, Hampshire. A considerable number of people seemed to have seen it at one time or another, including a gamekeeper, and it approached a travellers' encampment but shied off when the dogs began to bark.

These are just two recent sighting of a misplaced animal that have come to light at the time of writing but it is typical of hundreds, if not thousands, of similar observations of large exotic animals, variously described as pumas, cheetahs, lions, etc. When people see these incongruous creatures, and even take photographs of them, then their obvious impossibility is not the only oddity.

Sometimes they exhibit amazing abilities, e.g. being able to jump over unusually large obstacles. In one case a 'puma' leapt over a woman and the horse she was grooming. Dogs, even large ones, are usually terrified when one of these odd beasts is near, which is not the normal reaction of dogs when faced with big cats.

An article on the continuing reporting of big cats in the UK (*Mail on Sunday Review*, 21 August 1994) suggested that their presence is the result of the Dangerous Animals Act 1976, which prompted private owners of big cats to release them to fend for themselves. It is a tempting theory but does not add up, if only because of the inadequacy of food supply.

It has often been pointed out that the frequent kills which any roaming big cat would have to make seldom occur. It has been estimated that a puma, for example, needs 300 lb of meat a week to survive, which would entail it killing the equivalent of 250 roe deer a year. Even if it supplemented its diet with rabbits, one large cat would still have to despatch thousands of rabbits just to keep alive.

However dense the woodland in the localities where these animals have been seen, surely, at some time or another, the remains of these apparent feral animals and their kills would have turned up – and yet this has not happened. The odd ones that have been shot or captured have usually been traceable to an escapee but the numbers are much smaller than one would expect if the number of sightings is taken into account.

Even so that does not preclude these creatures killing, and they have been seen to do so, but, seen or not, they often do not eat what they have killed – or they only partially eat it. In some cases, it may not even have been the killer who ate the remains. Certainly, there is insubstantial evidence to show that, in areas where these animals have been seen, there was sufficient consumption of livestock, etc. to keep the animal alive.

Many more cases than can possibly be covered here are cited in *Alien Animals* (Bord J. & C., 1985). Ohio was visited in the spring of 1977 by a creature that mauled sheep so badly that very few survived. Several farms were visited; 57 sheep were mauled over a 2-day period at one farm while, at another, almost all the penned sheep were similarly savaged and most died. The creature responsible showed considerable intelligence because it set off half-a-dozen steel muskrat traps without being caught and it was so strong that it ripped the gates off the sheep pens, leaving fang and claw marks on the wood. The depredations of this 'animal' went on through March into May and there were sightings of a cat-like creature. At one stage, when cornered by two policemen and two county officials, it started to walk towards them in a docile manner before suddenly turning and moving at incredible speed to disappear into the nearby woods.

That same year, another strange creature was killing or maiming pigs in Bay Springs, Mississippi, by either biting off their ears or tearing them out by the roots. It was described as being bigger than a German Shepherd dog and, despite its size, was capable of 'jumping further than any dog could jump'. The strange behaviour of this predator was outclassed by the fact that, among the wounds inflicted, there were 2–3-in cuts in the back of the neck, which were made cleanly as if by a surgeon's knife. This has echoes of the cattle mutilation cases described in chapter 18.

There was a case in Illinois which parallels the cases of electro-magnetic interference reported, where cars' engines die in the presence of UFOs. In this event, the driver of the car (Mike Busby) got out to see what had suddenly made his engine die, only to be immediately confronted by 'a large black cat-like creature with greenish glowing eyes' that came out of the Shawnee National Forest alongside the road. This apparition, however, was walking on its hind legs and was 6 ft tall. It hit him with the pads of its forepaws and then grappled with him, inflicting wounds on his arm, chest and abdomen. A passing lorry startled the animal and it retreated into the forest but the driver of the lorry was able to confirm Busby's description. There are several other instances of 'cats' that walk upright and more or less attack people.

The UFO-like elements in these events point to creatures that have been in some way 'created' and which, perhaps, are only in a 'devel-opmental' stage. When, as has been reported on numerous occasions, the animals have eyes that generate light, we cannot be dealing with ordinary terrestrial animals. We must consider whether these entities are being 'sown' in an area as mobile (and presumably controllable) monitors. Their eyes project light so that what they are looking at can be illuminated in the dark. The light, while intense enough to occasion comment in those who see the creature, is not all that strong and is, perhaps, merely a largely unwanted side-effect of the much more powerful invisible rays that are being projected onto the scene. The eyes are, in effect, acting as surveillance cameras, relaying information about us to a UFO elsewhere. This could explain why so many witnesses have mentioned how the animal stared straight at them for what seemed like a long time.

Then, of course, there is the problem of continuity. When an animal is seen on and off over a span of years we must remember that genuine terrestrial animals are born and need two parents. That entails there being not just one big cat in an area but two of different sexes. It means that young cats have to be protected and nurtured for many months before they can fend for themselves. What is odd about the 'puma' sightings is that the animals all seem to have been fully grown specimens. Cubs have been sighted but they are a rarity and they may have been the young of genuine terrestrial animals, because there is always the possibility of a few, albeit very few animals escaping from wildlife enclosures. Yet such animals have to die and someone, somewhere, is going to find the remains.

Newspapers for 2 August 1995 carried a report of the skull of a predator with large fangs being found by three brothers in the River Fowey, near St Cleer, Cornwall. The Assistant Curator of Mammals at London Zoo identified it as that of a leopard or puma and the animal had, according to him, been dead for 3–4 months. It was soon shown, through the discovery of a tropical beetle within the skull, that the animal had certainly not died in the UK.

However the 'Beast' did not lie down. Newspapers of 9/10 August 1995 carried photographs of a large cat-like creature which had been video'd by amateur cameraman, Wayne Broad, on Monday 7 August, near his home at Pawlett, Somerset. The video footage occupied several minutes and it was estimated that the beast was some 6 ft long, including its long sweeping tail, and stood 3 ft high.

In the previous July, a Ministry of Agriculture investigation concluded that there was no evidence that the Beast of Bodmin Moor existed. They said that, despite this new discovery, their inquiry would not be re-opened and, of course, we know why. The Men from the Ministry are fully conversant with the animal mutilation cases in the UK and around the world and do not wish to be drawn into what they know is another fruitless search for non-existent real animals.

Even one skull of a real animal is not sufficient to explain the other sightings. It simply confirms what some have said, that the Dangerous Animals Act did lead to the odd exotic pet being freed to fend for itself and for the odd remains to be found. Even so, we have to ask: Where are the carcases of these cats which are sighted so many, many times and in so many places?

Often the descriptions, while superficially resembling a puma, leopard or lion, on closer examination do not exactly fit any known terrestrial species. For example, in June 1969 (Bord, J.&C. 1985), a Colonel Haines was driving on a sunny day near Witheridge, 10 miles west of Tiverton, in Devon. He was able to watch a creature by the roadside for 3 full minutes, from a distance of only 15 ft. He described it as being like a small leopard (many of which he had seen in Malaya).

It had a brown head, large, black, prominent eyes and a nose extraordinarily like a pug. Its left ear was pricked, but the other hung down as if torn. Its ribs were bright, pale chestnut, turning to a sort of dirty gingery brown, and its hindquarters were darker still. On its hindquarters were three black spots about the size of a penny and along its spine was a ridge of hair, about 2 inches in length, which waved in the breeze. Its body was smooth-haired and thin. Its tail, long and thin, looked like a piece of dirty rope. Its legs were very long for its body, and pale fawn in colour.

There had been similar sightings in the area 2 years earlier and the Colonel was able to confirm from witnesses that his description tallied with theirs. But what had happened to the creature in the intervening time?

The so-called Beast of Exmoor terrorized the Devon/Somerset borders in 1983 and was described as a large black or brown creature that looked more like a dog than a cat. At the same time, however, a great number of sheep were killed in the vicinity and these killings were, of course, blamed on the Beast. Casts of its footprints showed claws and cats walk on their pads, with claws retracted. *If* the Beast killed the sheep, then it apparently did so in a cat-like manner but its $3\frac{1}{2}$-in footprints resembled those of a dog. I say 'if' because one wonders whether the notion of the Beast was introduced to supply an 'alibi' for the sheep killings, which were actually in the same vein as the cattle mutilations described in chapter 18.

When we look at the fossil record of today's dog, we find that the dog's early ancestors had retractable claws like a cat. The earliest known was *Miacis*, a ferret-sized animal with five-toed paws, which, while it fed like today's dogs, lived mainly in trees. *Miacis* existed over 50 million years ago and evolved, via *Cynodictus* and *Tomarcus*, into *Canis* some 25,000 years ago. From the dawn-dog, *Miacis*, also came cats, hyenas, civets, weasels, raccoons and bears. Could it be that those who sow the strange cat/dog creations we see today are working on old 'blue-prints', so that what appears is based on one of the ancestors of both today's cats and dogs?

On a previous occasion, at the end of August 1994, when the so-called Beast of Bodmin Moor was caught on video, pictures of mutilated, but not eaten, sheep were shown on television. The Beast of Exmoor has been terrorizing that part of southwest England on and off for many years but it is no more surprising that nothing has been found, any more than it was in the past.

Despite a contingent of the Royal Marines being called in to make a search, nothing was ever found of the Beast of Exmoor and, in the usual manner of these visitations, they abruptly ended. It is the sudden cessation of sightings that makes it quite evident that we are not dealing with a normal set of flesh and blood animals. This becomes even more obvious when, in another Illinois case, six people were travelling in a car when a tan and grey puma-like animal suddenly materialized alongside it. Strange as that may sound it is even odder that only some of them could see the creature, even though they were all in a position to do so.

When people with firearms are 'attacked' by 'pumas' and other animal-like manifestations, it is remarkable that, while shooting usually results in the creatures' retreat, the bullets do not seem to harm them. The same kind of reaction occurred with the humanoids in the Kelly, Kentucky, visitation described on page 22.

Australia has also had puma-like cats preying on livestock since 1956, in one case despatching 340 sheep on one farm during a 2-year period. As elsewhere, despite massive hunts, nothing was found.

It is rare for the evolution of strange creatures by UFOs to be observed but no less than ten large black hairy dogs were seen to emerge from a UFO that landed in a cemetery in Savannah, Georgia, in September 1973. In other cases, typical UFO sightings have been so regularly and closely accompanied by the sightings of odd animals that the link seems too obvious to be coincidental.

Then there are the sea creatures. Many reported sea serpents could simply be unknown terrestrial species for, considering the vastness of the oceans, they would for the most part be able to remain out of sight of Man. For example, five Army personnel out for a day's fishing off the coast of Nova Scotia in May 1833 signed a statement that they had all witnessed an 80-ft long serpent swim by their boat not more than 200 ft away.

Two men who rowed across the Atlantic, John Ridgeway and Chay Blyth, encountered a monster 35 ft long in July 1966. It was probably a creature from the murky depths because it was outlined in phosphorescence and it is well known that deep-sea creatures often carry such 'neon lights'.

However, stranger water creatures have been seen creatures – ones which parallel the the 'cats' above in terms of impossibility. The most famous of them is, of course, the Loch Ness Monster. This creature has been seen on an estimated 10,000 occasions, which means that very few can doubt that there is something observable in the Loch. The number of high-tech expeditions mounted to find the creature show that there is sufficient evidence to justify the outlay of considerable funds on trying to locate and record the beast for posterity. Yet, despite all the cameras and sonars, no one has, as yet, managed to get convincing evidence of the creature's existence. It is as elusive as the extra-terrestrial animals mentioned already. It is there and yet it isn't. It seems to want to reveal itself to some but not to others. You feel it is playing cat and mouse with all those who pit their wits against it.

I say 'it' but, if it is a terrestrial creature, then surely I should say 'them'. Loch Ness has been cut off from the sea for millennia and therefore 'Nessie' would have had to breed if this were truly a terrestrial phenomenon. Sightings have occurred for hundreds, even thousands, of years and no one would suggest that a normal flesh and blood creature could exist alone for such an immense time.

Loch Ness is, at 900 ft, deep enough and murky enough for the sceptics to be able to cling to their crumbs of doubt that the Loch Ness monster is anything other than some creature left over from a previous age. But why has no bloated carcase of a dead Nessie ever been found floating on this much frequented loch?

If Loch Ness is sufficiently voluminous to enable a large creature to hide in its depths, there are other totally impossible places where such monsters have been seen. Take Lough Nahooin in Connemara, Ireland. This small stretch of water is some 300 ft long by 240 ft wide and 20 ft at its deepest point. Following a sighting, by the Coyne family on 22 February 1968, of a 12-ft long water creature that had a 'pole-like head' and a flat tail, the lough was strung.

The Coyne family were treated to a 'display' by this creature which lasted as long as an hour, and they only stopped watching it because it was getting dark. Yet the investigators netted nothing, despite the use of a fish-stunner to frighten the creature into the waiting nets. Stephen Coyne, the man of the household and the one who had first seen the creature, said that he had seen a similar creature some 20 years earlier in the same lough. Once again we have the impossibility of a large water creature being able to sustain itself for even a short period on the fish in a small lough like this, let alone for 20 years. More information about this and other phenomena of the little lakes of Connemara is contained in *Creatures From Elsewhere* (Brooke-smith, 1984).

The phenomenon of 'impossible' water monsters akin to the Loch Ness Monster is a worldwide one. Janet and Colin Bord (1985) give a list of 300 locations, including Africa, Australia, Canada, England, Ireland, Japan, Norway, Scotland, South America, Sweden, USA, the former USSR, Wales, etc. but why, they ask, do monster hunters invariably fail to capture the creatures? Why do monsters so often appear to those who are not actively seeking them? Why have ciné cameras jammed in the presence of monsters, or why have they appeared after cameras have been put away? Considering the number of sightings, there are miserably few photographs and those which exist are inconclusive evidence.

The situation with regard to all these strange creatures runs parallel to the UFO scene. There are very, very few good photographs of UFOs. Time and again, people who have cameras handy fail to use them and afterwards cannot understand why. Only a few UFOs have been captured on film and this is probably because the UFOnauts wanted us to do so. Those who go looking for UFOs rarely see them, whereas they appear to surprised witnesses who, until then, probably never believed the things existed.

The idea that entities such as Men in Black can only exist in our dimension for a relatively short time (see page 38) may also be the case with alien creatures. It is rare for sightings to last for very long and the Coynes' sighting is a rarity.

It is difficult for us to comprehend stages of being that hover between true physicality and true spirituality. We may be able to accept ghosts and can believe in a spirit world that lies beyond our five senses but things that can be produced by manipulation of the 'spiritual continuum' are very difficult to come to terms with.

However, mediums have demonstrated on many occasions that a human being in contact with the spirit world can produce physical entities. Photo 15 shows a Polish medium, Franek Kluski, materializing a large bird of prey. He was able to produce this same manifestation on several occasions in 1919 and a creature resembling a Big Hairy Man (BHM) also appeared. Madame David-Neel (1936) was able, after a few months' isolation for thought and the performing of rites, to materialize a monk – what she called a *tulpa* – and this entity took on a life of its own. It joined the party when she went on tour in Tibet and a herdsman actually saw the tulpa in her tent and took it to be a real lama. Eventually, however, it began to escape her control and became, as she put it, a 'day-nightmare'. Only after 6 months of hard mental struggle was she able to dissolve her, by then, unwanted phantom. It was more than just a projection of herself and once created was tenacious of life.

It is now becoming more and more clear, through our study of UFO-related phenomena, that those who visit us from elsewhere have at their command abilities which we consider the province of trance-mediums and their circles. They are working with the spiritual continuum in a natural way. What to us is a more or less one-off occurrence, which takes extreme concentration and dedication on the part of a gifted person, is for them an everyday event. In *UFO Quest* (Watts, 1994) I proposed the term *molographic* for those entities which have more substance than if they were merely a kind of holographic projection.

In holography, a visual image is projected which appears to be three-dimensional and in which objects appear to move relatively to each other, as in real life. Now assume that we can clothe this holographic image in real matter and, because it is now composed of material molecules rather than ephemeral light energy, we can refer to it as being molographic.

I believe that many alien creatures are advanced forms of molographic image. For instance some Bigfoot creatures have been seen to disappear suddenly in a 'flash of light'. In others, the entity has just dissolved in front of the witnesses. There were BHMs about in Pennsylvania in 1973–74 and, in more than one sighting, only a part of the creature could be seen, either the head and torso or the lower appendages (Brandon, 1978).

Some of these creatures, however, have attacked and killed domestic animals, crashed into cars or even struck and injured people, so they are more than wraiths. We cannot imagine how this is achieved at our state of knowledge but evidently it can be done, and is being done, all the time, all over the world.

The one aspect which links all these reports of alien creatures is remoteness. This suggests that those who are sowing them across the Earth wish to come and go undisturbed, and also invisibly, and so the creatures are made to appear as natural as possible. However, as we have seen, they are only superficially natural and, when we investigate further, we continually find oddities which indicate that they cannot possibly be terrestrial in origin. This desire to manifest themselves only where they will not be disturbed is shared by the UFOs.

In *Challenge to Science*, Jacques and Janine Vallée (1967) have plotted the positions of all the unexplained landings that they investigated in France in 1954 and show that the vast majority were in spots remote from populated areas. This also suggests that the sightings were not a psychotic phenomenon, which might be experienced by anyone, because there was not a single report of a landing in the densely populated areas of Paris and its surroundings, where a third of the French population live.

The creation and sustaining of a creature such as a Bigfoot or a lake monster may be a relatively simple matter for those with the kind of collective mind that some of our space visitors appear to possess. It may be possible to leave behind an advanced molographic entity

(AME), with certain, but not all, of the characteristics of a real Earth creature, and for that AME to function independently for some time before being whisked back to whoever sowed it in the first place.

The investigation of the visitations of UFOs has shown us that AMEs which look like and appear to function as real people are part of the phenomenon. We have seen this in the cases of John (see page 35) and Kathy Davis (see page 116) and there are many more.

Thus, in our advancement into the greater world of the Universe, we will have to accept that many of the things we thought were simply psychic phenomena are actually, to many of those who patrol the Universe, second nature. We do not know why they want to visit strange animals on us and arrange for some but not others of us to see them but that will not stop them being here for us to see, nor will it obviate their 'reality'.

TWENTY

PAST, PRESENT AND FUTURE

I BELIEVE THAT the year 1947 was meant to be a breakthrough year for the Civilizations. Surely it was more than coincidence that private pilot Kenneth Arnold's sighting of nine discs, flashing in the sunlight over Mount Rainier in June 1947 should have suddenly awakened the world to UFOs? In an interview with Ed Murrow, Arnold is reported to have said (Randles & Whetnall, 1987): 'I never could understand why the world got so upset about 9 discs, as these things did not seem to be a menace.'

Looking back on it now, I am on the side of Arnold. Why those discs, and why then? During World War 2 all major combatants had experience of 'foo fighters' – small discs formatting with, and possibly 'observing', their aircraft. There were the ghost missiles that plagued Scandinavia in 1946 (Buttlar, 1979) but no such visitations hit anybody's headlines. In fact, Jacques and Janine Vallée's research (1967) showed that the 30 years 1916–1946 were characterized by a dearth of reports. It seems that 1947 was the year in which a new chapter in Earth's history was opened.

This contention is further strengthened when we realize that it was only just over a week later that the Roswell 'crash' occurred. Arnold's encounter was 24 June and the craft came down during the night of 2/3 July 1947. It would seem that a hidden purpose may have lain behind these incidents.

Then, in 1952, 'They' allowed George Adamski to take good, detailed pictures of one of their craft and backed it up by having a young boy, Stephen Darbishire, snap the same type of craft in England (Cramp, 1954). Also in 1952, the Council of Nine contacted humanity through Dr Vinod and opened perhaps our first direct link with those who have shaped our destiny over the millennia.

Then, probably because he was comfortable with the idea of ET space travel, Adamski was contacted directly on 20 November 1952. It is possible that the being who spoke telepathically with Adamski on that occasion was a representative of the Civilization Altea, who manifest themselves in the form of fair humans. But the world was not ready for any of these events. Someone had jumped the gun.

It has become ingrained in us through science-fiction writers, that beings from space are able to do almost anything they choose. The book I have referred to many times, *The Only Planet of Choice* (Schlemmer, 1974), is so called because it tells us that, on the contrary, it is we who have freedom of choice. However because of our hierarchical mode of thinking, it is extremely difficult for us to realize that those who could control our destiny totally are, in fact, most reluctant to intervene. To me, one of the most amazing revelations in *The Only Planet* was that the Nine do not consider themselves greater or better than us. Like highly intelligent and responsible parents, they allow us, their children, to make our own mistakes. Only if we should be so stupid as to stumble into the fire and really risk the collective life of the planet are they prepared to make a direct intervention.

So, if the modern UFO visitation was spawned by them, then their intervention was undertaken on the best available information as to what our reactions might eventually be. In fact, as usually happens, while the humble and powerless people, such as George Adamski, were ready to accept the advances being made, the powerful saw in the visitors the most potent risk to their power and prestige that they had ever encountered. Thus their reaction was what we unfortunate earthlings have come to expect – confrontation and prodigious efforts to silence those who were trying to tell the truth.

However, we cannot bypass the thought that maybe things have gone deeper than a simple attempt to debunk the idea of visiting spacecraft over which the most omnipotent powers have no control. Are we now beginning to see that the powers that be, far from being disbelievers, have actually been laying plans to parley with the 'enemy'?

The research carried out by Timothy Good and others makes it very possible that this is what has happened. Nevertheless, whether or not it is on our terms or on theirs we, who are outside the fold, are not yet able to establish. Some observers are even suggesting that the seamier side of UFO visitations, e.g. artificial insemination of abductees and spates of animal mutilations, have been given the wink and the nod by our own side in exchange for information on the advanced technology of the saucers. Personally, I find that hard to believe but, if it has happened, I wonder what kind of guarantees we have that the game will be played fairly on both sides?

It may be impossible, as yet, for us to assess the way in which the ETs' minds work. If the captured EBEs (Extra-terrestrial Biological Entities) were, for example, very advanced robots of the kind we already (via science fiction) call androids, they could just be channels for the promulgation of whatever information their lords and masters wished to convey. This might very possibly be disinformation to suit their own agenda. We have already been warned by the spokesman for the Nine that the Greys should be treated with extreme caution. There are EBEs who are here for the good of mankind but the Greys seem to be here for their own ends. I feel that we are playing with cosmic fire if we start thinking that they are just odd-looking human beings and will react like human beings. Do Greys have a conscience? Or are they, as Whitley Strieber suggests, part of a 'hive' in which each EBE is a small part of a great collective consciousness? We have received information via Phyllis Schlemmer that some of the Civilizations are organized in this way, i.e. all the entities on one planet are an integral part of a whole and act and function in unison. We cannot comprehend what life must be like for such entities and so we will always be at a disadvantage when dealing with them.

Thus we can only hope that anyone who strikes bargains with these space entities is fully aware of the implications, not just for themselves, but for the future of mankind as a whole.

Yet, despite everything, mankind is making progress – and how things have changed in a mere 50 years! In that time our view of Planet Earth has gone from being an island in apparently empty space, occasionally visited by strange events in the sky, about which no one had very much information or even ideas, to a gradual realization that we are not alone in the Universe. We are now having to consider the implications of confronting and living beside many more space races. When the Soviets put Yuri Gagarin into space and the USA launched the Moon-landing programme, they ushered in a world revolution – probably with no idea of the outcome.

Earth people, wittingly or unwittingly, went to join those for whom our local space was 'home' and, to those trusting souls gathered around their television sets, went about it in the frame of mind that we were going into a void. Nothing could have been further from the truth.

In his book *Secrets of Our Spaceship Moon* Don Wilson (1979) gives a resumé of the then available information about the Apollo missions' encounters with UFOs and says: 'This summary ... indicates that nearly every Apollo astronaut and mission encountered UFOs on or around the Moon'. The public did not get wind of any such encounters because the radio signals were sent directly to the spaceflight centre at Houston and then rebroadcast. In this way, Mission Control could delete whatever they chose and stringent precautions were taken to ensure that the communications could not be received by anyone else, as those of the earlier Gemini and Mercury flights had been. This indicates that the spaceflight programmers were fully aware that the Apollo astronauts would see UFOs and would report them. It was for this reason that the television pictures were not live in the accepted sense but suffered a delay, so that any UFO reports or other sensitive issues could be intercepted. Berlitz and Moore (1980) give a good chronological resumé of UFO contacts with the Mercury, Gemini and Apollo spacecraft.

Thus the whole truth about our first small step into the realms of the space denizens has never been told and no shots of UFOs, either in space or on the Moon, were beamed into our living rooms. So, for the vast majority of the millions who watched the American astronaut dramas unfold, space was as empty as they had always been led to believe. There is no lie as good as a governmental lie.

However, just as with the rest of the saga of the visitation by ETs, one day the truth will out. How the U-turn will be accomplished I do not believe anybody knows, including those who have stifled the information. But, however long it may take, there has to be a day of reckoning. UFOs have been coming here since time immemorial and they will be coming here for an equally long time into the future. So maybe the powers that be believe the lid can be kept on the boiler for a considerable time yet. That is unless something spectacular occurs, such as an overt landing in the Spielberg *Close Encounters of the Third Kind* tradition. Tom has said that such an event cannot be ruled out but indicates that it would be a last resort. In the interim we shall be subject to the same régime of visitation as we are now experiencing.

In *Alien Liaison*, Timothy Good (1992) quotes a physicist, Bob Lazar, who claims to have inside information on, among other things, the US Government's relations with EBEs, and the briefing papers which detailed what had been learned from the ETs themselves. Lazar said that he personally had difficulty with one idea he read there, that 'humankind is the product of periodic genetic corrections'. Yet this is just what we have been told by contactees and through channelled information. So the same story seems to be coming even from what may well be members of the 'opposition' and therefore it looks like fact.

Lazar also told of 'an extremely classified document dealing with religion, and it's extremely thick'. 'But why,' asked the hard-headed physicist Lazar, 'should there be *any* classified documents dealing with religion?'

The answer seems to me to be quite simple. Religion is, or should be, about soul matters and that is what our visitors from elsewhere are adepts at and are interested in. In *The Only Planet*, Tom is quoted as saying:

It was necessary in the beginning to have a structured form of religion. What was in error was those religionists that began to have control over others and to make *themselves* important instead of the understanding.

And we know where that has led us: to a flight from established religion and to empty churches because those who can think for themselves recognize that the dogma and ritual of churchmen is not what true religion should be about.

If you read Tom's answer to the question 'What is God?' you will realize how far from the truth the synods and pronouncements of prelates have driven us. Tom defines God in this way:

It is unified, infinite intelligence, supported with pure love. And it grows with pure love. It is absolute faith and absolute love. That is God.

There are very many men and women of religion who have struggled to preserve and communicate the simple message of love and humility that Jesus the Nazarene was reincarnated to deliver but they are so often beaten by the system. For the last 2,000 years, people who declared themselves to be the representatives of God have been devising and perfecting a system of control over others that is quite totalitarian. Thou shalt believe and if you dare not to then awful things will happen to you. Many churches unfortunately deal in fear when they should be dealing in love and therefore any statements of the truth from those who come from elsewhere, and are impartial, are, to these churches, a threat. That is why documents relating to information from ETs on soul matters have been highly classified; the wrath of the established churches, as expressed through their more militant devotees, is something which governments do not wish to confront. After all, churches are ostensibly the upholders of the faith and they have a primitive power. Do not prelates crown kings?

When I read *The Only Planet of Choice*, I knew at once that here was primal truth. There were no hidden agendas, no dogmas to follow slavishly, and I saw a great light dawning. Here was a great leap forward to our eventual integration into the family of the Universe. I knew I was being led further along a path which would eventually enable me to better appreciate the position of human beings on Earth in the great scheme of things. Strangely, while at one point we were warned to be careful of the Greys, it is from the Greys that Whitley Strieber obtained his insights into the same soul matters that are the subject of his two books *Communion* and *Transformation* (Strieber, 1987 & 1988).

In the concluding chapter of *Transformation*, Strieber summed up the important things that he learned from his experiences at the hands of his 'visitors'. He believes them to be an admixture of the physically real and the psychically real. His experience leads him to see how easily they can move from one realm to the other but he cannot help concluding that their psychic reality is their true reality and that they only manifest physically in order to deal with us. It is the same mode of thinking that made the Hawk come in the shape of a bird to accelerate mankind's development. That was how we 'children' could understand and maybe accept something we would not otherwise comprehend.

He accepts their proven ability to enter the mind and to use this mastery to perform feats that certainly look, to us, like magic. He is sure, as I am, that we have a soul separate from the physical body and he sees the soul as 'some form of conscious energy possibly electro-magnetic in nature'.

Personally, I feel that, while it is evident, from the medical profession's use of cerebral electrodes, that the mind uses EM waves to perform many of its functions, there is more to soul than some assemblage of EM 'images'. At a deeper level than the electromagnetic there has to be a spiritual continuum whose laws are different from those of electromagnetism. This, as we have already said, must be another aspect of the Cosmon Continuum of R.D. Pearson (see page 65).

Just as our physical body is designed to operate in a physical world so soul is the 'body' of the spiritual continuum. The physical body is mortal but the soul is immortal. It can be changed but not destroyed. Once a soul starts its long journey through its many lives, it will develop with its experiences but it cannot die (Currie, 1995).

Finally Strieber's, to date, apparently unique experiences lead to the conviction that being afraid of those who visit us from elsewhere is useless. He believes that we must accept our fear of this unknown and not suppress it. Only in that way can we come to terms with the reality of the experiences that stem from the UFO phenomenon.

I was surprised to read in *The Celtic Shaman* (Matthews, 1991) that the path of the novice shaman starts with facing your worst fears. Shamanism is perhaps the oldest 'religion' in the world and yet its discipline asks its neophytes to do voluntarily what Whitley Strieber's 'visitors' forced upon him. Maybe novice shamans need to do this because we are so hemmed in by the paraphernalia of modern existence that we can no longer see the wood for the trees. Indeed, Matthews tells his erstwhile shamans to imagine themselves to be in a great forest clearing (or a cave) which is so vast as to disappear into the dim distance while providing a high canopy, like a cathedral roof. Here they must surround themselves with a circle of light for protection and, when they feel secure, they must summon the things which they fear most, one by one, and confront them. Within a difficult discipline that must be one of the most demanding things to do thoroughly and honestly. Yet there are societies on Earth today, e.g. the Hopi Indians, who embrace such basic and primeval concepts as part of their daily lives (Waters, 1977).

So the story that comes from people like Strieber, and that which comes through psychic communication via spokesmen, such as M, R and Tom, is the same. Many, if not all, of those who visit us are here to help us lift ourselves out of the pit of slavish adherence to the religious legacy of the last two millennia. You cannot converse in any way with those who engineered the original bases of our religions unless you throw off the yoke of the Establishment. That is what clouds the verities. Christ came with a simple message: love thy neighbour and expel false doctrines. It is clerics out for power and control who have so besmirched that message. Muhammad preached the same doctrine and yet we now find his words so twisted that his more extreme devotees can, in his name, kill others who disagree with them. This is of course what so-called Christians did in the not too distant past (and some still do) and sectarian violence in countries throughout the world continues such slaughter in the name of God.

There is a dichotomy here however. Western religion developed in a way which allowed the suppression and exploitation of our fore-fathers so that we, today, could emerge into a world that may look on the ideas coming to us from space without fear of persecution. Christianity has been the cohesive force which has underpinned the morality to which we still basically adhere and, when the time was right, has allowed the development of the scientific age. Other religions have stifled such enlightenment so that they still, in many ways, dwell in the Middle Ages, although they are not averse to accepting e.g. cars, aeroplanes, air conditioning, all of which have been developed by the Western world under the aegis of a religious system that they profess to abhor.

However, there may be grounds for hope in the twentieth-century's flight from established religion. A large proportion of the public have been able to stand back and look at what they believe in. I have a sneaking suspicion that the religious vacuum that now exists has possibly been engineered. If not, it is an extremely fortuitous occurrence because so many people are now able at least to countenance the idea that beings from outside Earth could have a greater monopoly on the truths of existence than human beings.

With time, mankind will have to accept that ETs formed human history; produced a beautiful and coherent planet into which a developing human species could be sown, just like the flowers of the field; nurtured its creation through its many vicissitudes; and cried over it when, due to the free will with which it had been endowed, it destroyed all that had been so carefully nourished and subtly supported. Again and again they restarted the experiment, led by re-incarnations of the old leaders, only to find that the 'children' could not function on their own once the 'teachers' had left them to their own devices. Eventually, 2,000 years ago, they decided that, despite its drawbacks, the only recipe had to be one that was based on slow, painful development. To help Western humanity through its ordeal, they created the foundations of certain religions so that, despite the Dark Ages, through which their devotees would have to travel, they could one day struggle through to what could prove to be a new Golden Age where the common man would live in greater splendour than any king of the Middle Ages.

And what if we collectively change too slowly in the coming years? Will it be necessary for the Council of Nine to intervene via one or more of their executive Civilizations? We are told that this is a possibility. So what form would such a visitation take?

It would be in physically real spacecraft – ones that could be touched. The ETs would come down from carrier craft in orbit, just as in the waves of sightings we were subjected to in the 1950s and the 1960s. Fear would be nullified by a form of beam but, because of the publicity given to UFOs over the last 50 years, most people would not be abjectly afraid of what was happening. Any military personnel who attempted to intervene in a war-like way would be reduced to impotence simply by one of the ET representatives raising their hand. It would be similar to the way a priest raises his hand when pronouncing the Benediction and possibly that act is meant to have the same calming effect on a congregation.

The landings would be spread over a period of days but they would occur all over the planet. Some of the representatives of the Civilizations would remain as teachers but the others would then go on to perform similar tasks in other parts of the Universe. It is described as the culmination of a major project that has occupied thousands of years and could take place in the near future, simply because mankind is coming out of the Dark Ages and is now aware that it is not alone in the Universe.

Many people, maybe most, in the developed countries, realize that Earth is not the be-all and end-all of creation. We are an important but not pre-eminent planet and God is not wholly and solely concerned with us and our welfare. We have indeed begun to grow up and are beginning to accept that there is no benevolent old man called God sitting up in the heavens with whom we can intercede directly. We have to take responsibility for our own salvation. We do not have to give up all the benefits of modern civilization but what we must do is to bring compassion and love to our everyday contacts with others. At the same time we must, as a matter of urgency, set in motion really effective measures to save the basic ecological framework of Earth. Although largely ignored, this has been the constant message from our space visitors for decades and we disregard it at our peril.

Today a vision of what could be hangs before our avid gaze but it cannot be achieved by greed and avarice. Only by common global cooperation and a great effort of will to put aside our desire for wordly wealth and aggrandizement can the new Golden Age be attained. There has to be rejection of materialism and the promotion of humility and love and it is in some ways ironic that it is taking visitors from space to make us realize that.

BIBLIOGRAPHY

Adamski, George, *Inside the Spaceships* Spearman, 1956.
Agee, Doris, *Edgar Cayce on ESP* Doris Agee, Aquarian Press, 1989.
Bartholomew, Alick (ed.) *Crop Circles – Harbingers of World Change* Gateway Books, 1991.
Berlitz, Charles, and Moore, William, *The Roswell Incident* Granada, 1980.
Bord, Janet and Colin, *Alien Animals* Panther, 1985.
—— *Life Beyond Planet Earth* Grafton, 1992.
Bowen, Charles (ed.), *The Humanoids* Spearman, 1969.
Brandon, Jim, *Weird America* E.P. Dutton, 1978.
Brookesmith, Peter (ed.), *Creatures From Elsewhere* Chartwell Books, 1984.
Buttlar, Johannes von, *The UFO Phenomenon* Sidgwick & Jackson, 1979.
Cayce, Hugh Lynn (ed.), *Edgar Cayce on Atlantis* Howard Baker, 1968.
Cerealogist, No. 5, 1991 (11 Powis Gardens, London W11 1JG).
—— No. 9, 1993 (11 Powis Gardens, London W11 1JG).
—— No. 13, 1994 (Hearne House, North Wootton, Shepton Mallet, Somerset BA4 4HW).
Charroux, Robert, *The Mysterious Unknown* Spearman, 1972.
—— *Lost Worlds*, Souvenir Press, 1973.
Childress, David H., *Vimana Aircraft of Ancient India and Atlantis* Adventures Unlimited Press, 1991.
Churchward, James, *The Sacred Symbols of Mu* Spearman, 1960.
Cramp, Leonard, *Space, Gravity and the Flying Saucer* Werner Laurie, 1954.
Currie, Ian, *You Cannot Die* Element Books, 1995.
David-Neel, Madame, *With Mystics and Magicians in Tibet* Penguin, 1936.
Davis, Beth (ed.), *Ciphers in the Crops* Gateway Books, 1992.
Delgado, Pat, and Andrews, Colin, *Circular Evidence* Bloomsbury, 1989.
Dodd, Anthony, 'The Invisible Predators' *UFO Magazine*, July/August 1995.
Donnelly, Ignatius, *Atlantis, The Antediluvian World* Samson Low, 1882.
Downes, Wesley (ed.), *Essex Ghosts and Hauntings* No. 5 Wesley Publications (61 Lymington Avenue, Clacton-on-Sea, Essex, CO15 4QE) 1995.
Downing, Barry, *The Bible and Flying Saucers*, J.B. Lippincott, 1968.
Drake, Raymond, *Spacemen in the Ancient East* Spearman, 1968.
—— *Spacemen in the Ancient West* Spearman, 1969.

Dudley, Marshall, and Chorost, Michael, *The Discovery of Thirteen Short-lived Radionucleides in Soil Samples from an English Crop Circle* Centre for Crop Circle Studies, 1992. (Available from M. Dudley, 40 Monitor Lane, Knoxville, Tennessee 37922.)

Duplantier, Gene, *The Night Mutilators* SS and S Publications (17 Shetland St, North York, Willowdale, Ontario, Canada, M2M 1X5), 1979.

Edwards, I.E.S., *The Pyramids of Egypt* Penguin, 1949.

Fiore, Edith, *Abductions. Encounters with Extraterrestrials*, Sidgwick & Jackson, 1989.

Fix, William, *Pyramid Odyssey* Mayflower Books, 1978.

Fuller, John, *The Interrupted Journey* Dial Press, 1966; Souvenir Press 1980.

Geller, Uri, *Uri Geller – My Story* Robson Books, 1975.

Good, Timothy, *Above Top Secret* Sidgwick & Jackson, 1989.

—— *The UFO Report 1992* Sidgwick & Jackson, 1991.

—— *Alien Liaison* Century Arrow, 1992.

—— *Alien Update* Arrow Books Ltd, 1993.

Goodman, Jeffrey, *Psychic Archeology* Wildwood House, 1978.

Hadingham, Evan, *Circles and Standing Stones* Heinemann, 1975.

Hamblin, Dora J., *The First Cities* Time Inc., 1973.

Hilton, Alan, 'Abduction' *Skylink*, No. 4, 1993a (Forge Cottage, Perch Lane, Lamberhurst Quarter, Tunbridge Wells, Kent TN3 8AU). 'Abduction' [cont'd] *Skylink* No. 5, 1993b.

Hinton, Geoffrey E., 'How Neural Networks Learn From Experience' *Scientific American*, September 1992.

Holroyd, Stuart, *Alien Intelligence* David & Charles, 1979.

Hopkins, Budd, *Intruders* Sphere, 1988.

—— *Selected Articles on the UFO Abduction Phenomenon* Intruders Foundation (PO Box 30233, NY 10011), 1991.

Howe, Linda M., *An Alien Harvest. Further Evidence Linking Animal Mutilations and Human Abductions to Alien Life Forms* Quest Publications (15 Pickard Court, Temple Newsam, Leeds LS15 9AY), 1989. [Videotapes available from above and Linda Moulton Howe Abductions, PO Box 538, Huntingdon Valley, Pennsylvania 19006–0538, USA]

Hynek, J. Allen, *The UFO Experience* Abelard-Schuman, 1972.

ICUFON, *Livestock Mutilation Wave over the United States* Intercontinental UFO Galactic Spacecraft Research and Analytic Network Inc. (NY), 1985.

Jessup, M.K., *The 1956 UFO Annual* Arco, 1956.

Keel, John, *Strange Creatures From Time and Space* Spearman, 1975.

Keyhoe, Donald, *Aliens From Space* Panther, 1957.

Langford, David (ed.), *An Account of Meeting With Denizens of Another World 1871, Loosley* David & Charles, 1979.

Leonard, R. Cedric, *Quest for Atlantis* Manor Books (NY), 1979.

Leslie, Desmond, and Adamski, George, *Flying Saucers Have Landed* Werner Laurie, 1953.

Lorentzen, Coral and Jim, *UFOs: The Whole Story* Signet Books, 1969.

Lowther, William, '4000 Year old White Tribe of China' *Mail on Sunday*, 20 March 1994.

Marinov, Stephen, 'New measurements of the Earth's Velocity with the help of the "Coupled Shutters" Experiment' *Int. Glasnost Journal on Fundamental Physics*, Vol. 1, No. 1, 1992.

Matthews, John, *The Celtic Shaman* Element Books, 1991.

Michell, John, *The Flying Saucer Vision* Sidgwick & Jackson, 1967.

Michell, John, and Rickard, Robert, *Phenomena. A Book of Wonders* Thames and Hudson, 1977.

Muck, Otto, *The Secret of Atlantis* Collins, 1978.

Nagaitis, Carl, and Mantle, Philip, *Without Consent* Ringpull Press, 1994.

Negev, Avraham (ed.), *Archeological Encyclopedia of the Holy Land* Weidenfeld & Nicolson, 1972.

Pearson, R.D., *Origin of Mind* 1992 (Available from Michael Roll, 28 Westerleigh Rd., Downend, Bristol, BS16 6AH).

—— *Key to Consciousness: Quantum Gravitation* 1994 (As above).

Proctor, Richard A., *The Great Pyramid: Observatory, Tomb and Temple* Chatto & Windus, 1883.

Puharich, Andrija, *Uri* Lab Nine Ltd, 1974.

Randles, Jenny, *The UFO Conspiracy* Blandford Press, 1987.

Randles, Jenny, and Whetnall, Paul, *Alien Contact* Thames and Hudson, 1977.

Roberts, Anthony, *Atlantean Traditions in Ancient Britain* Rider, 1975.

Sandan, N.K. (trans.), *The Epic of Gilgamesh* Penguin, 1970.

Schlemmer, Phyllis, *The Only Planet of Choice* Gateway Books, 1994.

Scully, Frank, *Behind the Flying Saucers* Holt (NY), 1950.

Shuttlewood, Arthur, *The Warminster Mystery* Tandem, 1967.

Smythe, Charles Piazzi, *Life and Work at the Great Pyramid* Edmonton and Douglas (Edinburgh), 1867.

Stanford, Ray, *Socorro Saucer* Fontana, 1978.

Strieber, Whitley, *Communion* Century, 1987.

—— *Transformation* Century, 1988.

—— *Majestic* Macdonald, 1990.

Sugrue, Thomas, *There is a River* Reinhardt & Winston, 1942.

Temple, Robert, *The Sirius Mystery* Sidgwick & Jackson, 1976.

Tomas, Andrew, *We Are Not the First* Souvenir Press, 1971.

Tompkins, Peter, *Secrets of the Great Pyramid* Allen Lane, 1973.

Trench, Brinsley le Poer, *The Sky People* Spearman, 1960.

Vallée, Jacques, *Anatomy of a Phenomenon* Spearman, 1966.

Vallée, Jacques and Janine, *Challenge to Science – The UFO Enigma* Spearman, 1967.

Waters, Frank, *The Book of the Hopi* Penguin, 1977.

Watts, Alan, *UFO Quest* Blandford Press, 1994.

Wilson, Don, *Secrets of Our Spaceship Moon* Sphere, 1979.

Zink, David, *The Stones of Atlantis* W.H. Allen, 1978.

INDEX